✺ THE LOGIC AND RHETORIC OF EXPOSITION

THE LOGIC
AND

HOLT, RINEHART AND WINSTON, INC.

NEW YORK · CHICAGO · SAN FRANCISCO · TORONTO

RHETORIC
OF EXPOSITION

✺ REVISED EDITION

Harold C. Martin, HARVARD UNIVERSITY

Richard M. Ohmann, WESLEYAN UNIVERSITY

❉ *Preface*

SOME BOOKS, Bacon said, are to be swallowed, some to be chewed and digested. Some, he might have added, are to be revised; and no doubt he would have done so had he been speaking of the writer rather than the reader. This is a revision. The book it revises, published five years ago, has had enough use for its flaws to become obvious and its strengths to become known. Before the flaws widen into fissures, the publishers have asked that the strengths be preserved by some reconstruction. That accounts for the fact that this revision is not simply a surface rewriting, a face-lifting job, but a revision that often reaches all the way to the foundation.

The original book was offered as "a helpful way of bringing average and better-than-average students to a recognition of their responsibilities as speculative and critical writers." Its purpose has not changed. Nor has its structure, which the original Preface described in these words:

> The first part of the book adapts a few important matters in logic to the immediate purpose of the writer of expository prose. The subjects chosen for treatment—definition, assertion, proof, and persuasion—are those which seem to uncover and help to remove the principal difficulties of the young writer trying to find solid ground in the mist and muck of new intellectual experience. The second part of the book presents the familiar matters of rhetoric in a manner intended to lead the student to something better than desultory acceptance of imposed dicta about form. The concluding section, that concerned with mechanics, footnotes, and bibliography, is abbreviated to the matters that most frequently need correction in students' essays.

What has changed, and sometimes changed radically, is the matter inside the frame. By and large, the changes are intended to increase the relevance of that matter to the process of writing. In some instances, they clarify; in some, they elaborate; in a few, they correct. They are also intended to make the book more enjoyable to read—not by making it easier, but by making it sharper in its discriminations and more succinct in its style.

In this revision, old indebtedness continues to members of the staff of General Education A, the freshman course in exposition at Harvard—

those still part of the staff and those now teaching in various colleges and universities in the United States; to Dudley Shapere, Clifton Orlebeke, and Max Bluestone, who gave invaluable advice during the preparation of the original edition; to Professor Martin Steinmann, Jr., of the University of Minnesota, and Professor S. O. A. Ullmann, of Union College, who read all or sections of the first text and made helpful suggestions. New indebtedness is gratefully acknowledged to Thomas Nagel of Harvard University for helpful comment on the revised chapter, "Proving," and to Professor Don Cook of Indiana University, Professor Roger Slakey, of Georgetown University, and Professor R. T. Lenaghan of the University of Michigan for constructive suggestions that were utilized in the revision as a whole.

The present text reflects the congenial collaboration of two teachers who, through other publishing ventures, have found that two cooks, one in charge of salt and one in charge of pepper, can make a better broth than either does alone.

H.C.M.

R.M.O.

Cambridge, Massachusetts
Middletown, Connecticut
February, 1963

✸ Contents

PART TWO

❖ THE LOGIC AND RHETORIC
OF EXPOSITION

❄ Introduction:
Experience and
Language

When we write, we translate experience and thought into arbitrary symbols which we call words. To write at all, we must have had experiences and we must be able to use one or more sets of symbols. To write well, we must understand the experiences we have had and we must be able to manipulate words so that they give the reader a clear sense both of the experiences which they translate and of our reflections on and attitudes toward those experiences. For that reason, a book that proposes to help people to write well must concern itself with ways of knowing experience as well as with ways of expressing it. Such a book must face, like the head of Janus, in two directions at once: toward the old, the experiences we have had or are having, and toward the new, the fresh communication of the experiences themselves.

There is a paradox in this matter of knowing and telling, however, which is of first importance. For a reason hard to understand, we do not seem to have a full grasp on experience itself until we have symbolized it in some fashion; we do not *know* until we have *told*. The telling may be done, of course, by many kinds of symbols—words spoken or written, musical notes, paints brushed on canvas, and so on. But whatever the kind of symbol, it appears to be true that we do not really know our experiences until we have expressed them. Yet it is also certainly true that when we express, we express *something;* that is to say, we do not use words at random when we begin to write about an experience but instead seem to be directed by our *un*expressed consciousness of the experience to choose certain words and ignore others.

1

One attempt to resolve this paradox appears in the common remark, "I know what I mean, but I can't find the words to express it." There is something attractive about this simple account of a baffling matter, but the account is probably a misstatement or at least an overstatement. It would be more accurate to say, "I know very vaguely what I mean, but so vaguely that I can't find any words inclusive enough to represent the notion I have of what I think I know." Put in those terms, the resolution of the paradox is closer. If we begin to describe an experience by testing one series of words after another, rejecting or altering as we do so, gradually the vagueness of our understanding diminishes as "wrong" words are eliminated and as "right" or "nearly right" words are accepted as proper symbols of the experience. We are directed by a vague understanding of the experience to words roughly suitable for its expression; by testing a variety of words which are roughly suitable, we refine our understanding of the experience. Thus we come to know the shape of experience through the process of using words to describe it. There is, then, a serious observation behind the superficially laughable question: "How can I know what I mean until I hear myself say it?" As we say or write words, as we set notes on a scale, as we blend pigments on canvas, we discover the complete nature of our experiences. We have had the experience before we begin to express it; we *know* or understand it only when we find means to transform it, internally or externally into some symbolic pattern.

A reader may be inclined to ask at this point if it is always true that telling and knowing are inseparable and interdependent. It is hard to give an answer to such a question because so little is known about the way of knowing anything. Still, it is clear that some experiences are either so violent or so simple that their expression requires no reflection at all. If we bark our shins against a table in the dark, we say, "Ow!" almost as quickly as we pull back our leg from the offending piece of furniture. If, like Archimedes, we suddenly discover what we have long been trying to find, we give a shout of delight. Both ejaculations may be called "noises," and they are certainly expressive noises. Yet neither is informative enough by itself to communicate more than a very vague notion of the experience from which the ejaculations spring. An enraged child expresses his rage *un*symbolically by crying; an enraged man may do the same, but because he is an adult and therefore richer in experience he is more likely to seek fuller means of expression. He knows that his rage has causes and probable effects and he uses language to convey his awareness of those causes and effects to the world around him. In giving expression to complexities of which the child is not aware, the adult necessarily and instinctively tries to understand the complexities himself in order that the symbols he uses may properly represent the subtlety of his feelings. Here he encounters the two obstacles mentioned above: the difficulty of knowing himself and the difficulty of choosing symbols that will adequately and accurately represent what he comes to know. It is awareness of these obstacles that may lie behind the proverbial maxim to count ten before you speak. If, instead of blurting "noises," you take the time necessary to analyze an irritating experience, you are more likely to understand the experience and therefore to comment or to act on it intelligently and informatively. In one sense, then, words not only discover and express experience but put some restraint on it as well; they fit one experience into the whole range of experience of which we are aware and prevent it from exercising an unmanageable control over us.

There are some people for whom the thought of restraint is infuriating or even profane. They feel that only the rush of words that seems to be stimulated by an experience is to be respected and that interference and analysis destroy the vitality and "truth" of the experience itself. Now there is certainly some truth in the contention that analysis may affect the flow of inspiration; if there were not, philosophers since the time of the Greeks would not have speculated about such matters as inspiration and intuition. If truth lay entirely in the uninhibited flow of "inspired" utterance, however, the same men would not have given their attention to analysis. It is clear that one of the problems of this book, and one of the principal problems of a writer, is to consider the relationship between spontaneous expression and controlled expression and to use the resources of both wisely.

Besides those who believe that only spontaneous expression properly represents experience and those who believe that experience is not even fully known until it has been analytically expressed, there are some who claim that expression is either impossible or, if not impossible, is detrimental to experience. In Ernest Hemingway's *The Sun Also Rises,* the leading character advises another who wants to explain her delight in a particular experience. "You'll lose it if you tell it." Followed to its logical conclusion, that advice implies the death of all communication, of all art, perhaps even of all but ecstatic self-knowing. It is probably true that some experiences are incommunicable because pictures of our experiences undoubtedly do often exceed in their variety and intensity any symbols we are capable of devising for their expression. Yet symbols are always helpful in reducing the amount of the uncommunicable in experience by fixing some portion of it, so to speak, in a frozen state, thus permitting us to turn our attention to the portions that remain still fluid and uncontrolled. In physics, the "law of the variable function" depends on a procedure by which all but one of the parts of a process are controlled so that the one left free may be observed without interference. Such a degree of regulation is possible only for simple experiences, but it is certainly one of the functions of symbols to control some parts of an experience while we attempt to observe other parts with undivided attention. Thus, confronted by an unusual experience to which we have reacted in ways we do not ourselves fully understand, we begin to work out of our confusion by labeling parts of our reaction: "Well, at first I was shocked. No, not exactly shocked, but surprised, I think. And the surprise was partly fear, or perhaps I should say 'dread.' Then. . . ." In such fashion as this, we blunder about with words, trying one after the other in the hope of reaching terms capable of translating a private affair into a public form.

Unlike the symbols used in mathematical computations, the words we use in this effort to translate our private experience of the world into terms that others can understand are themselves variable and indefinite. Words change meaning over the years and, even at a given moment, do not mean precisely the same to all who use them. In writing, then, there cannot be absolute control either of experience or of expression. Moreover, because the use of words and the knowledge of experience interact, there cannot be perfect communication. If we could say, "First we experience, then we know, then we express" and could take "then" to mean "consequently," we might hope for a formula or a foolproof procedure like that which Jonathan Swift satirized in his account of the writing-machine in the laboratory at Laputa; and modern electronic "brains" often seem, to the layman, to have solved the problem entirely. But Swift's writing-machine and the electronic calculator have this limitation in common: both require that the raw material of experience be translated into some kind of symbolic form before they can begin to work on it at all. The human being, on the other hand, can do his own translating; in fact, he gains command of experience only when he *does* do his own translating. Although his "translating" is never perfect, it is one of the principal glories of the human being that he has found so many means of sharing with others such a large measure of the necessarily private response each man has to all that touches him.

It is wise to begin the discussion about writing by openly facing these difficulties because writing is a serious matter for all who seek a liberal education. It is the principal means by which the educated man tries to discover and transmit the truth about himself and about the world as he understands it. If we cannot fully resolve the paradox with which we began—experience as necessary to symbols and symbols as necessary to a knowledge of experience—we can at least say that, in practice, we do find it possible to communicate. This we find it possible to do because we have the conviction that we know, and because we instinctively distinguish between knowing and having an experience, which is to say that we do recognize something external to our own mental processes. If this separation is an illusion, as some claim, it is a necessary illusion, natural to our existence and apparently important to our lives. We must assume the separability of events from knowledge of events in order to write at all; we must recognize the interdependence in order to write well.

This book is built on the premise that writing is a way of coming to know as well as a way of communicating what is known. It recognizes that perfection in both processes is beyond human attainment, but it assumes that the proper role of writing in a liberal education is that of moving toward perfection in each. Moreover, it takes as axiomatic the proposition that the two processes, though in fact indivisible, can be separately analyzed, as well as the further proposition that attention in practice to one will result in improvement not only of the one practiced but of the other as well. For the purposes of teaching, it goes beyond simple division of the processes to suggest that students who are intent on improving their writing will generally achieve success most rapidly if they begin with some analysis of the process of coming to know and then move on to study and practice of the means by which we express what we know. This order is the reverse of the one often practiced, but it is adopted here in the belief that analysis, far from deadening the nerve ends, makes them increasingly sensitive and increasingly reliable in what they report. The words we use when we write are not simply blown through us by the winds of the Muses; they come out of the turbulence of our minds. And the reins that analysis puts on the wild chargers of the imagination alone make it possible for the chariot to move swiftly and well. Stephen Spender has observed that the poet's use of rhyme does not so much stifle as stimulate thought and feed inspiration. Analysis does much the same service for prose. Even so, it is only half of the process by which we transform thought and feeling into language. In practice, analysis works in tandem with experimentation in forms of expression; neither does well without the other. Both, then, are proper subjects of study for the person who is concerned about the improvement of his own writing and about a deeper appreciation of the writing of others.

❖ PART 1

❋ *Defining and Describing*

ONE OF THE PARADOXES of learning is that a beginner must accept much before he can understand anything. Each of us works with certain "givens," as they are called in geometry, and builds his structures of knowledge and belief in the confidence that those givens are more or less unassailable. What child could doubt that parents know everything, that the world is full of solid objects, or that there is a stern but kindly God? Yet, for the child, growing up means gradually beginning to question and to reinterpret such postulates as these, and learning, finally, that some of them are precisely the propositions that continue to challenge the intelligence of wise and thoughtful men. The process is sometimes disillusioning, but there is comfort in the apparent fact that the path to large and firm truths must lead through partial truths and misconceptions. Physics could hardly have produced an Einstein without first producing a Newton, or for that matter, an Aristotle and a Ptolemy.

Among the most central of our givens are words themselves, and their meanings, with which the child has a special concern. A perceptive study by Jean Piaget, *The Language and Thought of the Child,* shows that a large part of early speech is monologue in which the child works out, in more or less dramatic fashion, the significance of the objects and persons that he encounters. For no reason apparent to an observer, he repeats words and phrases over and over, as though to fix identities firmly in his own mind and to guarantee their authority in his own little world. Much of his verbal activity is *naming,* or what he will later come to call "defining"—attaching a set of characteristics to a word in order both to set it off from other words and to place it among them. At the same time, he organizes the nonverbal world under these verbal headings, giving it a coherence and neatness it could not have for him without words. Perhaps because words sustain so much of his familiarity with the world, he becomes remarkably tenacious about them by the time he is

9

seven or eight. Everyone knows the confusion and annoyance, even ex-
asperation, of discovering that people from other parts of the country call
doughnuts "crullers," milkshakes "frappes," or some such piece of nonsense. Why can't they use the right names? For the child does tend to
think of words and their meanings as absolutely, finally, almost magically
linked. His feelings on being confronted with a new usage or a foreign
language are likely to be somewhat like those of Jim, the runaway slave
in *The Adventures of Huckleberry Finn*:

> "Why, Huck, doan' de French people talk de same way we does?"
> "No, Jim; you couldn't understand a word they said—not a single
> word."
> "Well, now, I be ding-busted! How do dat come?"
> "I don't know, but it's so. I got some of their jabber out of a book.
> Spose a man was to come to you and say *Polly-voo-franzy*—what would
> you think?"
> "I wouldn' think nuff'n; I'd take en bust him over de head. Dat is, if he
> warn't white. I wouldn't 'low no nigger to call me dat."
> "Shucks, it ain't calling you anything. It's only saying do you know how
> to talk French."
> "Well, den, why couldn't he *say* it?"
> "Why, he *is* a-saying it. That's a Frenchman's *way* of saying it."
> "Well, it's a blame ridiculous way, en I doan' want to hear no mo'
> 'bout it. Dey ain' no sense in it."

Jim is obstinate, but not unusual, in his conviction that there is only one
right way to say a thing—witness the perennial jokes that depend for
humor on foreign or dialectal accents.

So jealously guarded are the conventions of word and meaning, not
only by children but by whole dialect communities, that this portion, at
least, of our given knowledge would seem heavily fortified against uncertainty and challenge. Yet troubles do arise in our use of words, serious
troubles that can become deeply imbedded in political or ideological
controversy, or sabotage any kind of intellectual machinery. A recent
school of philosophers, headed by the late Ludwig Wittgenstein, has
contended that most philosophical problems are simply "mental cramps,"
caused by malfunctioning of language. And a whole field, *semantics*, has
grown up around the theoretical and practical difficulties that beset
human beings when they use words; extremists within this movement
have even argued that war, neurosis, prejudice, and many of the most
onerous problems of human conduct have their roots in linguistic misunderstanding. Without acquiescing in such zealous overstatements, and
without airing the philosophical controversies that surround meaning,
we can still set it down as certain that no one aspiring to rationality in
thought, speech, or writing can afford the child's unquestioning confidence in words and meanings. Words need loving care and attention,

especially in the hands of the writer, whose whole enterprise depends for success upon the clarity, precision, and integrity with which he uses them. Defining, therefore, far from being a sterile academic exercise, is a necessary preliminary to writing even when the final draft will contain no definitions. In many, many undertakings so much hangs on the meanings of words that definition had best be brought out into the open.

1) THE USES OF DEFINITION

William James, the American psychologist and philosopher, once described an argument between two groups of people on a camping trip. Here is the problem they debated: a man is standing a few yards from a tree, and part way up the trunk, on the other side from the man, is a squirrel. The man moves around the tree trying to see the squirrel, but the squirrel keeps moving around the trunk, staying just opposite the man. Clearly the man goes around the tree, but does he go around the squirrel? One group said yes, one said no, both were equally convinced, and the argument, like the man and the squirrel, progressed in circles. James pointed out that the disagreement was not factual, but verbal. If "to go around something" means to progress in a circle around it, regardless of what *it* does in the middle, then the man does go around the squirrel. But if "to go around something" means to move from the front of it, to one side, to the back, to the other side, and finally to the front again, then the man does not go around the squirrel. Not all James's friends were content, but it seems clear that James had attacked the problem in the best possible way. If he did not "solve" it, in the sense of proving one side right, he at least *dis*solved the problem by showing that it was an unrewarding one unless couched in other terms. And of course he did so through definition.

The example is a trivial one, but the moral is not. Many puzzles of greater consequence create perplexity partly or entirely because of such confusions. Take for instance the old teaser as to whether a tree makes a sound if it falls in a deserted spot out of the hearing of man or animal. Or the still more ancient philosophical question about the reality or unreality of objects. Instances abound in more practical matters, too. Are viruses alive? That depends partly on the definition of "alive." Is Algeria entitled to independence? Any discussion of the issue must include a definition of political rights. Is such and such a law unconstitutional? The answer may hinge partly on the meaning of "unconstitutional," and it will almost certainly depend upon the definition of words in the Constitution and in previous court opinions. Whenever the facts are certain but the controversy still lumbers on unfruitfully, it is wise to take a fresh look at the key terms of the controversy and at their meanings. Students and others who like firm answers may weary of the rejoinder, "It's all a matter of definition." And indeed, the call for definition can be tedious, question-begging, and sophistical: not every dilemma will be resolved by a clarification of terms. But clarity of terms is essential to every important argument, and definition offers a powerful means of brushing away intellectual cobwebs.

Many questions, like those in the preceding paragraph, cannot even be intelligently posed without definition. Hopeless to ask how much poverty there is in the United States unless there is some acceptable definition of poverty. Especially in problems of classification, definition is a prerequisite. Thus, in deciding which organizations were subversive, the Attorney General's office first had to define "subversive," implicitly or explicitly (it defined the word too loosely, to many people's taste). A well-known House committee decides at intervals whether certain activities are "un-American." The censors, and sometimes the courts, are asked to determine what books and movies are "obscene" or "blasphemous." As these decisions have serious practical consequences, so do the definitions they incorporate. Meteorologists cannot say how many *hurricanes* there were last year without definition; nor can critics decide when the *novel* arose as a literary form; nor teachers which students have done *satisfactory* work; nor the man on the street whether what he is about to do is *wrong*. Problems of all sorts, including many that students write about, are likely to become manageable only after a certain amount of defining.

Dilemmas, questions, and problems of classification often call for definition as a means to an end; some difficulties faced by the writer call for definition as an end in itself. Perhaps he is uneasy about the popular use of a certain word—as the architect Richard Neutra was about the verb "own." Neutra thought it absurd to speak of a man as owning a house that was built, not for his individual needs, but to the specifications of a mass-produced stereotype, a house with no privacy in a row of identical houses, a house with a thirty-five-year mortgage. Ownership should imply more psychological control and more personal involvement than that, he argued. His problem was specifically one of definition, or rather of redefinition.

Similarly, a writer may wish to propose a new definition of a term in common use, even though the conventional definition is not so much wrong as incomplete or puzzling. This happens often in science: in a sense, men knew for a long time what electricity was, but scientists could not rest content with the layman's definition. In humbler pursuits, too, conceptual reform often comes with redefinition. There was a revolution in social work and penal practices when theorists began to think of a

criminal not as an inherently bad man, but as the product of his environment. And definitions of education continue to proliferate, though everyone knows what education is, after a fashion. To define such terms is to
attack conceptual and practical matters at their center.

Now and then the writer encounters a phenomenon, a complex of
events, a way of behaving or thinking, which has persisted for some
time and been vaguely noticed, but which has never been isolated,
fenced in, and given a label. If he wishes to concentrate his attention on
such a phenomenon, to analyze it, and to understand it, he will save a
great deal of inconvenience and verbosity by *naming* it. There have
always, no doubt, been people who washed their hands every ten minutes,
or couldn't stop chewing their nails, or just had to touch every other
lamp post, but the psychologist who gathered such quirks and oddities
together under the heading "compulsive" did a service to his colleagues
and to users of the language generally by providing a shorthand term
and a definition. And innovation of this sort can often be much more
than a procedural shortcut. Freud, by coining and applying "repression,"
the "Oedipus complex," the "id," the "death wish," and other terms,
opened the door on a whole new way of understanding the human mind,
though the patterns of behavior referred to by his neologisms were
probably as ancient as the family. To name and define is to reinterpret,
as well as to reduce complexity.

Sometimes, too, naming and defining are ways of overcoming newness
and strangeness. History sometimes repeats itself. But it also dazzles the
observer with novel arrangements of people and institutions, which only
become "thinkable" as names and definitions are minted and pass into
currency. "Cold war," "iron curtain," "balance of terror"—terms like
these, though they sometimes lead to oversimplification, have helped
postwar Americans to orient themselves within the turmoil of move and
countermove brought on by the rise to power of Soviet Russia and the
development of atomic weapons. Similarly, an obscure social upheaval
assumed new clarity and shape for outsiders when Jack Kerouac labeled
and defined the "beat generation." (In fact, one doubts that the movement itself would have flourished so briskly without the rallying point
of a title.) The chance to make the new familiar through language does
not present itself only to public men and novelists; even a student
grappling with an assigned theme is likely to find that some obstacles
melt away if he confronts them with name and definition.

The need for defining may also arise, not from the encounter with
experience, but from the necessity of making words behave properly.
Perhaps the writer wishes to introduce a technical term, say "entropy,"
one with which his readers may be unfamiliar. Clearly, if the word is to
perform its function for him, he must define it before he proceeds. Or

perhaps he wants to restrict the meaning of a common word to suit his purposes. It is within his rights, in an essay on traffic deaths, to use the word "accident" to mean "collision caused by a driver's carelessness or miscalculation" (thereby excluding murder, suicide, mechanical failure, etc.); but, if he takes this liberty with the word, he has an obligation to spell out for the reader just how much he has narrowed down the usual meaning, an obligation to define "stipulatively," as we shall call it. Again, it often happens that a writer imports a term from another field and uses it metaphorically or analogically in his own. Thus Matthew Arnold christened the English middle class "Philistines," and literary critics have come to speak of the "tension" in a poem between two attitudes, image clusters, patterns of structure, and so on. Since a metaphor or analogy never creates an exact equivalence, the writer who first takes such a leap must make it clear how much and how little of the original meaning he has carried along with him. These are procedures which will from time to time concern every writer except the most slavishly conventional; in bending language to one's special purposes it is often expedient to define.

Definition has a common use, too, in studies of other writers' thoughts. It would be difficult to describe the theme of Book I of *The Faerie Queene* without knowing what Spenser meant by "grace." Such concepts can be so central to the outlook of a man or an age that they deserve full-scale definition. Whole books have been devoted to the idea of progress, Shakespeare's concept of nature, the notion of romanticism, and so forth. In literary criticism, intellectual history, and philosophy, a great deal depends on understanding precisely how men have used their favorite terms, for the structures of human belief are accessible to the student only through scrutiny of the words men use to express those beliefs.

And (to make an end of this survey) defining serves the writer well even when he does it privately, never committing his definition to paper. For his very competence with language will be in part a consequence of adequate control over words and meanings. To say this is not simply to say that a writer should have a "big vocabulary." Although his vocabulary is immense, he may still confuse "infer" with "imply," or fail to understand the subtle distinction between "ethics" and "morality." He may commit stylistic blunders such as writing "this mistake and other ideas"— which he might avoid by simply defining "mistake" and "idea" for himself. He may overlook the difference in suggestiveness between "obedience" and "servility." And in general, his style will be flabby, wavering, and unpersuasive unless he is attuned to the intricacies of meaning that surround his words. Nor can his thought be lucid if it must wallow in vague and ambiguous language. The writer who protests, "You understood me, even if I didn't use the right word" is fooling himself and shirking the arduous job of writing plainly. Similarly, the writer who claims, "I know what I mean, but I can't put it into words" is mistaking a half-formed intuition for a fully explicit thought. Of course all writers, to one degree or another, possess a "feeling" for the words of their native languages; but even the most accomplished poet or novelist must frequently stop and ponder the appropriateness of this or that word. The neophyte will never grow as a writer without a constant effort to master the words he half-knows, and to study those with which he is barely acquainted: in short, a constant effort to define, if only for himself.

2) *DEFINING OR DESCRIBING*

The reader may have noticed that under the heading of definition we have included at least three different sorts of activity. In common parlance, one defines *words*. That is, the definer proffers a word or combination of words which serve as a near-equivalent of the word in question, plus some rules of usage. Definitions of this kind are what we might call *formal* (philosophers call them *nominal* definitions); they place the word to be defined in its proper context of linguistic conventions, and in their pure form they seem to have little to do with the world outside language. On the other hand, surely the man who asks for a definition of "existentialism" or "organism" is not asking simply for a verbal stand-in. He wants to know something about the real world, about the characteristics that distinguish existentialism from other schools of thought or an organism from other conglomerations of matter. He wants a *descriptive* definition (a *real* definition, in philosophical terms).

A little analysis will show that the distinction is far from rigid or absolute. To define "pique" as "an emotion like anger, but less strong— akin to annoyance" is to define both descriptively and formally, to give information both about linguistic conventions and about emotions. Which category a definition belongs to depends not so much on the form it takes as on the need it answers. The definition above might be considered formal in response to the question "What does the word 'pique' mean?" and descriptive in answer to the question "What is pique?"

The issue is further complicated by the fact that some definitions seem to be of a third type: they point to facts about the meaning associated with a word in someone's mind. Such definitions might be called *mentalistic;* they would be likely to occur in answer to the questions "What did eighteenth-century critics mean by 'decorum'?" or "What is Plato's concept of justice?" or to the question, "How do most people understand the word 'pique'?" Mentalistic definitions are usually recognizable by their having reference to particular users of language, but they, too, shade imperceptibly into the other types.

That there should be three kinds of definition, and that they should overlap and blend into one another is not surprising, given the nature and use of language. For words take their meanings from three different but interlocking relationships, which might be schematized like this:

1) word ——— other words

  (relationships such as synonymy, antonymy, inclusion, exclusion, grammatical substitutability, syntactical function, etc.)

2) word ——— world

  (relationships such as applicability to certain objects or circumstances, reference, appropriateness, etc.)

3) word ——— speaker, writer, and audience

  (relationships such as using the word "*x*" to mean *y,* understanding *y* by the word "*x,*" being reminded of *y* by the word "*x,*" etc.)

Around these relationships and their relevance to what we know as "meaning," disputes have flourished for centuries. But communication goes on unimpeded by philosophical uncertainties, and so does most defining. On the whole it is safe for the writer to leave semantic theory unexplored, as long as he makes sure, when he defines, what kind of question he intends his definition to answer. He should know whether the problem is mainly one of descriptive defining, formal defining, or mentalistic defining, or of all three. If he can be clear about this to himself and his reader, he will not trip over philosophical hurdles.

3) CONVENTIONAL DEFINING

What we have said about the various needs that press a writer to define and about the complexities of meaning should make it abundantly clear that defining may require more than a word, more than a sentence or paragraph, more even than an entire volume. Even in the face of such elaborateness, much can be done to make defining efficient and comprehensible. If it could not, men would move blindly in the welter of experience, and, moreover, would find themselves frequently unable to transmit to others or receive from them any account of experience at all.

But of course defining is, to begin with, a procedure with a firm place in daily life and ordinary discourse. A conventional (and highly useful) pattern of definition has grown up, one that may conveniently serve as our starting point. Roughly, the pattern is that of an equation, an equivalence between an unknown and something known, between an *x* and a *y* where *y* is something that is already familiar. This is the pattern most often found in dictionaries—an assertion of the sameness in meaning conveyed by two or more words:

> **institution,** n. 1. an organization or establishment for the promotion of a particular object, usually one for some public, educational, charitable, or similar purpose. 2. the building devoted to such work. 3. a concern engaged in some activity, as a retail store, broker, or insurance company. 4. *Sociol.* an organized pattern of group behavior, well-established and accepted as a fundamental part of a culture, such as slavery. 5. any established law, custom, etc. 6. *Colloq.* any familiar practice or object. 7. act of instituting or setting up; establishment: the institution of laws. 8. *Eccles.* a. the origination of the Eucharist, and enactment of its observance, by Christ. b. the investment of a clergyman with a spiritual charge.
>
> *American College Dictionary*

Even conventional definition, as the example shows, can be a highly refined procedure; and, as our experience with the use of dictionaries, especially the best dictionaries, makes clear, it is not always so illuminating as might be hoped. For one thing, a good dictionary presents many y's for the x whose meaning its user wishes to know, and he is sometimes perplexed as to which he is to choose. More than that, the y's themselves may often be as unfamiliar to him as the x from which he begins. If, for example, he finds that an equivalent for "profuse" is "prodigal," he may plunge further into darkness; conversely, if he finds "imperturbable" equated with "not perturbable," he gets nowhere at all. Reliable dictionaries, of course, have many ways of obviating the awkwardness illustrated by the equivalents, or synonyms, for "profuse" and "imperturbable." Yet their best devices will often not be helpful enough unless the user understands the nature of the process of defining.

A definition has two initial components: the term-to-be-defined (*definiendum*) and the defining term (*definiens*). In the example given above, "institution" is the *definiendum,* and each part of the lengthy series of words and phrases following it is a *definiens,* a defining term. It is immediately apparent that the *definiendum* is usually limited to a single grammatical unit, generally to a single word. To ask, "What is an ecclesiastical institution?" is probably to imply that one already knows what "institution" means and wants only to know what it means when it is modified by the word "ecclesiastical," or it is to ask for two definitions, one for each word in the *definiendum.* Certainly it would be bizarre to ask for a definition of "all the ecclesiastical institutions in seventeenth-century Italy which were neither corrupt nor moribund," or any such oversized *definiendum.* The simplicity required in the *definiendum,* however, is neither expected nor desired in the *definiens.* In it one may properly anticipate more than one word, more than one grammatical unit, more than one logical division.

Consider this simple definition: "A gig is a two-wheeled, horse-drawn passenger vehicle." The *definiens* is composed of four informative expressions: "two-wheeled," "horse-drawn," "passenger," and "vehicle." Of the four, one is a noun, and refers to a class of objects meant to include the referent of the *definiendum*. If it alone is used ("A gig is a vehicle"), there is indeed a definition, and for some purposes that definition may be adequate. That it may not be, this colloquy makes apparent:

Inquirer: What is a gig?

Respondent: A gig is a vehicle.

I: Oh, I understand. A gig and a wagon are the same thing.

R: Not at all. A gig is designed to carry passengers.

I: Well, a wagon may carry passengers.

R: Yes, but a gig is designed especially to carry passengers, and a wagon is designed to carry freight rather than, or in addition to, passengers.

I: Well, then, a gig is a special kind of wagon.

R: No, it's really not a wagon at all. Its particular function is different. A wagon carries passengers only incidentally. That is not what it is designed to do.

I: I think I understand you now. A gig is a carriage.

R: That's more like it, but there is another difference I forgot to mention. Most carriages have four wheels and a gig has only two.

I: Is a gig, then, like a bicycle?

R: Not at all. For one thing, the two wheels on a gig are joined by an axle and operate in parallel; the two wheels of a bicycle are placed one behind the other and are connected not by an axle but by a rigid frame which permits one to follow the other or, as a matter of fact, one to precede the other. Besides that, I said passengers, not passenger.

I: My brother and I often ride together on a bicycle.

R: True, but a gig is *designed* to carry more than one passenger, and a bicycle is not.

I: *Must* there be more than one passenger in a gig?

R: No, there need not be, but a gig is designed to accommodate more than one, though generally not more than two or three without crowding. It has only one seat, and a carriage has one or more.

I: Now I know what you mean. When I was in Japan I rode in gigs, but the name used for them there is "rickshaws."

R: A rickshaw is a different thing because it is pulled along by a human being. A gig is pulled by a horse.

I: Could an ox draw it—or a dog?

R: Neither one, I think. An ox requires a yoke, and a gig has shafts; and the shafts are too far apart and too far raised from the ground to be attached by harness to a dog. At any rate, a gig is designed to be drawn by a horse.

I: I conclude, then, that a gig is a vehicle for one or more passengers, operating on two wheels joined by an axle, and drawn by a horse. Why didn't you say so in the first place?

In short, the task of definition is far from complete when only the class term has been supplied.

The example is not so preposterous as it may seem in the form of a dialogue. The backing and filling illustrate quite accurately the mental process of framing a definition, and it is to avoid such roundaboutness in exposition that a pattern of formal definition is useful. Compressed, the *definiens* turns out to have two parts: in addition to the *class term* (vehicle), it needs one or more *distinguishing* terms to set it off from other objects (wagon, carriage, bicycle, rickshaw) in the same class. The defining term, then, is a composite. It names (a) what the referent of the defined term has in common with other objects (class term) and (b) what differentiates it from other objects in the same class (distinguishing terms).

If the Respondent had first answered the Inquirer's question by saying, "A gig is a thing," the process would, of course, have been even longer. From this one may infer that the class to be used in the defining term should be as limited as it can be without excluding "gig," the *definiendum*. The limitation can be stated in this way: the class word of the *definiens* should be of the order of generality *next above* the *definiendum*. To find that class word may in itself be no easy matter, but unless it, or one near it, is found, the definer makes for himself exactly the kind of difficulty the Respondent would have had with the Inquirer had he started with "thing" instead of with "vehicle."

Selection of the distinguishing terms presents similar difficulties. The Respondent might have described the vehicle as "made of wood and metal," for instance, but had he done so he would have added little that is helpful, since wood and metal are markedly less specific properties of the object he has in mind than are its two-wheeledness or its limited carrying capacity or its mode of locomotion. On the other hand, if the Respondent had added the distinguishing term, "with red leather upholstery," he would have erred in the direction of being *too* specific, for not all gigs are so nattily equipped. The general rule for choice of distinguishing terms is that they should be the ones that most strikingly set off the object referred to by the *definiendum* from other objects in the same class.

One more part of the definition requires attention. What of the equation sign between the *definiendum* and the *definiens*, of the word "is" in the original definition of "gig" and in the definition finally arrived at? Considering the false leads and the tediousness of that definition, one might say that it more nearly represents an intention than a certainty. The definer intends, when he is done defining, that the expressions on each side of the word "means" or the copula ("is") will balance perfectly, like the two pans of a scale in which one might measure out a quantity of potash by putting a metal weight of known quantity in one pan and sifting potash into the other until the indicator of the scale rests at dead center. Since measuring an amount of potash is very much simpler than measuring words, it is natural to regard with suspicion this indication of equivalence between the two sides of a definition. Indeed, it is not uncommon to hear people say that there are no such things as synonyms or synonymous expressions in language and that precise definition is, therefore, impossible. For the practicing writer such an assertion is academic, to say the least. He is much less concerned to know whether or not a precise definition is possible than to know what degree of precision is necessary for the answer demanded by the question "What is x?" Potash, too, can be more or less accurately measured in truckloads, on a feed-store weighing scale, or in delicate balances in the laboratory.

If uneasiness about the copula persists, one may be tempted to look on it less as a statement of equivalence than as a command, as though the definer were saying not "x is y" or "x means y" but "Use x to mean y." This restricted kind of definition—*stipulative definition,* as it is usually called—is very useful and must eventually be examined with care. For the present, however, it is best to confine attention to those definitions that assert, rather than command one to accept, an equivalence between terms and, by inference, between the objects to which they refer.

We have taken nouns ("gig," "institution") for our sample *definienda,* and indeed, the writer will more frequently have cause to define a noun than one of the other parts of speech. But notice that the conventional method of definition serves as well for verbs, adjectives, and adverbs, with slight modifications:

> To *gerrymander* is to set the boundaries of political districts in a way strongly favorable to one party, by arranging them in grotesque and complicated shapes.
>
> *Arrogant* means proud and confident to excess.
>
> *Decidedly* means pronouncedly, definitely.

In dealing with adjectives and adverbs, the definer is likely to offer one or more near-synonyms, rather than a class term and several distinguishing terms. And with pronouns, auxiliary verbs, articles, prepositions, and so on, the conventional method breaks down more seriously—consult dictionary entries for some of these words to see what subterfuges are necessary. Still, nobody but a lexicographer has much occasion to define "the," "could," "in," and the like, and for most practical purposes the standard form is adequate:

$$\textit{definiendum} — \genfrac{}{}{0pt}{}{\text{``is''}}{\text{``means''}} — \text{class term} + \underbrace{\text{distinguishing terms.}}$$

definiens

4) LEXICAL DEFINING

Most people have widest acquaintance with the definitions that appear in dictionaries, that is, with *lexical* definitions, and these bear special consideration. The task of a lexicographer, contrary to popular belief, is mainly one of reporting, not prescribing. He is concerned with recording the actual meanings and uses of words, noting, to be sure, which uses are colloquial, slangy, characteristic of the uneducated, and so forth, but not dictating the way language *should* be used. He presents the meanings of a word that have had or still have currency, those that various men at various times and for various purposes have used. An abridged dictionary records as many meanings as suit its purposes and size; an unabridged dictionary purports to record all the meanings that have sound claim to attention, all that have had enough currency at any time to be considered a legitimate part of the language.

One of the editorial consultants of the *American College Dictionary* (abridged) reports that he and his colleagues tabulated 832 meanings of the word "run," but that they included only 104 of those meanings in the desk dictionary which they helped to compile. The reason for their making so drastic a reduction is obvious enough, but the grounds on which they chose one meaning rather than another for inclusion may be less evident. They might, of course, have excluded all meanings no longer current, but to do so would have been to reduce the usefulness of the dictionary for anyone dealing with the writing of past centuries. They might have limited their choice to meanings common in the general use of language, barring all technical usages. Or they might have made more or less arbitrary choices, setting down the meanings they approved or those which the etymology of the word seemed to justify. The inadequacy of any of those criteria is readily apparent. What lexicographers actually do in such a case is attempt to determine which meanings are most common in general discourse, and then to make special provision for technical, rare, purely colloquial, and dialectical meanings. If they have done their work well, the meanings they record are all proper, the equivalences true equivalences, and the definitions "good" ones.

Unabridged dictionaries are of two kinds: (1) those that record the full range of meanings detected by lexicographers, arranging them in groups to indicate similarity; (2) those that attempt to locate the earliest appearance of each meaning and to record its persistence at subsequent periods. Both kinds may, and generally do, document the meanings they list by brief quotations. The foremost American unabridged dictionary is *Webster's New International,* a large one-volume work which not only contains a much greater number of meanings for each word than an abridged dictionary but also defines a much greater number of words. Even more extensive and elaborate is the *Oxford English Dictionary*, the great historical dictionary of the English language. Its thirteen folio-size volumes make it possible to scan in one place the entire history of a word, and it is for that reason an invaluable resource for students and scholars alike. Some idea of its approach to the problem of defining can be gathered from a greatly abbreviated account of its treatment of the highly ambiguous word "nice," a word so variously used today that one would be hard put to answer quickly a demand for its definition. Since the OED is a dictionary built on historical principles, it is appropriate to rephrase the defining question to read not "What does 'nice' mean?" but "What did, and does, 'nice' mean?" A few (perhaps one-sixth) of the answers to that question are set down here:

Foolish, stupid, senseless. *Obs.* (Common in 14th and 15th c.) **a.** Of persons.

> 1387) Trevisa *Higden* (Rolls) VI. 23 He made the lady so mad and so nice that she worshipped him as the greatest prophet of God Almighty.

Wanton, loose-mannered; lascivious. *Obs.* **c.** Of dress: Extravagant, flaunting. *Obs.*

> 1563) *Homilies* II. *Idolatry* III. (1640) 72 An Image with a nice and wanton apparell and countenance.

Slothful, lazy, indolent. *Obs. rare.* **b.** Effeminate, unmanly. *Obs. rare.*

> 1598) Florio, *Paranimpha* . . . an effeminate, nice, milkesop, puling fellow.

Fastidious, dainty, difficult to please, esp. in respect of food or cleanliness; also in good sense, refined, having refined tastes.

> 1782) Cowper *Mut. Forbearance* 20 Some people are more nice than wise.

d. Precise or strict in matters of reputation or conduct; punctilious, scrupulous, sensitive.

> 1887) Baring-Gould *Red Spider* xvii, I should get it back again . . . and not be too nice about the means.

Not obvious or readily apprehended; difficult to decide or settle; demanding close consideration or thought; intricate. **b.** Minute, subtle; also of differences, slight, small.

> 1870) Howson *Metaph. St. Paul* ii. 41 When we desire to appreciate the nicer shades of meaning.

Agreeable; that one derives pleasure or satisfaction from; delightful.

> 1837) Maj. Richardson Brit. Legion ix. (ed. 2) 220 The Commandant, whom I subsequently found to be a very nice fellow.

The soundness of such definitions is beyond dispute simply because the cited text is evidence that the word once had the meaning attributed to it by the lexicographer (historical lexicographers do occasionally make mistakes in definition, but their citations give the dictionary user a chance to spot any lapses). The importance of appreciating the historical "truth" of a definition is more apparent for reading, of course, than it is for writing. A man writes, for the most part, with his own age in mind, and he defines words with the assumption that his readers will know that he means their definition to be taken as referring to his and his readers' present existence. If for any reason he prefers to use a word in a manner no longer common, he prefixes to his use of it a reminder: "When I call Miss Grundy a spinster, I use the word *in its now almost forgotten sense,* not of an unmarried woman past her prime, but of one who makes her living at the spinning wheel." But the reading of books from other periods is not made easy in this way. In dealing with them, the reader must always be aware that meanings do change and that his understanding of a passage depends on his knowing the words in it as their author knew them. To read "humorous" in these lines from Kyd's *Spanish Tragedy* as though it means "amusing" is to miss the point altogether:

> *My Lord, be not dismay'd for what is pass'd;*
> *You know that women oft are humorous.*

Kyd's use of "humorous" is conventional for his time, and a check on the meaning of that word in the sixteenth century will provide the information needed to make the passage intelligible. Meaning in this instance, however difficult it may be to come at, is literal. When it is more than literal, when, for instance, a pun is involved, the reader may have to resort to historical knowledge of other kinds, to etymology, for example, as in these lines from Milton's *Paradise Lost:*

> *As we erewhile, astounded and amaz'd*
> *No wonder, fall'n such a pernicious highth.*
> (1, 281–2)

Both "pernicious" and "astounded" are serious puns; both mean what they still mean today in common usage, but both have additional meanings drawn from their Latin ancestry. "Astounded" comes from *ex-tonare* and refers to being struck by, or hurled out by, thunder, a reference to the battle in which Satan was cast out of heaven by God. "Pernicious" comes from *per-nex* and means "through death" or "death-giving," a description of the "highth" much more impressive than one is likely to understand if the word is taken only to mean "bad" or "undesirable."

Now if historical definitions are either true or false, it might seem that they should provide no particular complexities. Faced with the problem of knowing what is meant by a word in an old text, one might think it necessary only to determine the range of meanings possible for the word, as of the time in which it was used and of the context in which it appears, and then make a choice among those meanings. Yet it does not take much reflection to discover that the procedure is not so simple as it sounds. Even if the choice among many meanings could be made without difficulty, another characteristic of words—*connotation*—makes them so elusive that even the best dictionary cannot nearly exhaust their meanings.

5) DENOTATION AND CONNOTATION

When a man says "I'm going home now," the person to whom he addresses his remark understands it well enough if he knows that home is "the place where a person (or family) lives; one's dwelling place; specifically, *a*) the house, apartment, and so on where one lives or is living temporarily; living quarters. *b*) the region, city, state, and so forth where one lives." (*Webster's New World Dictionary*, meaning 1). This definition, like most dictionary definitions, gives the *denotation* of the word, that part of its meaning which is essential. Another way of putting it is to say that this denotative definition names a characteristic (it might have named more than one) which all homes share: a place simply is not a home if no one lives (or has lived or is about to live) there.

But a man who says to his host, "This place is a second home to me," does not mean that he is settling in permanently. The host would have good cause to become alarmed, that is, if he understood "home" in its denotative sense alone. For the speaker is drawing on the *connotations* of "home" in expressing his gratitude. He may have in mind such things as warmth, intimacy, security, comfort, familiarity, and peace, or even such things as spaciousness, the presence of children, a cat, the sound of a lawnmower, the smell of cooking, a creaking stair. To be sure, peace is a stranger to many actual homes; the air may crackle with tension, and there may be elevators instead of stairs. Lacking every one of these attributes, a place is still a home as long as people live there, however miserably. Yet the word "home" does suggest security, comfort, and children; these connotations have fastened onto it firmly and are there for the writer to draw on or to ignore at his peril.

The distinction between denotation and connotation may become clearer with another example. Take this definition: "Mother" means "female animal parent." "Female animal parent" is what we loosely call the "denotative meaning" of the word "mother." How far from being complete it is, one has no trouble in discovering. In the 1930's, for instance, Gertrude Stein and Virgil Thomson wrote an opera about the great suffragette, Susan B. Anthony, and to it they gave the title, *The Mother of Us All*. Now it does not even occur to us to take only the denotative meaning of "mother" in this instance. We recognize readily enough that the word "mother" in the title is used figuratively, that it is meant to imply that, in one or more ways, Susan B. Anthony stands in relationship to those who have followed her as a female animal parent stands in relationship to her offspring. What we do is desert, or minimize, the denotative meaning and jump directly to one or more of the connotations of "mother." And, although those connotations are many, we are not very likely to go wrong in making the jump. We may have to see, or read, the opera to know which ones of the many connotations Miss Stein had in mind, but, for this word, at least, the range of possibilities has more similarity than dissimilarity: protector, inspirer, lover, encourager—such are the connotations that immediately come to mind. Perhaps Miss Stein had no more than a slight extension of the denotative meaning in mind, a "parent" not of children but of ideas or conceptions of freedom and human independence. When a man speaks of the "mother country" or of the "fatherland," he recognizes in the same way that the words we use have connotative as well as denotative character. When adolescents say that they no longer want to be "mothered," they are protesting not against parenthood but against activities which they associate with it. In ordinary discourse, then, connotative meanings are projections beyond denotative meanings, neither better nor worse but different.

How extensive can the projections be? Clearly the question has no firm answer, but one thing seems certain: no one who speaks and writes can expect his audience to respond to connotations that rise from his own purely personal experience. His mother may have spoken with a lisp or carried a pocket full of lemon drops or been a good automobile mechanic, so that the word "mother" always reminds him of these things, yet they are not connotations of the word. Some people associate colors with numbers, but orange is not a connotation of "four." Connotations, properly speaking, include only those associations with words which are part of their public accompaniment, the range of suggestiveness that can be called upon in communication. For everyone, some words have *private* connotations, and the writer may occasionally wish to exploit such meanings for a special purpose, or even to mention them in a definition. But when he does he should be aware that he has stepped over the boundary of language as a public domain, and into the formless no-man's-land of introspection and word-play, where the reader cannot follow him without instructions.

Private associations aside, connotations are capricious enough on their own account. Some words, for instance, lend themselves more readily than others to the development of connotative meanings. Why that is so, it is not easy to say. Familiarity undoubtedly plays an important role in the process, but that role is not definitive: "house" is a familiar enough word, but it has few connotations, compared to "home." Nor is the historical development of a word necessarily the determinant of its connotative activity: "egregiously" derives from the Latin *e-* plus *grex, gregis,* meaning "out of the herd" or "outstanding." Through the seventeenth century it was used primarily as an adverb of admiration and praise; gradually, perhaps through irony at first, the word began to mean "outstandingly" in a pejorative, or unflattering, sense. Today it is almost exclusively used to mean "monstrously" or "flagrantly" or "outrageously."

The example just cited suggests that connotations may have an effect on denotations, that what is more or less vaguely suggested by a word may in time affect the "meaning" of the word itself. For the writer, this fact is of less importance than the fact that connotations do cling to nearly every word he uses. By remembering this he can save himself some blunders—those, for instance, that often accompany the effort to achieve gentility by using euphemisms such as "facilities" for "toilet," and (in public school jargon) "exceptional" for "retarded," or for plain "stupid." And he must recognize that, even in the act of defining, he deals with the volatility of language, with its power to suggest more than it states. Defining is, in part, a procedure for reducing vagueness in statement; it calls for precise selection of defining terms, and there is no possibility of precision without respect for the connotative, as well as the denotative, activity of words.

6) STIPULATIVE DEFINING

The statement that defining is a procedure for reducing vagueness is itself a definition, but it is an imperfect one. A definition may do more than reduce vagueness; it may also resolve, or remove, ambiguity. The definition of "institution" in an earlier section of this chapter offers many meanings for the word, some of them quite different from others. Since all of the meanings are proper ones, it is clear that the use of the word "institution" in a sentence might very well produce confusion for the reader or hearer. For that reason there must be devices for indicating a choice among the many meanings—devices, in short, for eliminating ambiguity. One of those devices deserves special attention.

It has already been mentioned in connection with the copula or sign of equivalence in a definition. In its usual form, a definition is a statement and is, therefore, either true or false. It is either true or false that "gig" means "a two-wheeled, horse-drawn passenger vehicle." But it is also either true or false that "gig" means "a narrow, light ship's boat for oars or sail," "a wooden box used to draw miners up and down a pit or shaft," "an instrument used for spearing fish," "a textile machine which raises nap on cloth," and "a top." Actually, "gig" means all of those things; each of the definitions is a good definition, each of the defining statements a true statement. Yet it is obvious that, in a given sentence, "gig" is not likely to mean more than one of the things named above.

To make clear which of the meanings is meant, a writer must sometimes resort to *stipulative definition*. And to indicate the kind of defining he is about to do, he may find it necessary to make an explicit announcement: "By 'gig' let us mean 'instrument for spearing fish,' " or "Understand 'gig' to mean 'top'." The need for stipulative definition may occur wherever a word has several distinct meanings, and it is particularly valuable wherever a writer needs to distinguish between conventional and technical meanings of a word in common use.

Because stipulative definitions provide a convenient way for keeping discussion on a single track, they often tempt expositors more than they should. It is sometimes possible, for instance, to win an argument by insisting on a stipulative definition of a key term at one stage of the argument and then using different, and perhaps more inclusive, definitions at another stage. And it is also possible to confuse an opponent by stipulating so unusual a meaning for a key term that he cannot accustom himself to it in time to assemble his forces for reply. That is approximately what happens in a famous colloquy between Humpty Dumpty and Alice:

"I don't know what you mean by 'glory,' " Alice said.

Humpty Dumpty smiled contemptuously. "Of course you don't—till I tell you. I meant 'there's a nice knock-down argument for you!' "

"But 'glory' doesn't mean 'a nice knock-down argument,' " Alice objected.

"When I use a word," Humpty Dumpty said in rather a scornful tone, "it means just what I choose it to mean—neither more nor less."

"The question is," said Alice, "whether you *can* make words mean so many different things."

"The question is," said Humpty Dumpty, "which is to be master—that's all."

Alice was too much puzzled to say anything, so after a minute Humpty Dumpty began again. "They've a temper, some of them—particularly verbs, they're the proudest—adjectives you can do anything with, but not verbs. However, I can manage the whole lot of them! Impenetrability! That's what I say!"

"Would you tell me, please," said Alice, "what that means?"

"Now you talk like a reasonable child," said Humpty Dumpty, looking very much pleased. "I meant by 'impenetrability' that we've had enough of that subject, and it would be just as well if you'd mention what you mean to do next, as I suppose you don't mean to stop here all the rest of your life."

"That's a great deal to make one word mean," Alice said, in a thoughtful tone.

"When I make a word do a lot of work like that," said Humpty Dumpty, "I always pay it extra."

"Oh!" said Alice. She was too much puzzled to make any other remark.

LEWIS CARROLL, *Through the Looking Glass*

Humpty has solved the whole problem of defining with admirable facility and forthrightness, but perhaps he ought to pay extra not only to the words he finds so manipulable but also to Alice, who is in the uncomfortable position of having to make sense out of his conversation. The trouble with Humpty's stipulative definitions, if they can be dignified by such a name, is that they are entirely capricious and absurd. They will probably not be the same tomorrow, or an hour from now, as they are at this moment; and, no matter what they are now or later, they have meaning and usefulness only for Humpty. Most stipulative definitions are neither less permanent nor less public than lexical definitions; they are simply definitions chosen from the range of lexical definitions, and so chosen in order to exclude meanings inappropriate to the immediate purpose.

Some stipulative definitions, however, do stray away from all the accepted meanings of words, and they may on occasion do so with good reason. A writer sometimes finds himself wanting to talk about a phenomenon for which there is no convenient name; yet perhaps the concept he has in mind is close to one for which a word exists, and rather than coin a new term, he prefers to stretch the familiar one to meet his needs. Thus physicists use the term "work" in a sense related to some of its ordinary meanings, but considerably more precise (see page 32). And chemists define the word "salt" in an expanded sense to include, not just sodium chloride, but many similar compounds as well. For obvious reasons this kind of stipulative defining occurs most frequently in technical writing. The scientist or technologist is particularly interested in creating a vocabulary that conforms to his refined and deep insights into the workings of things, and he needs definitions far more exact than any established by casual usage. At the same time, his investigations often *begin* with the layman's vocabulary and concepts; besides, he may wish his findings to become incorporated in the stock of common lore and common speech. Hence he adapts a familiar word to his purposes, and, if his work is influential enough, his newly established meaning may take hold and persist alongside the other meanings of the word. If not, the stipulative definition can at least serve its purpose of the moment: to make discussion compact and precise. The same purpose often justifies stipulative defining in less exact fields, too. Literary critics imported the word "theme" from music criticism and employed it, of necessity, in a rather different sense. A central concept in existentialism is that of the "absurd"—though the absurdity referred to is far more consequential than the everyday incongruities and tomfooleries which the word ordinarily calls to mind.

Both stipulative defining and extensions of meaning without any explicit defining seem almost inevitable when a writer presses toward new knowledge or new firmness of thought. In any event, these resources are available to all; language is man's servant, not his master (Humpty was right, in a sense), and it must always be flexible enough to tolerate useful changes and accretions. The writer should remember, though, that when he defines stipulatively he lays certain obligations on himself: first, to guard against stipulations that contradict the whole weight of established usage, as Humpty's do; second, to make certain that his innovations are justifiable (nothing is more annoying to a reader than having to cope with dozens of bizarre or capricious innovations); third, to be consistent in his use of the words he defines stipulatively; and fourth, to see to it that his reader knows precisely how far he is departing from ordinary usage. If he observes these cautions, the writer can make stipulative definition a tool for full and rich expression of thought, even for discovery.

Since this book is concerned with writing in all its stages, from the puzzling over of a problem to its final delineation in clear and forceful prose, an additional word about the usefulness of stipulative definition is pertinent. Even when a person is only communicating with himself or "inquiring," stipulative definitions are often valuable. A problem in which all the terms seem to have more meanings than the writer can conveniently cope with at once may force him to limit one or more of the terms to a single meaning, arbitrarily chosen, in order to make any headway at all in the solution of the problem itself. If, for example, part of his problem is to decide whether or not *Pride and Prejudice* is a "sociological" novel, he may temporarily stipulate that "sociological" means "concerned with the solution of social problems." Having made a decision on the basis of that definition, he may stipulate that "sociological" means "concerned with depicting as exactly as possible a social problem" and then proceed to another decision. Next he may decide that "sociological" means "concerned with presenting a picture of society, or of a part of it, in a given time and place," and go on to a third decision. What he would *not* do, of course, and what Humpty Dumpty did do with his words, is stipulate that "sociological" means "divided into three parts" or "enjoying custard pie more than ice cream."

7) DEFINING IN THE NATURAL SCIENCES

More than once in the preceding pages, some mention has been made of the particular needs of "technical" writers. Although those needs are, in the main, fairly obvious, it is worth while to speculate briefly about the different demands on words, and therefore on the definition of words, that are made in the various intellectual disciplines. For the sake of convenience, the discussion makes use of a three-part division of those disciplines which has wide general acceptance: the natural (or physical) sciences, the social sciences, the humanities.

The natural sciences deal, insofar as such dealing is possible, with the world apart from man's experience of it. That is, they try to find out what is constant in the world, and to do so they try to separate matter from the sensations it produces in sentient beings (or, as in modern physics and in perception theory, to formulate laws that "build in," or allow for, the role of the observer). In order to make their measurements as precise as possible, they regularly attempt to reduce the world to quantities of this or that. In the little essay that follows, an English scientist discusses the way in which the common word "hard" is made useful for scientific measurement by strict exclusion of connotative meaning and careful transformation of denotative meaning into quantitative form.

WHAT "HARD" MEANS

In the last article I wrote about the way in which ordinary words change their meaning as they are used in science and technology, taking as an example the word "hot." All adjectives start as descriptions of qualities. They end up as descriptions of quantities, if they are taken over by science. A word like "big" or "long" is entirely relative. A mile is a long swim but a short walk, because an ordinary man often walks a mile, but seldom swims a mile. A man is large compared to a cat, and small compared to an elephant, and so on. This sort of contradiction does not trouble anyone but philosophers, because we are accustomed to measure lengths, and we all know what a foot or a mile means.

But we are in much greater difficulties with some other common adjectives such as "hard." Of course we use the word metaphorically, as when we talk of a hard question, meaning one which is difficult to answer, or hard X-rays, meaning rays which penetrate easily through matter. But I want to deal with the word in its ordinary sense, as when we say that iron is harder than butter. Everyone will agree that this is true. But it is not so easy to decide which of two pieces of iron is harder, and as a matter of fact there may be no definite answer to the question. When we come to accurate measurement, we find that the word "hard" has dozens of slightly different meanings.

The most usual test of hardness in steels is that of Brinell. A very hard steel ball of 10 millimetres diameter is pressed onto a steel plate for 30 seconds with a load of 3 tons. The hardness number decreases with the depth of the indentation.

Another test of hardness which generally agrees pretty well with the Brinell test is the weight which must be put on a diamond point in order that it should just produce a visible scratch when pulled sideways. But as soon as we use moving bodies to measure hardness things become very complicated. For example at a relative speed of 30 feet per second a disc of "soft" iron was cut by a steel tool: at 100 feet per second the disc cut the tool itself, and at 300 feet per second the disc cut quartz. In the same way hardness varies with temperature.

If we compare an ordinary hardened carbon tool steel and a high-speed tool steel at ordinary temperatures, the former is probably a little harder by the Brinell test. But at a dull red heat the high-speed steel is still hard, while the ordinary tool steel is about as soft as is copper at room temperature.

Hardness is also used as a measure of the amount of wear which a material will stand. But here again the details are very important. We may want to test how a metal stands up to rolling friction without lubricant. This is essential in tests of rails, and wheels of railway vehicles. Or we may want to know how a metal stands up to sliding abrasion, either with or without a film of oil. One steel may stand up better to rolling friction, and another to sliding friction. Here their differences in hardness probably depend on the fact that metals sliding over one another actually melt at the point of contact, so their properties at high temperatures become important.

Within a century or less we shall probably be able to calculate the various kinds of hardness with great exactitude from a knowledge of the forces between atoms. At present we can only do so very roughly. Probably the physicists of the future will be able to specify the different kinds of hardness very completely in terms of a few numbers.

It would be possible to deal in the same way with the meanings of various words such as toughness, elasticity, and brittleness, which are applied to solids. None of these can be expressed by a single number.

The properties of liquids are a good deal simpler than those of solids, and the properties of gases are simpler still, though anyone concerned with the design of aeroplanes finds even gases quite complicated enough. And when we come to such a property of material systems as life, the complications are of course vastly greater. Scientists are reproached because they cannot say in simple terms what life is. It is easy enough to point out differences between a dog or a cabbage and a stone or a machine. It is much harder to draw the line when we get down to the agents of smallpox and other diseases, which behave in some ways as if alive and in others as if dead. But if anyone reproaches science because it cannot yet give a complete account of life, it is a fair reply to ask him what he means by hardness, and how he would tell if one thing is harder than another.

J. B. S. HALDANE, *A Banned Broadcast and Other Essays* (London: Chatto & Windus, 1946).

Another definition, this time of the equally common word "work," makes the point even clearer by showing how the definition that is useful to the natural sciences may actually contradict ordinary usage, though not so blatantly as to call into question the choice of that word rather than another one.

WORK

We feel we have been doing more "work" when we have lifted 20 lb from the floor to a bench 1 ft high, than if we had lifted only 10 lb: and we feel it takes more work to lift 10 lb from the floor to a table 2 ft high, than to a bench 1 ft high. Such qualitative judgments may have been the starting point for the following quantitative definition:

The *work* done by a force F lb, constant in magnitude and direction, when it has moved its point of application a distance D ft along its own direction, is the product $F \times D$:

$$\text{Work} = \text{force} \times \text{distance}.$$

The unit of work is the foot-pound (ft-lb), a derived unit:

$$W \text{ (ft-lb)} = F \text{ (lb)} \times D \text{ (ft)}.$$

Note that this is a definition, not a physical law. Note also that it contradicts some of our experiences. If we lift 20 lb through 3 ft twenty times in succession, the definition says we are doing the same "work" each time, namely, 60 ft-lb, whereas we know our work gets harder as the task progresses. The same would be true if we tried to climb the stairs in the Hancock Building. The fact is that physics uses some of the words of the English language, "work" for instance, in a new and specialized sense entirely its own. Also we must not make physics say more than it does: "physics" is concerned with measurements of length, time, force, and derived quantities; it says nothing about sensations. Scientists know very little as yet about "biophysics" in general, and physiological fatigue in particular. (They are working at it, just as Leonardo da Vinci and Simon Steven and Galileo were working at understanding mechanics.)

PHILIPPE LECORBEILLER, *Natural Sciences I Syllabus* (Harvard University, 1951).

8) DEFINING IN THE SOCIAL SCIENCES

All critical writing, within or outside the natural sciences, aspires to precision in its definitions, and it would be foolish indeed to conclude that precision is unachievable except by the means congenial to science. There are other means of reaching toward exactness in definition, and it is with such other means that the social sciences and the humanities must do most of their work. The following passage from a work in sociology provides a good illustration:

Hardened institutional fabrics may . . . disintegrate and routine forms of life prove insufficient for mastering a growing state of tension, stress, or suffering. It is in such crises that Weber introduces a balancing conception for bureaucracy: the concept of "charisma."

Weber borrowed this concept from Rudolf Sohm, the Strassburg church historian and jurist. Charisma, meaning literally "gift of grace," is

used by Weber to characterize self-appointed leaders who are followed
by those who are in distress and who need to follow the leader because
they believe him to be extraordinarily qualified. The founders of world
religions and the prophets as well as military and political heroes are
the archetypes of the charismatic leader. Miracles and revelations, heroic
feats of valor and baffling success are characteristic marks of their stature.
Failure is their ruin.

> H. H. GERTH and C. WRIGHT MILLS, introduc-
> tion to *From Max Weber: Essays in Sociology*
> (New York: Oxford University Press, 1946).

The writers define the word "charisma," as Weber used it, by several
means: they indicate its provenience from the work of a church historian
and jurist, they refer to its etymology ("meaning literally 'gift of grace' "),
they explain in what situation Weber uses the word ("to characterize
self-appointed leaders who . . ."), they add examples of people who possess
the quality represented by the word they are defining ("founders of
world religion and . . . prophets as well as military and political heroes")
and, finally, they list achievements of those who possess it ("Miracles and
revelations, heroic feats of valor and baffling success . . .").

The main reason that defining in the social sciences is very different
from that in the natural sciences is quite obvious: the complexity of
relationships which the social scientist sets out to describe is often greater
and is not so readily reducible to simplicity. If the chemist needs to define
"catalyst," he can do so entirely in terms which have concrete and particular reference. But the social scientist who must define "prejudice" or
"motivation" or "progress" is faced both with the connotative activity of
words and with a phenomenon so intricate that it almost defies analysis.
Therefore he must refine as much as words will allow him to do and then
resort to supplementary devices of example, comparison, and so on to
finish the job.

9) DEFINING IN THE HUMANITIES

What is true of the social sciences is true of the humanities as long as
one is thinking of critical efforts to determine the meaning of a term.
Both areas of knowledge are most commonly treated in words rather than
in mathematical symbols or in operational demonstrations (like the
Brinell test cited by Haldane), and both must therefore rely on controlling rather than on ignoring the connotative activity of language.

In some ways, the problem in the humanities is even more difficult
than it is in the social sciences because so large a part of the critical
vocabulary used in discussing works of art is metaphorical. For each of
the arts there is a vocabulary that is particularly appropriate ("mass" in

sculpture, for instance, and "euphony" in poetry), but the specific vocabulary has never been adequate to meet critical needs. The tendency to borrow the words appropriate to one art for the description of another is therefore almost irresistible, and such borrowing immediately raises problems of definition. The word "texture" used to describe a piece of cloth is immediately comprehensible; used to describe one aspect of a painting, it calls up much the same response; but used to describe a passage of poetry, it obviously requires an imaginative translation from imagery of feeling to imagery of hearing. In the same way a translation from the imagery of hearing to the imagery of seeing is necessary when the word "tone" is used to describe painting. If these "translations" are left entirely to the whim of the reader, confusion is bound to occur, and it does indeed occur in some criticism. The careful critic may be unwilling, nonetheless, to abandon the suggestiveness of such words and will find himself constrained, therefore, to make stipulative definitions for them. These stipulative definitions he should reinforce as the social scientist reinforces his definitions—by example, allusion, comparison.

Our remarks may have implied that definition outside the natural sciences is always arduous, complex, and potentially vague. Not so. Clarity and conciseness are within the range of any practiced and intelligent writer, whatever his particular discipline. Perhaps it will be best to illustrate defining in the humanities with an example that is simple as well as adequate, though the *definiendum* is used metaphorically in literary criticism:

> *Atmosphere* is the mood pervading a literary work, setting up in the reader expectations as to the course of events, whether happy or (more commonly) disastrous. Shakespeare establishes the tense and fearful atmosphere of *Hamlet* by the terse and nervous dialogue of the opening; Coleridge engenders a strange compound of religious and superstitious terror by his manner of describing the initial scene of "Christabel"; and Hardy, in *The Return of the Native,* makes Egdon Heath an immense and brooding presence which reduces to pettiness and futility the human struggle for happiness for which it is the setting.
>
> M. H. ABRAMS, *A Glossary of Literary Terms,* based on the original version by Dan. S. Norton and Peters Rushton (New York: Holt, Rinehart and Winston, Inc., 1957).

Abrams begins with a compact definition in conventional form; the first sentence alone pins down the term rather neatly. But the examples are by no means superfluous. The first two suggest two different ways of building atmosphere (dialogue and description). The third indicates how important a function atmosphere can have in a literary work. And all three explain the concept further by illustrating the language critics use to speak of atmosphere ("tense and fearful," "compound of religious and superstitious terror," "immense and brooding presence"). The only way for a reader to go much beyond the understanding offered by this brief definition would be to make his own extended study of atmosphere in literary works. If the final test of a definition is that, at its conclusion, both the definer and the person for whom the word is being defined are in agreement about its meaning, then successful definition is possible in any field of inquiry.

10) *PATTERNS OF DEFINITION*

Such examples make it possible to move away from the somewhat confining formula of conventional definition and look at the process of defining in the fullness that is valuable in writing. This is not to suggest that the standard formulation is useless; in one way or another, a definer is constantly pressed back to it, not only to make clear to others what he means but to make meaning clear to himself. It is only to say that good exposition employs methods that are various beyond the power of any simple formula to describe. Many of the means of definition appropriate to expository writing have already been illustrated, but a brief discussion of them, in orderly fashion, will perhaps be helpful.

The simplest in form is also the one most common to an abridged dictionary: *definition by synonym*. Putting aside the claim that no two words mean the same, one can recognize in synonyms an essential device for conveying meaning. To say that "heroism" means "bravery" does not indeed exhaust the possibilities of meaning for the word "heroism," but it directs the mind effectively toward one range of possible meanings. Anyone who knows what "bravery" means, but not "heroism," would at least be led part way to understanding by such a definition. And, after all, *no* definition could take him all the way: only a full acquaintance with the behavior of the word could do that. Synonyms are useful in defining, and the search for semantic perfection should not make the perfectionist lose sight of that fact.

Where synonyms do not satisfy because the *definiens* is as little agreed upon or as hard to pin down as the *definiendum, definition by analysis* will help. This is the kind of definition used in the discussion of "gig" above, one in which the *definiens* includes mention of the class of objects to which the *definiendum* belongs and of the characteristics that distinguish it from other members of that class. Like definition by synonym, it, too, is commonly found in abridged dictionaries, though much less elaborated than a writer may wish to make it in his own work. In definition by analysis, the definer comes closer than in any other means to the search for full meaning that is the primary end of the use of language as an instrument of inquiry. The resources of the analytic definition are exhausted only when there remain no more questions to ask, no more distinctions to make. It may do its job adequately in one sentence or may fail to come to the end of it in a volume. Whether a sentence or a volume is needed depends on the purpose the definition is meant to serve and on the perceptiveness of the definer.

Another means, very close to analytic definition, is that in which the *definiens* contains a class word and distinguishing characteristics but in which the distinguishing characteristics depend on a relationship with other members of the class. To define the "pre-Cambrian" as the "earliest geological period" is to define *synthetically;* so, also, is to define "electron" as "one of the smallest particles of matter." Synthetic definitions are concise, but often they fail to supply as much information as one would wish. Think how much more a novice would need to know about the pre-Cambrian age or about electrons in order to achieve genuine understanding. The synthetic definition is incomplete, but it is at least emphatic— it calls attention to just one characteristic of the thing in question, and if that characteristic is important enough, such a definition can be highly economical.

Earlier in this chapter we mentioned the frustration caused by definitions such as " 'imperturbable' means 'not perturbable.' " Still, *definition by negation* sometimes has its uses. Remember, for instance, how much of it proved necessary in the dialogue on "gig." Similarly, it may be important revelation in some contexts that the crocodile is not (technically) an amphibian. But notice that such definitions do their work only when the audience already knows rather a lot about the things or concepts involved—knows, for instance, what the biological characteristics of amphibians are. Negation is, at best, a helpful aid to definition, never more than a way station.

The four methods of definition reviewed so far—by synonym, by analysis, by synthesis, and by negation—all fit the pattern of equivalence ($x = y$). One other kind of definition lies at the edge of this group; it may be called *definition by likeness* (by comparison, simile, or analogy). One of Robert Frost's most impressive sonnets begin with the line

> *She is as in a field a silken tent,*

and goes on to explore the simile. Of course the value of the definition hinges on the power of the image to suggest, of itself and through connotations developed in the poem, important qualities of "she"; fragility, resilience, strength, sensitivity, serene aloofness, surprising stability. This may be a roundabout way to define, or it may strike to the heart of the matter. That depends on the skill and discrimination of the writer, who should be secure in his mastery of connotations before he attempts this sort of definition. But in less imaginative forms, definition by likeness is within the reach of every writer, and highly pertinent, for all its indirection. The ways in which marriage is like an armed truce, or a pretty girl like a melody, or a peccary like a pig, are important and illuminating, even though no comparison will match up *definiendum* and *definiens* point for point (if it did, it would be an equivalence, and the word "like" would be out of place). Moreover, it is important for the definer who chooses this method to spell out the ways in which, say, a peccary is *not* like a pig—to supplement comparison with negation. Definition by likeness is never complete, but it can be dramatic, suggestive, and vivid.

Of the methods of definition that remain to be discussed, some may lend themselves to expression as equivalences, but that form does little justice to their nature. Essentially they focus attention in a certain way, or suggest operations to perform, or illustrate the *definiendum* in action. Consider first the least important of these methods, *ostensive definition,* or definition by showing. It is much more common in speech than in writing, since it must be accompanied by a gesture, or the equivalent: "What is a cam shaft?" "That, right there." The writer may, however, get the same result by using pictures or symbols: "This is an ampersand: &." Or he may direct attention to the thing in question through verbal instructions: "If you look for a minute at a bright light and then close your eyes, what you will see is an after-image." The speaker or writer, in defining like this, does not offer an equivalent for the *definiendum,* but points to an instance, from which his audience can generate its own definition.

This method is closely related to *definition by example,* the difference being that one who defines by example mentions or describes an instance, rather than actually showing one. "What is a *Bildungsroman?*" "Well, things like *Great Expectations, The Red and the Black,* and *A Portrait of the Artist as a Young Man.*" "Oh, you mean a novel about growing up." "Yes, that's it." The definer does not specify the properties of his *definiendum,* but leaves that task to the audience. Of course, his several examples may have more than one characteristic in common, some of which are irrelevant to the term being defined, and for this reason definition by example is most reliable when accompanied by a standard analytic definition. However, it can stand alone if the audience knows the object, but not the name of it: "Lepidoptera are lunas, monarchs, fritillaries, swallowtails, and so on." Definition by example relies upon the fact that every class has what logicians call an *extension*—a set of individual members—as well as an *intension*—a set of shared characteristics, or a definition, which unites the members. When a writer produces examples, he is listing part of the extension of the class, but his purpose is to guide the reader to an understanding of the intension. The best way to do this, obviously, is to spell out the intension, and use the examples as supplementary material. But if, for some reason, the writer wishes to let his examples carry the whole burden of definition, he has two responsibilities. First, he should offer enough examples to allow correct generalization (he might even list the whole extension, if the class is a small one); and second, he should make sure that his examples are typical and illuminating (for defining purposes, Beethoven's Seventh Symphony is a much better example of romantic music than his Fourth). These cautions should not obscure the unequalled usefulness of examples in defining. Not only do they give body and clarity to a writer's definitions; they are indispensable aids to persuading, since a concrete instance often captures the reader's interest and imagination when a generalization fails to do so.

The other kinds of definition without equivalence do their work by revealing the object or the word in action. *Definition by function* is an extremely common type, especially useful when the object, person, and so on, is known primarily for what it does: "A detergent cleans"; "A podiatrist studies and treats disorders of the foot." Closely related, but often more complex, are what scientists call *operational definitions,* definitions which express the meaning of a term by listing the operations one must perform in order to see if the term applies. An example is the Brinell test of hardness, mentioned by Haldane. Or take these simple instructions: "Measure the three sides of a triangle; if they are equal in length, the triangle is equilateral." (Notice that measuring the three angles of a triangle will produce the same result; the terms "equilateral triangle" and "equiangular triangle" are operationally equivalent.) Many of the terms in science can be operationally defined—"mass," "precipitate," "relativity"—and scientists tend to prefer such definitions because they make it possible for any investigator to confirm the results of another, and because they incorporate, not only knowledge, but the means of arriving at knowledge.

Definition by context is akin to operational and functional definition, but the definer, instead of describing the behavior or use of things, illustrates the behavior or use of the term itself. The quotations drawn from the *Oxford English Dictionary* to illustrate meanings of "nice" are examples of definition by context; they show the word in action, giving thereby a richer insight into its meanings than analytic definition alone. Partly, the meaning of a word is a function of its interaction with other words: What adjectives apply to "proposition"? Can "astonish" have an inanimate noun for direct object? If one does not know the answers to these questions, he will not be able to use the words appropriately, nor will he fully understand them. "Famulary" means "of or pertaining to servants," so says the dictionary. But what does one *do* with the word? Does one speak of "famulary duties"? "famulary men and women"? "famulary quarters"? "famulary virtues"? Can something be "exceedingly famulary"? Only definition by context could resolve these problems. It goes without saying that children first learn words largely from contextual appearances, and though this method is cumbersome in itself, it is often an indispensable aid to defining, even in prose that is far from childlike.

There are more ways of defining than these ten, but these are perhaps the most important. And indeed, it may seem that ten are too many. How is the writer ever to get on with his business if he must ponder such a battery of methods every time he wishes to define a term? Actually, the matter is not so complex as that. As we have indicated, the various patterns of definition have their peculiar virtues and flaws; each is particularly appropriate in some contexts, and quite out of place in others. The very needs which lead the writer to define will in part determine which method or methods he selects, as will his rhetorical purpose, his relationship to his reader. The important thing is for him to have the patterns at his command and to understand how each of them works. Once he has achieved this much mastery, framing a definition will become more a matter of solving individual writing problems than a matter of memory and labored choice.

11) PERSUASIVE DEFINITION

Definition does not usually occur in isolation except in dictionaries and glossaries. Normally it fits into a rhetorical plan, a pattern of argument, a demonstration. How this happens was detailed at some length in the section on the uses of definition, of which there are many legitimate ones. It is worth while to mention here a common argumentative use of definition whose legitimacy is questionable, since it masquerades as what it is not. Suppose that a writer defines "true democracy" as "a form of government which gives people a political voice proportionate to their economic contribution." Now there are many forms and theories of democracy, and this may well be one of them. The definition is faulty, not so much because it is false, as because it claims more than it deserves, and because its actual purpose is persuasion rather than definition. Here is how it works: The terms "democracy," and, *a fortiori*, "true democracy," have many favorable connotations in our part of the world. To call a government a democracy is to praise it. Hence, if the writer can reserve the label "true democracy" to just one political system, he may convince his reader that the system is the *best* one. But to do such a thing, of course, is outside the province of definition, which can only describe objects and record the uses of words. The writer who defines democracy as above is conducting a political and moral argument under the guise of definition, and if he wins the argument, he will not have done so legitimately. He has also sinned, incidentally, by defining stipu-latively without saying so. Such stratagems are called *persuasive defini-tions,* and both writer and reader should guard against them.

Notice that such definitions can be negotiated in other ways, as, for instance, when a writer defines "democracy" so as to exclude socialism, thus denigrating the governments of Great Britain, Sweden, and so on. Or he may define a term with *un*favorable connotations, say "fascism," so as to include what he does not like—say, the participation of big business in government. Persuasive definitions have a greater power to deceive than one might imagine, perhaps because they always traffic in highly emotional issues. But a writer of integrity will not distort his appeals in this way.

12) FORM IN DEFINITION

After a writer has successfully thought out the purpose and means of his definition, he may still encounter snags in the actual wording of it, even if he uses the neat form of equivalence that is common to most definitions. One requirement of that form is that the terms on both sides of "is" or "means" be of the same grammatical class: a noun on one side of the equation demands a noun on the other, an adjective demands an adjective, and so on. The following definitions, though adequate as far as meaning is concerned, illustrate breaches of form:

> Rent is paying money to an owner for the use of his property.
>
> Cramming is when you study very hard immediately before an examina-tion.
>
> "Flagrant" means something openly outrageous or illegal.

A simple correction in each preserves the proprieties of expression:

> Rent is money paid to an owner for the use of his property.
>
> Cramming is studying very hard immediately before an examination.
>
> "Flagrant" means openly outrageous or illegal.

Despite its neatness, the invariability of the formula $x = y$ may make it disagreeable to the writer. To avoid the mechanical balancing of *definiendum* against *definiens,* he may resort to several other patterns. He may, for instance, compress a definition in this fashion: "A square joins four equal straight lines at right angles so as to form a complete enclosure." This is the same as the analytic definition. "A square is a geometrical figure in which four equal straight lines meet at right angles so as to form an enclosure," but substituting an active verb for the copula and class term of the analytic definition considerably reduces formality. Another way of reducing formality and providing variety is to use the grammatical structure known as "apposition." This also has the advantage of reducing emphasis on the definition so that the forward movement of the discourse is not interrupted:

> Paul used the Greek term *agape*, a word meaning "brotherly love," to distinguish a kind of Christian love which he believed to be entirely different from love as the unrelieved search for fulfillment discussed in Plato's *Symposium* and deeply rooted in subsequent Greek thought.

In *"agape*, a word meaning 'brotherly love,'" there is a definition (by translation) which is presented as an appositive. The reader gets the explanation of *agape* which the definition supplies without having his attention drawn away from the principal focus of the sentence (a contrast between two concepts of love). If the writer had wished to provide the Greek equivalent for "love as the unrelieved search . . ." as he did for "brotherly love," he could have used the same device as for *agape*, or he could have set the word *eros* in parentheses after "fulfillment." If his intent had been to follow this paragraph with a discussion of the Platonic concept, he might have wished to emphasize the term for it, preparatory to beginning a discussion. To do so, he could have separated the definition from the preceding sentence in this way:

> . . . entirely different from the Platonic concept of love. That concept, given the name *eros*, was the embodiment of the human faculty of desire, of yearning, of lust to possess. It included every manifestation of powerful longing from the most sensual to the completely sublimated.

In this example of a definition to which importance has been lent by its presentation in an independent sentence, one can see also the most common device writers have for making definitions fully effective—that of adding definition to definition until a complex series of equations is established for the *definiendum*.

13) CHECKS ON DEFINITION

The various ways in which a definition can be presented give the writer no excuse for failing to clarify as he goes along, unless, of course, his purpose at a given point in the discourse is to mystify or to create suspense by withholding information. He may use one means of definition only, or many; he may set down his definition with all the starkness of a mathematical equation or with the unobtrusiveness of an aside. Which means and which manner he uses will depend on his intent and on his assessment of his readers' needs.

Once the writer understands the nature of the defining process and knows how to handle definitions deftly in the regular flow of discourse, he may still need to check himself occasionally to make sure that his definitions will hold up under careful scrutiny. The process of writing is such that a writer is often carried along by his own words, the words seeming at times to come almost of themselves. So great is their impetus at such times that the writer may neither wish, nor be able, to check the rush of words. He will be convinced that the words say what he means to say and will not dare to test them at the time of the writing for fear of shutting off the flow itself. When he comes back to his work and looks at it soberly and critically, however, he may find inadequacies and contradictions where he would earlier have sworn that completeness and harmony reigned. At such times—and they are common—system is the best buckler against despair. If he can ask a series of questions about his terminology, if he can systematically test his definitions, he may swiftly discover the weaknesses and discrepancies and remedy them; if he cannot, he must write and rewrite until the sentences satisfy his inner ear. Both methods work, and most writers make use of one or the other as occasion demands.

A system of checks on what one has written is essentially negative. Like a mechanic checking an automobile engine to discover the cause of sluggish operation, the writer eliminates one by one the possible causes of disorder until he has found and corrected the faulty mechanism. This hunt for the causes of trouble is seldom as orderly an affair as a book will make it out to be, but that is true of the entire process of writing. In any case, a list of common faults in defining is helpful, even if the writer never applies the checks systematically.

OVERINCLUSION • Complete confidence about the meaning of some words, and equal confidence that others are sure to understand them as the user does, often make the writer rather summary and careless in definition. For example, to define "patriotism" as "the feeling a man has for his country" is less than enough simply because men have many feelings about their country which are far from patriotic. This is the fault of overinclusion, of failing to qualify the class word in the *definiens* as much as it needs to be qualified. In the example given here the addition of qualifying phrases to "feeling" will correct the deficiency: "Patriotism is the feeling of partiality, respect, love, and pride which a man has for his country."

OVERRESTRICTION • At the other extreme, a definition may suffer from overrestriction, from being so closely confined by the class word or the qualifiers in the *definiens* that not all of the things to which the *definiendum* may properly refer are covered by it. "Kings are rulers by hereditary right" is an overrestrictive definition of the word "king" since it makes no provision for rulers who have taken thrones by force or who have been elevated to them without any hereditary claim at all. Both overinclusiveness and overrestriction can be detected by sampling, that is, by asking if all the examples one can call to mind have the attributes named or implied in the *definiens*.

DUPLICATION • It is sometimes convenient and useful, though often dangerous, to define a term simply by using a second term which has a different linguistic history but the same meaning. The definition, " 'Liberty' means 'freedom,' " uses a word of Latin origin on one side of the verb and a word of Germanic origin on the other. Where definition is needed because the *definiendum* (the word itself) is simply unfamiliar to the reader, this kind of definition may be valuable: " 'Prophylaxis' means 'cleaning' " is an example. Where definition is needed because the *definiendum* stands for something which the reader actually does not know, a definition of this kind is of little help. In general it is best avoided except in the act of translation ("Rot" in German means "red" in English) because it may appear to give information without actually doing so.

CIRCULARITY • A definition which uses the *definiendum,* or a variant of it, in the *definiens* is said to be circular. Most instances of circularity occur not in a single sentence ("Freedom is the state of being free") but in a series of sentences long enough so that the repetition of the *definiendum* is not immediately noticeable:

> *Freedom* is not easily defined except by reference to what it is not. The closest one can come, in positive terms, may be to call it "independence of action." Independent action is that which is free from coercion or control by any external agent whatsoever.

AMBIGUITY • In any writing, the danger of ambiguity is always great because words shift and multiply meanings so rapidly and because there is sometimes actually an accidental identity between the appearance or sound of words having very different meanings and origins. Think, for instance, of the differences in meaning between "herd" and "heard," or "foul" and "fowl," or between the two meanings of the word "mean," one from Medieval French, the other from Old English, in this sentence: "The average man is the mean man of the population." Definition is often thought of as the means of eradicating ambiguity, and it is true that stipulative definition, at least, does have that as its main purpose. Lexical, or historical, definition, however, does not so much eradicate as describe the essential ambiguity of words because it indicates all or a large number of the meanings which a word may have. Yet, despite the fact that definitions can seldom divorce themselves from ambiguity, there is a sense in which they must attempt to avoid it. The examples given above deal with *semantic* ambiguity, that deriving directly from the meanings of words themselves. Another kind of ambiguity, that known as syntactical, is more likely to plague the definer because it results from the careless handling of punctuation or of the order of words. To define a "willful abstainer" as "one who does not do something because he does not wish to" is to produce such ambiguity: in this instance, a simple cure is effected by placing a comma after "something." The definition "In gin rummy, a discard is a card placed by a player of no value to him in the center of the table face up in return for a card previously drawn from a face-down stack also in the center of the table" has all the words needed to make an accurate definition but they are arranged so badly that their meaning is ambiguous.

OBSCURITY · The person who defines stipulatively usually does so in order to clarify or restrict meaning. It is only a short step from stipulative defining of the right kind to another kind that is less defensible, the stipulation of bizarre and newly invented meanings for words in common use. The writer who insists on the privilege of making up his own definitions for words which, in ordinary discourse, have different meanings from the ones he attributes to them runs several risks. If the word for which he makes a private definition has strong connotations, nothing he can do will relieve it of them, no matter how he defines it. Moreover, because the writer, like his readers, is accustomed to using words with their conventional meanings, he is very likely to be caught off guard in any extended passage of writing and to find, too late, that he has used an important word both in a private sense and in the sense common to everyone. Should he be skilled enough to escape both dangers, he faces a third, that of developing a vocabulary so special and private that a reader needs a special lexicon to make use of his works. It is safe to say that a writer must have rare talents to find and keep readers willing to make such an effort for him. In most cases, such private defining is less the product of special insight than of laziness or pretentiousness; when either is the cause, the reader is fully warranted in leaving the writer to weave his web in splendid isolation.

These formal checks on one's defining are mechanical aids only. Good definitions can come only from some understanding of what is involved in the defining process. Enough has been said here to suggest the ramifications of that process and to indicate the respect it deserves from a serious writer.

EXERCISES

1) Describe the faults in each of these definitions; then write a better one.

    a. When a group can maintain conformity, it is called equilibrium.

    b. Network: anything reticulated and decussated at equal intervals, with interstices between the intersections (from Dr. Samuel Johnson's *Dictionary of the English Language*).

c. Literature is the embodiment in words of a great religious or mythical system.

d. A recluse is an eccentric.

e. The real traitor is the man who criticizes his country in intemperate words.

f. Verse is prose cut into lines of equal length.

g. Osmosis is where one thing filters into another.

h. The policy of containment can best be described as one in which the idea is to contain the spread of something uncontained.

i. In underworld parlance, a rod is a gat.

j. What Weber means by "charisma" is leadership.

k. Sculpture is the representation of human or animal figures in marble.

2) Common words often lose precision through overuse. When that happens, the only recourse for the careful writer is to indicate by definition the meaning he wishes to convey. Remembering the summary of cautions to be observed in defining, prepare a careful definition of each of these terms:

a. liberal (politics)

b. communism (economics)

c. friction (physics)

d. motivation (psychology)

e. shock (medicine)

f. middle class (sociology)

g. theme (poetry)

h. romantic (music)

i. space (architecture)

j. structure (fiction)

3) Often a definition can be *reinforced* by distinguishing the object referred to from others with which it might be confused. Define the first word in each of the groups below, making proper distinctions between it and the others in the group:

a. planet, star, sun, asteroid, meteor

b. sonnet, ode, quatrain, rondeau

c. capitalism, socialism, communism

d. rectangle, parallelogram, trapezoid

e. deviation, difference, variation

4) Invent a word to serve as a noun or adjective expressing some substance or quality for which there is not at present a proper word in English. (It has been noted, for example, that there is no dignified but unpretentious word in English meaning "the regular male companion of a young, unmarried female"—what is rather embarrassingly

called a "boy friend.") Without defining the word you invent, use it in a paragraph until its meaning becomes clear. Then write a definition.

5) One of Santayana's essays begin with this sentence: "Patriotism is a form of piety." What kind of definition is this? What obligation does it lay on the definer? How would you meet the obligation?

6) Throughout the chapter on definition the process of defining is treated with an eye to ordinary discourse. Following the principles of that treatment, develop an extended definition of an abstract word: "honor," "virtue," "pleasure," "wealth," "vanity."

7) How does the following definition work? Is it possible to deduce from it an analytic definition? What is gained and lost by the attempt?

> July 3, 1943
>
> We received a letter from the Writers' War Board the other day asking for a statement on "The Meaning of Democracy." It presumably is our duty to comply with such a request, and it is certainly our pleasure.
>
> Surely the Board knows what democracy is. It is the line that forms on the right. It is the don't in Don't Shove. It is the hole in the stuffed shirt through which the sawdust slowly trickles; it is the dent in the high hat. Democracy is the recurrent suspicion that more than half of the people are right more than half of the time. It is the feeling of privacy in the voting booths, the feeling of communion in the libraries, the feeling of vitality everywhere. Democracy is the score at the beginning of the ninth. It is an idea which hasn't been disproved yet, a song the words of which have not gone bad. It's the mustard on the hot dog and the cream in the rationed coffee. Democracy is a request from a War Board, in the middle of a morning in the middle of a war, wanting to know what democracy is.
>
> E. B. WHITE, *The Wild Flag*

8) In the *Nature of Prejudice* Gordon Allport develops a definition for the word "prejudice" as he intends to use it in his book. He begins with a dictionary definition (a. below); from analysis of it he discovers the need to develop another (b. below); and finally he alters the second definition to make it serve his particular purposes (c. below). Examine the three definitions and then explain the effects of each change.

    a. thinking ill of others without sufficient warrant

    b. a feeling, favorable or unfavorable, toward a person or thing, prior to, or not based on, actual experience

    c. an avertive or hostile attitude toward a person who belongs to a group, simply because he belongs to that group, and is therefore presumed to have the objectionable qualities ascribed to the group.

9) How would you go about defining these words, given the stated purpose or problems?

    a. genius (you want to analyze the role of genius in public life)

    b. realistic (you are faced with a disagreement as to whether *Moby Dick* is realistic)

    c. syndrome (you want to decide whether a certain journalist is justified in using the word to describe President John F. Kennedy's style of speaking)

    d. lip-service (you want to analyze a new attitude of college students toward social issues, an attitude for which there is as yet no convenient name, and "lip-service" comes close without being quite right)

10. How near do the following pairs come to being exact synonyms? What are the differences between the two members of each pair?

    a. gourmet—gourmand

    b. confident—optimistic

    c. meaning—sense (of a word)

    d. persuade—cajole

    e. policeman—officer (cf. cop)

    f. fate—destiny

    g. right—good

    h. vacillate—waver

    i. stream—brook

    j. unintentional—inadvertent

    k. correct—proper

    l. suggest—imply

11. Describe the connotations of each word in the following list. Then state its denotation, and try to think of other words with the same denotation but different connotations.

    a. grubby

    b. hair-splitting

    c. physician

    d. congenital

    e. epistle

    f. yokel

    g. discriminating (adj.)

    h. comprehend

    i. independent

    j. innocent

    k. brothel

    l. foe

    m. darling (adj.)

    n. reiterate

12. Choose ten of the words from Exercises 9, 10, and 11, and construct a definition for each. In every definition, use *three* of the ten methods of definition proposed in this chapter. Make sure that you use each method at least once.

❋ *Asserting*

WORDS DO NOT add up to prose unless they are strung together in sentences. To be sure, the writer will get nowhere *without* a firm mastery of words and their meanings, but such control does not in itself guarantee sound exposition. After the last definition has slipped into place in his mind, he must still wrestle, joggle, and nudge the words into sentences, the basic units both of grammar and of expository prose. That doing so is generally an arduous task, any serious writer will testify, however slim or vast his experience. Even if he knows his subject thoroughly, as well as its vocabulary, he may encounter vexatious obstacles when he tries to give his thoughts the form which sentences impose. For sentences must measure up to standards: it is always fair to ask of a sentence, "How *good* is it, or how good for the writer's purpose?" Phrased this way, of course, the question is so general that it can be of little use to the writer himself, or indeed to the reader. Fortunately, it breaks down under scrutiny into at least four narrower questions of evaluation: "Is it grammatical?" "Is it gracefully and efficiently formed?" "Does it cooperate well with the sentences that come before and after?" And, roughly, "Is it adequate in its content?" Questions of the first sort concern pure linguistic form, and we shall not consider them, except in passing, in this book; they are the grammarian's province. The second question is one of style, and the third concerns both style and argument; these we shall discuss in other chapters. Here we mean to consider questions—and there are many—like the fourth one, questions about what sentences say, and how the writer may judge that "what."

1) SENTENCES THAT ASSERT AND SENTENCES THAT DO NOT

But first we must limit our scope still further. Exposition draws from time to time on sentences of every type, but some types, common in conversation, fiction, and drama, appear only rarely in expository prose, and, moreover, when they do appear, usually perform functions rather tangential to the central one of exposition. For the most part, these sentences can be distinguished grammatically from the ones that bear the burden of expository writing: they are *questions, commands, resolutions, interjections,* and *wishes.* These sentence classes have grammatical features too complicated to discuss here, but all are readily distinguishable from the grammatical type that is overwhelmingly preponderant in exposition: declarative sentences, or statements, or, as we shall usually call them, *assertions.* That assertions do occupy a central place in expository prose is almost too obvious to bear mentioning. It is only when one asks *why* they predominate that the differences between sentences that assert and sentences that do not begin to seem important.

One way to get at those differences is to consider the responses that the various kinds of sentences provoke in the listener or reader. A *question,* typically, calls upon him to make an answer—to supply information. Since answers are verbal responses, it makes little sense for the writer to ask for them as if he were face to face with his reader (though of course he may ask *rhetorical* questions, questions that imply their own answers, or to which the writer himself provides answers). Getting verbal responses is not a main purpose of exposition, as it is of talk and letter writing; hence questions play a minor role in expository prose.

Commands, too, call for the hearer or reader to do something in response, namely, obey the command. Of course it is often polite for the hearer to respond in words as well; in answer to the command "Bring the can opener, please," he might well say, "Certainly—I'll be glad to." But his verbal response is only an assurance that he will later obey the command, and the initial speaker would have cause for complaint if all he got was the polite answer and no can opener. The main purpose of a command is to elicit action. Now writers do, sometimes, put pen to paper in the hope of encouraging readers to act, but the best way of achieving this result is hardly to set down a string of commands. The writer with such an aim will have more success if he explains the necessity for action, urges, cajoles, and so on. Commands, like questions, are most appropriate and effective in direct confrontations of two people. And the same is true of *resolutions* ("Let's go to the movies"). Whenever a writer uses commands, resolutions, or questions, he seems to be creating an "as if" intimacy, the intimacy of personal contact.

Interjections, a miscellaneous class of abbreviated sentences, are themselves usually responses, either to something that has just happened or to something someone has said. Some of them call for verbal responses or action—"Hello," "Goodbye," "Help," and "Ouch," for instances; but in the main they are simply means of expressing spontaneous feeling, or of letting off steam: "Oh," "Good Lord," "Rats," "Wow," and so on.

The circumstances that give rise to such exclamations are usually too ephemeral to be dealt with in exposition, and even if the circumstances are noteworthy, interjections themselves are such fleeting and trivial responses that they have little place in serious and reflective prose.

It is a little difficult to say just what the proper response is to a *wish* (we mean sentences like "Heaven help the poor Bulgarians" or "Would that Ezra were here"). Probably the wisher simply hopes that his hearer will share the wish, sympathize. In any case, wishes, like other nonassertive sentences, are rather out of place in expository prose, not because they demand a listener, but because their passive dreaminess is not generally to the writer's purpose.

These varieties of sentence are in no way inferior or illicit; they merely serve the purposes of speech more than those of expository writing. What is it, then, that exposition tries to accomplish? Its function is to transmit information, to convince, to persuade, to record the truth. And the response that the writer hopes to arouse in his reader is primarily one of *assent,* of agreement, of acceptance, whether or not that assent leads the reader to speak or to act. Thus the main vehicle of communication in expository prose is inevitably the assertion, for only assertions give the reader anything to assent *to.*

In its grammatical form, a simple assertion comprises two elements: the subject and the predicate:

> Shakespeare (subject) wrote plays (predicate).

> Shakespeare (subject) was born at Stratford (predicate).

The assertion as a whole claims that something (the predicate) is true about something else (the subject). Thus the sentence will have done its main job if it states something that is in fact true, and if the reader (or hearer) gives his assent to it. In other words, although one may react to assertions in any number of ways (see the beginning of "Proving" for some), the standard response to an assertion is something like "That's true," or "I see," or "Oh," whether uttered aloud or not. Of course the reader may also reject the claim of the assertion—"That's false," or "Nonsense," or "I doubt it"—and if he does, the assertion has fallen short of its goal. For this reason, the writer himself has a responsibility to test his assertions by asking "Are they true or false?" There are, to be sure, many other ways of weighing the content of assertions, and we shall discuss some of them later in this chapter; but the first and primary evaluative question must be one of truth or falsity.

The discussion suggests a simple definition:

> An assertion is a sentence that is either true or false.

We shall have to qualify this definition in due time, but for the moment it serves to segregate assertions from the other grammatical types of sentence, and to show why assertions are most pertinent to writing designed to produce conviction. Notice that it would be absurd to answer the question "Where is Church Street?" by saying "That's true." A question asserts nothing, and can be neither true nor false. Similarly, truth and falsity are irrelevant to commands, resolutions, interjections, and wishes. One may, it is true, assent (in a way) to "Pass the salt" or "Let's go now," but not by saying "That's true." Assertions are the only sentences that must pass the test of truth.

(Having maintained our definition for one paragraph, we must now draw back from it one step. It is not quite true that *all* assertions are either true or false. Consider sentences like "I refuse to come" and "I promise." It makes no sense for a listener to question the truth of such assertions; in saying "I promise" the speaker *has* promised, whether he lives up to his word or not. The purpose of these assertions—philosophers call them *performatives*—is to perform an action, such as promising, guaranteeing, objecting (in court), taking a woman to be one's lawful wedded wife ("I do"), and so on, and the question of their truth is simply irrelevant. But they constitute a minor exception, inasmuch as this is a textbook in composition rather than philosophy, and we shall let them pass with this brief mention.)

The adequacy of an assertion's content, then, is first a matter of its truth. This sounds simple enough. The question "Is it true?" can, after all, receive a limited number of answers: "Yes," "No," "Partly," "I can't tell," and perhaps a few others. But to arrive at one of these answers is often far from simple, for a decision as to the truth of an assertion may depend on any of numerous criteria. To put it another way, assertions can be classified according to the grounds upon which we judge them true or false, and according to the degree of certainty with which we are able to make that judgment. What the writer needs, therefore, in order to weigh his assertions, is an awareness of their credentials.

2) CONVENTION, FACT, OPINION, PREFERENCE

Such an awareness is probably second nature for most skilled writers, who, needless to say, do not stop to examine microscopically the underpinnings of every assertion. But for the less practiced, a breakdown of assertions into categories will be helpful, if not for constant, mechanical use, at least for storage in the back of the mind and for reference when needed. The scheme we shall propose has the advantage of being rooted in common sense and usage; it has the disadvantage of less than ideal rigor. The writer will not go far wrong with it if he takes it for what it is—a suggestive arrangement—rather than for what it does not claim to be—an airtight classification (which, incidentally, philosophers have pursued for centuries without notable success).

A simple assertion and two responses to it will provide a starting point:

> Melville is a greater novelist than Hawthorne.
>
>> 1) That's a fact.
>>
>> 2) Well, now, that's a matter of opinion.

In the two responses, the statement is classified as fact and as opinion. Now it is clear that, in this instance, the classification does not depend on the statement (since there is only one statement) but on something in the attitude of the respondent. The two responses might be altered to read (1) "I agree" and (2) "I'm not sure whether I agree or not." Or those responses may be a way of saying (1) that the statement is one that can be proved true and (2) that it is one that can probably not be proved either true or false. Since these responses contradict each other, one of them must be wrong. Yet no one reading the two responses is at all likely to be misled about them; nor is he likely to think one a wrong, another a right, response. Instead, he will recognize that they represent different aspects of a complex act of judgment.

Where simpler acts of judgment are called for, this kind of classification readily produces at least rough justice, as discussion of several assertions will show.

> Three feet make a yard.
>
> A *novella* is a short novel.
>
> Horses have manes.
>
> Churchill smokes cigars.
>
> These two are the most intelligent students in the class.
>
> More leisure leads to more contentment.
>
> Lemon pie tastes better than apple.
>
> Rousseau was a bad man.

Each of these assertions poses a different problem of verification, because they are unlike in several important ways. Some concern a whole class of objects; some are confined to particular members of a class. Some would appear to require very little in the way of verification; some, to require a great deal. Some seem susceptible of almost certain proof; others, impossible to prove at all. And, finally, some appear to invite tests of validity; others, to warn that such tests are irrelevant. Because these assertions are different in so many ways, a writer commonly uses signals to warn his reader about the differences, signals ranging from parenthetical remarks ("without doubt," "to be sure," "so far as I can tell," "in my judgment," "from one point of view," and so on) to the development of an informative tone of voice in the paragraph (that, for instance, of reassurance, of decisiveness, of hesitancy, of cautious speculation, of skepticism). In general, these signals are intended to make the distinctions which we commonly indicate by the loose, and more or less rhetorical, categories, *statements of convention, statements of fact, statements of opinion, and statements of preference.*

If we attempt to locate each of the sentences above in one or another of these four categories, we can get some notion of the issues involved. Clearly, the classification of any sentence is partly a judgment on it, particularly on its reliability or degree of certainty—certainty to the writer, certainty to the reader, and certainty irrespective of any one person. But certainty is primarily a matter of how we know, or how we would find out, whether an assertion is true or false. Hence the shortest way to the heart of our problem takes us directly to *verification.*

How would one set about to verify the assertion, "Three feet make a yard"? The question itself has an odd ring, for the assertion is so patently true as scarcely to need verification at all. The certainty with which we regard it issues, of course, from conventions—those conventions of measurement and of the English language. A yard, by definition, is three feet long; that is what the word *means.* It would be ludicrous for anyone, asked about the truth of the statements, to begin diligently measuring yardsticks to determine whether each of them measured three feet: what could he measure them with except other yardsticks or rulers? Likewise, no one would test the statement "A *novella* is a short novel" by counting the pages in actual *novellas.* Rather, if he were uncertain about the truth of the assertion he would investigate the linguistic practice of literary critics. Another way to understand the force of statements of convention is to imagine rebutting the statement "A *novella* is a long novel." The speaker has not made a mistake in fact, but simply failed to understand the word *"novella,"* and the way to correct his error is to explain the relevant convention. Assertions of this type, in other words, depend for their truth upon rules, regularities of usage, linguistic custom, and so on. One does not verify them through an appeal to experience, other than experience of this limited sort. Paradoxically, it is just because of this remoteness from experience that statements of convention tend to seem more certain than any other kind, for the other statements involve links between word and world, and such links are often puzzling, even with the simplest statements of fact.

The statement "Horses have manes" would require for complete verification the examination of, or a reliable report on, all horses now living and all that have ever lived or will do so; most of us would (and *must*) settle for less, it is true, just as testers of all kinds now draw conclusions from "sample populations." Whether or not we require reference to all horses, we are satisfied that it takes only the simple tests of direct observation to determine the truth or falsity of the statement. And it is that feeling of the simplicity or relative certainty of proof that leads us to treat such a statement without qualification and to refer to it as though it represented something about whose truth or falsity we could eventually reach an unassailable decision. Statements of this kind we conventionally call "statements of fact," meaning not that they are beyond doubt true but that we are sure that their truth or falsity can be readily and finally determined by reference to experience.

(In ordinary language, we occasionally distinguish between "factual statements" and "statements of fact," meaning, by the former, statements whose truth *or* falsity can readily be determined and, by the latter, those which are true. In this discussion, the two terms are not distinguished: a "statement of fact" may be either true or false, and it is different from other statements primarily because of its high susceptibility to tests of validity.)

If we treat "Horses have manes" as a statement of fact because we know that the proofs for establishing its truth or falsity are within our power to produce, we shall not hesitate to classify "Churchill smokes cigars" in the same group. Provided that we understand "smokes" to mean "sometimes smokes" or even "customarily smokes," we know that there are easy ways of finding out whether or not the statement is true. To be sure, the appeal to experience need not be direct; few of us are in a position to make *observations* of Churchill's smoking habits. But *reports* are easily accessible, reports just one step removed from observation. And even when the evidence consists of second-, third-, or tenth-hand reports, we still call an assertion a statement of fact if it has its origin in observation and if the reports come through reliable channels.

The statement "These two are the most intelligent students in the class" presents somewhat greater, but certainly no insuperable, difficulties. As soon as we get agreement on a means of measuring intelligence, we can proceed to test the truth of the statement. If the means agreed upon is a pencil-and-paper test, verification will be easy; if the means is a record of responses to all kinds of challenges and crises in actual experience, verification will be extremely difficult. Since by "intelligent" few people mean simply "good at tests," they are likely to think of the statement as one of opinion. The reason is in part our lack of confidence in actual tests; in part the complexity and unavailability of better tests; and in part the nature of the word "intelligent."

Obviously, "intelligent" is an ambiguous word; that is, it means different things to various people. What one will find adequate as the meaning of "intelligent," another will find inadequate or completely irrelevant. The more ambiguous the predication of a statement, the more difficult it will be to find generally acceptable tests of validity; the more difficult it is to find such tests, the more uncertain we are that any statement requiring them is sure to be found true or false by everyone. It is the increase of uncertainty that leads us to think of such statements as "statements of opinion" rather than as "statements of fact." There is no strictly logical difference between them: both kinds require reference to experience for verification. The difference lies either in the ambiguity of a term or in the difficulty of determining truth or falsity, or in both. Thus there can be little doubt that "More leisure leads to more contentment" is also a statement of opinion, for how is one to measure contentment? Certainly the tests would have to be complex, and probably unreliable to boot.

Another source of uncertainty in the classification of such statements is the connotative effect of words. For various reasons we respond favorably or unfavorably to certain words. Most words, indeed, besides directing us to consider something, influence us to take an attitude toward it as well. Suppose that a man regularly puts away all the money he earns except what he must spend on the necessities of life. Then consider these two statements about him:

He saves his money.

He hoards his money.

Whether we think of one as a statement of fact and of the other as a statement of opinion will depend partly on the denotation of the words "saves" and "hoards" but even more on their connotation, on the associations they raise in our minds. "Hoards" carries the sense of secret and greedy accumulation; testing the truth of the assertion which contains it would be difficult. Since "saves" means only "puts away," testing the truth of the statement is theoretically not hard at all, given access to the man's financial records and behavior. The connotative power of the key words may therefore lead us to place quite similar statements in different categories.

Within this class of assertions whose truth or falsity is determined by reference to experience, three subdivisions of some importance to the writer have so far been distinguished. The first, statements of convention, reflects the writer's certainty that no appeal to nonlinguistic experience could possibly overthrow his assertion. The second, statements of fact represents the writer's feeling of assurance that the test of truth or falsity can be readily determined and that there is already general agreement about the truth of the statement itself. The third, statements of opinion, reflects the writer's uncertainty about the possibility of producing satisfactory proofs of soundness and his recognition that disagreement is more

likely than not. This uncertainty sometimes is the result of the difficulty
of the procedures necessary for testing, sometimes of the ambiguity of
terms in the statement, sometimes of the connotative effect of terms in
the statement. The progression, then, has been from relative certainty to
considerable uncertainty.

To continue that progress is to move into another category common to
everyday discourse about statements, that of statements of preference. In
some ways, these are the most interesting statements of all to writer and
reader. The medieval proverb, *De gustibus non est disputandum* ("There
is no disputing about tastes"), reflects a popular view, shared by some
philosophers, that the grounds of choice, being subjective, are neither
logically defensible nor attackable. Yet, for the very reason that they are
subjective, that is, that they refer not simply to the data presented to our
senses but to our experience and judgment of it, we are likely to hold to
statements of preference or taste with singular tenacity. At the same time,
we recognize that there is no infallible means of testing the truth or
falsity of such a statement as "Lemon pie tastes better than apple," and
we do not try to do so. But if this statement is changed into "I like
lemon pie better than apple pie," it then becomes an autobiographical
statement, and not very different, as far as proof is concerned, from "These
two are the most intelligent students in the class." The tests which someone else would apply to determine the truth or falsity of our stated
preference for lemon pie (seeing which kind we eat when we are given
a choice, for example) are not different in kind from those he would apply
to detect the intelligence of students in the class.

In its original form, however ("Lemon pie tastes better than apple"),
the statement of preference means something more than "I like lemon
pie better than apple." It either assumes agreement among people of
"right" perception or it indicates that no agreement is expected and that
the statement is really one about the condition of the stater rather than
about lemon and apple pie. A proper feeling for the meanings of a
statement of preference will often lead a writer to qualify it ("Con-
noisseurs agree that . . .") or to overstate deliberately in order to emphasize the limitedness of intention ("Every man who has ever put fork to
pie crust knows that lemon pie tastes better than apple").

From the taste of apple pie to Rousseau's moral qualities is a long
leap, but according to our criteria the assertion "Rousseau was a bad
man" must also be called a statement of preference. Two men who both
know all the facts of Rousseau's life may nonetheless disagree as to
whether he was a bad man, and there is no final way to arbitrate the
issue, for standards of goodness and badness differ. Thus *ethical statements,* as these are sometimes called, and *statements of obligation* ("Men
ought to love their neighbors") are subcategories of statements of preference, along with *statements of taste* (the one about lemon and apple pie,

for instance). But to make this classification is by no means to disqualify or undermine these assertions; in point of fact, they are among the most important in human discourse. And certainly the person who calls Rousseau a bad man does not merely mean that he dislikes Rousseau; nor would he be willing to concede, in all likelihood, that the issue is undecidable or meaningless. Rather, he probably assumes enough shared attitudes and moral standards among human beings to encourage considerable agreement about Rousseau, given the pertinent facts. The assumption is unjustified in this case; the argument about Rousseau's morality swirls on. But a great many ethical statements and statements of obligation do seem relatively certain: Hitler and Caligula were evil; St. Francis was good; men should be kind; they should not murder; and so on. Society would be impossible if most of us did not share such beliefs and the premises that support them. The writer need not shrink from statements of preference; on the contrary, they will often be the main justification for writing. But he should bear in mind the uncertainties and disagreements that lie behind them and see to it that he is no more confident than the particular assertion warrants.

In a way this is the moral of our whole attempt at classification: the writer deals in assertions of several types, and each type must meet different tests of adequacy, of truth and falsity. To ignore these differences is to lose contact with the ethics of writing, and with the ground upon which successful communication takes place.

3) OTHER WAYS OF JUDGING ASSERTIONS

In the preceding sections we have said enough about judgments of truth and falsity to establish their central importance to the writer, as well as the importance of having satisfactory ways to tell whether this or that assertion is true or false. But our remarks may also have been disquieting to some. Not only does it prove impossible to label all statements with conviction as fact, opinion, and so forth: the very labels "true" and "false" are often difficult to apply. This is so partly because we simply lack information—no one knows (at this writing) whether the assertion "There is life on Mars" is true, although it is a plain statement of fact. But the more bothersome and interesting difficulties in determining the truth of statements have to do with the nature of statements themselves and of their relationship to experience. Words have multiple meanings and connotations; thus the assertions built from words often admit of several interpretations. And in any case, sentences do not match up to facts in neat one-to-one correspondences. So the truth or falsity of an assertion may be unclear. To complicate matters further, some statements are partly true and partly false ("France is a republic, but Italy is a monarchy"). In short, for a writer weighing assertions, the question "Is it true or false?" may be the begin-all, but it is scarcely the end-all.

And a little reflection will show that this question is not always the most illuminating one to ask. The writer who asserts, "Empiricism, more than any other science, causes reactionary developments," has obviously missed the mark, whatever that may have been. But to say that his statement is *false* is to deliver no insight whatever into the ways in which it goes amiss. Nor is it enough to call it *uncertain*. Truth and falsity, certainty and uncertainty: so far we have concentrated on these forms of evaluation. But assertions can be sick or healthy from other causes, too, and there is perhaps as much danger in overemphasizing truth as in slighting it. Philosophers, understandably, have always had an overmastering fondness for truth and falsity, but the writer needs more and sharper instruments of judgment in his critical workshop.

Fortunately, such criteria abound, and their use requires neither special technical training nor a recondite vocabulary. The assessment of statements is a common and necessary activity in daily life, and ordinary language has a rich supply of terms for this purpose. All we shall do is briefly mention a few of the most useful, to suggest the range of possibility.

A) MEANINGFUL AND MEANINGLESS • Before a statement can be judged either true or false it must qualify as meaningful; otherwise, of course, there will be no way to go about testing it. An assertion can be meaningless through grammatical disorder or through the inclusion of nonsense words. The most interesting examples, however, are statements in proper linguistic form which still somehow seem to defy verification, or even understanding. Two well-known examples are: "The Absolute enters into, but is itself incapable of, evolution and progress," and "Colorless green ideas sleep furiously." What predictions about experience could one make from either of these assertions? To be sure, context may give a kind of meaning to assertions that are in themselves meaningless. As a matter of fact the first of our examples comes from *Appearance and Reality,* by the philosopher F. H. Bradley, who undoubtedly thought he was saying something, given his use of "Absolute" and his whole philosophical system. The second—an example, devised by the linguist Noam Chomsky, of a grammatical but meaningless sentence—has been incorporated meaningfully in several poems. Moreover, the most empty assertion may be meaningful in other senses: it may have emotional significance, or suggest images. Still, there is an aura of futility in such assertions, and the writer will do well to avoid them.

Related terms: *significant, verifiable; nonsense.*

B) VAGUE AND CLEAR • Even though a statement is meaningful, it may be so loosely related to facts or experience that its truth is hard to assess.

If a writer asserts, "Considerations of objective phenomena dictate modifications of certain aspects of the domestic posture," he may mean that the country needs new farm laws to deal with the crop failure, or that it is time to get up and have breakfast, or any one of a number of things. But who can tell? The statement is so vague as practically to defy interpretation, and no writer should permit himself to stray this far from clarity, even if context throws some light on the confusion. Vagueness disables an assertion for its main task, to communicate.

Related terms: *inexact, indefinite, abstract; precise.*

C) AMBIGUOUS • Vague assertions wallow in a morass of obscurity; ambiguous statements have clear meanings, but more than one. Ambiguity is often syntactical: "Visiting relatives can be annoying"; "The war broke out and there were numerous rebellions after the serfs were freed." Or it may stem from ambiguous words: "Oscar Wilde valued *sensual* experience"; "The Governor was criticized for the *execution*." Context is a convenient antidote most of the time: "The Governor was criticized for the execution of his duties" (or "of the prisoner").

Related terms: *equivocal, indeterminate.*

D) MISLEADING • To call a statement meaningless, vague, or ambiguous is to say that its relation to the facts is unclear. The terms of evaluation to which we now turn point rather to *distortion* of the facts. The statement "During Eisenhower's administration there was an increase in serious crime" is both clear and true, but misleading in implying a causal connection. Assertions may also mislead by leaving out part of a complex truth: "Abraham Lincoln was a storekeeper." And indeed, the ways of misleading are plentiful and often subtle. No writer of integrity misleads intentionally, but in the grip of enthusiasm or affection for one's own thesis, it is easy to write assertions that angle in at the facts rather than meet them squarely.

Related terms: *slanted, deceptive.*

E) EXAGGERATED AND UNDERSTATED • One way of distorting the facts is to exaggerate, usually with the aid of words like "all," "never," "extremely," and "tremendous." For the statement "Women never reach the first rank in the arts" there is some basis in fact, and if it were limited to composing, painting, and sculpting, or if it read "do not generally" instead of "never," it would have strong claims. But it ignores Jane Austen, Sappho, Emily Dickinson, Jenny Lind, Sarah Bernhardt, and many others. The writer has marred a potentially valid point through overstatement. Likewise, "The League of Nations was a total and abject failure." As for understatement, it is not likely to offend so seriously, since it seems to proceed from caution rather than from flamboyance. Still, it, too, can lead to misrepresentation: the writer who refers to the Second World War as an "unpleasant skirmish" carries moderation to the point of euphemism, if not plain falsehood. Overstatement and understatement have their rhetorical uses, but the writer who employs them intentionally must make certain that his real purpose shows through the mask.

Related terms: *emphatic; magnification, hyperbole.*

F) OVERGENERAL · An exaggerated assertion describes the facts too strongly; an overgeneral one lays claim to more factual support than it actually has. Two examples will make the differences clear: "Asia is a primitive, agricultural continent" is an exaggeration; "Asian countries are not heavily industrial" is an overgeneralization, which could be saved by making an exception of Japan. (A writer may err in the direction of the specific, too, but when he does so he does not distort the facts; he simply wastes space or misses important generalizations.)

Related terms: *broad, loose, abstract.*

G) OVERSIMPLIFIED · An oversimplification is, of course, an assertion that pays too little heed to the intricacies of a situation—"Tragedy is a dead form in the twentieth century," for instance, or "Government spending causes inflation." Whatever the dangers of such assertions, they often prove necessary as a stage in inquiry or as a convenience. Many of the laws of science, not to mention those of the social sciences, are oversimplifications in that they leave out qualifications and exceptions for the sake of emphasizing a major principle. Every writer needs to oversimplify from time to time, and he may do so legitimately as long as he apprises the reader of his intention.

Related terms: *abbreviated, condensed.*

H) TRIVIAL · The faults we have considered so far all pervert the proper relationship between assertion and fact. Carried far enough, they can make an assertion *untrue.* The next two criticisms have little or no bearing on the truth of statements, but they are serious criticisms nonetheless. To call an assertion trivial is not to question its accuracy but, quite the contrary, to claim that it is so patently true as not to deserve mention. It may be trivial because the fact it refers to is minor ("The Nevada atomic testing grounds are closed to real estate development," in a paper on the evils of atomic weapons), or because it is obvious, unilluminating, or empty ("Children learn to talk by trial and error" as an explanation of language learning). With the notion of triviality we enter an area, of great importance to the writer, where truth and falsity have no place: namely that of emphasis, selection, and organization. An assertion is trivial, not in relation to the facts it describes, but in relation to *all* the facts and to the writer's purpose in treating them.

Related terms: *unimportant, obvious, insignificant.*

I) IRRELEVANT • To the argument that socialized medicine is wasteful and inefficient, the assertion "Both doctors and patients have a right to freedom" is simply not relevant. The charge of irrelevance is a grave one, for an assertion that is off the issue pulls no weight and may either confuse the reader or damage the argument. Even when there is no intent to deceive, irrelevance is a sign that the writer is not in full control of his material. This is not to say that digressions and asides are never permissible, but that the writer should understand that they are such, and clearly label them.

Related terms: *not germane, off the point.*

J) OBLIQUE • An oblique statement is one whose relationship to the facts depends on a special understanding between writer and reader about the use of words. Mention of obliqueness opens the whole Pandora's box of rhetorical figures, which belongs properly to a later section of this book, and here we shall only touch on the matter by listing the two main subdivisions of oblique assertions. In *metaphor,* the writer uses one or more words in a nonliteral sense: "A good editorial page is a court of justice before which public action stands trial daily." An *ironic* statement, on the other hand, calls upon the reader to reject the literal sense of the whole sentence, and substitute a contradictory one: "We can be grateful to the city fathers, whose judicious nonenforcement of fire regulations has so cheaply cleared our slums and so efficiently dealt with the problem of overpopulation." Needless to say, the fact that such assertions come at the truth by indirection does not necessarily count against them; so long as their force is clear, they can make an invaluable contribution to the persuasive power of expository prose.

Related terms: *indirect, figurative.*

K) TAUTOLOGICAL • Two criteria that have a more logical flavor conclude this catalogue. A statement is a tautology if part of it merely repeats another part, in the guise of adding information: "Penicillin cures because it has a therapeutic effect"; or "In my experience, every quadruped is a four-footed animal." To cure *is* to have a therapeutic effect, and the word "because" does not belong. Similarly, "quadruped" *means* "four-footed animal," and experience (except of language) has nothing to do with it. Notice that tautologies are rather like definitions, and if the writer offers them as such, he commits no sin. But when they masquerade as explanations or as discoveries about the world, they do not achieve what they claim.

Related terms: *redundant, circular, empty, analytic* (in a philosophical sense).

L) SELF-CONTRADICTORY • Precisely opposite to a tautology is a self-contradictory assertion—a statement of which one part conflicts with another, logically or otherwise. Statements of this kind are so obviously undesirable (consider "Iranians are mainly nomads, while Persians are mainly farmers") that we need say nothing more about them.

Related terms: *impossible, illogical, inconceivable.*

No mere primer of terms used in evaluating assertions can make it a mechanical task for the writer to decide when a given sentence is adequate to his purposes and to the facts. Sorting out truth from falsehood, clarity from obscurity, and distortion from precision is more complicated than separating good apples from bad. But even the novice at writing has a huge advantage on his side: since reaching the age of reason he has had constant practice in matching assertions up with experience, for on this activity the whole of rational thought and sane conduct depends. A list like the foregoing is no more than a codification of what intelligent speakers already know about the ground rules of statement. To apply this knowledge to writing should not be impossible.

4) CONTRADICTORY, COMPATIBLE, AND EQUIVALENT ASSERTIONS

Some of the criteria for weighing assertions led us away from the relationship between assertion and experience and toward that between assertion and assertion. There is a strong reason for giving more attention to this second relationship; the writer conceives what he has to say, not only against a background of facts, but in a context of other assertions, his own and those of other people. Therefore he had best understand clearly the possible connections between statements. This section and the two following ones will scan this crucial subject; the next chapter covers it even more extensively from another perspective.

The mention of self-contradictory assertions offers a starting point, for plainly this relationship can spread out to cover two separate statements. In the most elementary form of contradiction a simple "not" does the trick ("Life is good"; "Life is not good"). But such contradictions are less common and less interesting than those that involve different wording: "Alfalfa is a profitable crop" and "Among crops that bring little income to the farmer, alfalfa stands out," for instance. The example should make two things clear. First, two statements are *contradictory* if every state of affairs (say, high profits from alfalfa) that makes one true makes its partner false. And second, even direct contradictions often depend upon the interpretation of words—what one writer (or farmer) thinks of as a good profit may seem a small income to another. It is only common sense to say that the writer must have a keen sense of contradiction, both to know when he is contradicting an opponent and to avoid contradicting himself.

When two assertions do not meet each other in square, head-on opposition, but the truth of either one precludes the other's being true, they are often called *incompatible* rather than contradictory, and the distinction seems worth preserving. Thus the two assertions "Riggs is an orthodox Catholic" and "Riggs does not believe in life everlasting" are incompatible, though nothing in the sentences themselves (other than the name "Riggs") even suggests that they are about the same subject. Incompatibility depends upon what we know about the world outside of language—for instance, that orthodox Catholics believe in life everlasting. Another difference between incompatibles and contradictories is this: it is possible for two incompatible statements both to be false, but not so for contradictories (check this against our examples). In short, incompatibility is a rather looser relation than contradiction, but for this very reason it constitutes a greater danger to the careless writer, who may fail to notice that such and such a statement in the first paragraph is incapable of living in the same universe with the other one down near the end.

Two *compatible* statements, by contrast, may both be true. Notice that compatibility is an extremely weak relationship, for the two assertions in question may have no logical connection with each other whatsoever: "There is a fly on George's nose" is compatible with "Low tariffs stimulate trade"—but who cares? What we need is a slightly stronger relationship. One such is consistency; two statements are *consistent* with each other if the truth of one might be suspected from the truth of the other. If we know, for instance, that the assertion "Henderson likes abstract painting" is true, we know it is likely that "Henderson is an intellectual," for most people who like abstract painting are intellectuals (and vice versa perhaps). Since one of the writer's main endeavors is to piece together separate bits of information and fashion a coherent whole, the relationship of consistency merits his attention. A still stronger type of compatibility is inclusion. Assertion A is *included* in Assertion B (or follows from it) if the facts upon which A depends for its truth are part of those which make B true. Thus "Vermont has two senators" is included in "Every state has two senators," and "The Tasmanian devil is a mammal" in "The Tasmanian devil is a marsupial." The included assertion cannot be false if the other is true, though it may be true if the other is false. Inclusion has special importance, obviously, for the writer who is generalizing from particulars or deducing particulars from a generalization.

Two compatible statements *may* both be true; two *equivalent* assertions *must* either both be true or both be false. That is, any conceivable state of affairs in the world will either justify both or defeat both. Sometimes equivalence results from purely grammatical relationships: "Wellington defeated Napoleon"; "Napoleon was defeated by Wellington." Sometimes the connection is a little harder to see: "Ferocity and patience are qualities of the tiger"; "Tigers are ferocious, but not impatient." Equivalence does *not* entail exact sameness of meaning, as the last example clearly shows, for language has more and subtler functions than to unveil the truth. But the very fact that the writer is interested in those subtler functions should turn his attention to equivalence, since he cannot choose intelligently between alternate ways of saying the "same thing" unless he knows whether they are actually equivalent and differ only in rhetorical or emphatic features.

5) ASSUMPTIONS

If we shift our perspective a bit, we can discover another reason why relationships like inclusion and equivalence are of importance to the writer. When the truth of Assertion A hinges on the truth of B, the writer always has the option of leaving B unstated, especially if B states common knowledge or a widely shared principle. But B will lurk in the background as an *assumption,* even so. Statements of obligation, in particular, nearly always seem to lean on one or more assumptions. The statement "People in sedentary jobs should run a mile daily" probably assumes something like this: "Sedentary people should exercise," which in turn assumes that "exercise is good for sedentary people," and so on, back to some central principle such as "Men should maintain healthy bodies." Notice that the original assertion also has an assumption of another sort, namely that sedentary people *can* run a mile daily, a doubtful proposition at best. This assumption is subject to the usual tests of verifiability; the others are not. This statement of obligation, therefore, is a compound of the testable and the nontestable, and most statements of obligation are of that kind. They are truly statements, or assertions (that is, they are true or false), but some part of them resists empirical verification and refers one to basic assumptions which cannot be "tested" at all.

The role that assumptions play in writing and reading extends far beyond statements of obligation. One way to describe assumption would be to call them "what we take for granted" or "what we do not feel obliged to prove," or "what else must be true in order for this statement to be true." Certainly we "take for granted" fully as much as we make explicit in our writing. Most of the time we do not even give a thought to the assumptions from which we begin; we simply *assume* that others make the same assumptions as we do. When we do have any cause to doubt agreement, we may make the assumption explicit ("Assuming that legislative programs are to be judged by their enduring effects, the New Deal was largely a failure"). But very often writers assume agreement when there may not be any; in fact, they may make statements whose assumptions they neither have investigated nor would accept if they were to do so. To write in ignorance of one's own assumptions is to write irresponsibly.

The need to reckon with unstated assumptions does not usually arise with simple assertions like "Jefferson designed Monticello." When assertions are combined causally, however, the unstated assertion may be fully as important as any assertion explicitly stated. Consider this sentence:

> Jefferson was an extensive landowner and was therefore interested in securing the independence of the American colonies from England.

Underneath this sentence there is an unstated assumption to the effect that all landowners at that time and in that place were interested in securing the independence of the colonies. And behind that assumption there may well be another, more general, to the effect that all landowners everywhere and at all times are interested in securing the independence from foreign control of the political territory in which they hold land. The criteria for testing these assumptions are historical; if we apply such criteria, we shall have no difficulty in finding that the assumptions are false. We might say of the original sentence about Jefferson, then, that it is based on an *unwarranted assumption*. Such assumptions are a particular danger in expository writing, precisely because they remain behind the scenes; yet they deserve as much attention, both from the writer and from the reader, as explicit statements.

6) IMPLICATIONS

To talk about assumptions is to talk about the logical precedents of an assertion, about what must be true in order for that assertion to be true. Because it is a looking backward, a search for antecedent condition, the search for assumptions is not always easy: a particular statement may rest on many assumptions, each of which must be acknowledged if the writer is to feel secure about his statement. To appreciate the logical consequences, or *implications,* of an assertion is to ask, "If this assertion is true, then what other assertions are necessarily true?" If, for instance, someone says that maple trees always shed their leaves in winter and if he is able to demonstrate that the statement is true, then it is perfectly obvious that a particular maple tree in your front yard will shed its leaves when winter comes. The truth of the first assertion necessarily implies the truth of the second. This form of implication is the simplest of all, since the fact that a particular maple is part of the category of all maple trees makes the implication unmistakably clear.

In the ordinary course of reading and writing, however, implications do not appear so openly. Instead, they operate subtly, often by omission rather than by announcement. Frequently, they arise from a sudden or peculiar emphasis; sometimes juxtaposition produces them. In a recent political convention, one speaker praised by name all of the President's principal advisers except one, thereby implying by omission his disapproval or dislike of that one. Had he gone through the list and then made a pointedly offhand addition of that one name to his list, he would have achieved the same implication by emphasis. Or had he dealt with each name in ascending order of value and coupled the one name with others early in his list, in defiance of the man's actual status, he would have implied by juxtaposition what he actually did imply by omission. The use of implication is not confined, of course, to getting revenge on one's enemies; it is also a primary instrument of humor and of satire ("all the necessities of life—food, shelter, clothing, and a TV set"), and an important means of enlarging the significance of a statement without making it seem unnecessarily explicit.

"Enlarging the significance of a statement" points to an ampler meaning often given to the word "implication" in ordinary discourse, a meaning roughly synonymous with "suggestion." When Laborite Aneurin Bevan called an opponent "that Parliamentary doodlebug," he probably implied—in this loose sense of the word—that the opponent was unfit to hold office or, at least, a fellow incapable of constructive action. Implication, in this sense, may reach to the furthest limits of association; in the stricter sense described above it includes only those additional statements logically entailed by the statement made.

Implications and assumptions really represent the gap between all that a man means and the language he uses to express it. Without them people would be required to lengthen their assertions almost endlessly, and they would be deprived, as well, of many of the artful devices by which they convey subtleties of understanding and feeling which lose some of their character when they are put into words. A considerable amount of the effectiveness of our language derives from the fact that people do not need to express explicitly everything they would have their readers or listeners understand. Were it not for assumptions and implications, a simple command like "Shut the door" would have to be elaborated in this fashion: "There is a door here, and it is now open, and you are able to shut it, and I want it shut; therefore, I order you to shut it; and I am treating you as a subordinate by omitting any polite form of request." And an exclamation like "Fire!" would require expansion to "There is a fire here; it is a dangerous fire; I advise everyone to get away from it as quickly as possible." There is no doubt, then, about the usefulness of this mode of saying less than we mean to have our listeners understand; it is only the matter of determining precisely what is meant in addition to what is explicitly asserted that makes a problem.

Every extended piece of serious discourse is made up of a series of assertions, however disguised. If a writer had to deal with each as elaborately as this book suggests, he would never get done. Yet, if he is responsible about his work, he cannot ignore the one consideration about asserting which underlies all that has been said here: *a writer must know the nature of the assertions he makes in order to understand what meanings they can convey and what responsibilities they impose upon him.* If that consideration becomes important to him, he has the kind of command over language that prepares him to represent honestly the world as he understands it.

7) THE USE OF ANALYSIS OF STATEMENT IN WRITING

To conclude this chapter on asserting, it may be useful to point out two ways in which the skillful construction of assertions may be of practical help to the student in developing both the early and the final drafts of an expository paper.

As practical instruments of speculation, assertions are of great value primarily because they bring thought into focus. It is sometimes said that the greatest educational achievement is learning what questions to ask. The statement is true enough, but only because questions themselves, as noted above, often suggest assertions. A question such as "Did Napoleon's ambition really have anything to do with his smallness of stature?" implies a tentative assertion which might not have occurred to the listener at all if the question had simply been "What were the causes of Napoleon's ambition?" The point of the illustration is that it is really tentative assertions, not questions, that mark the inquiring mind, though the assertions may be cloaked in interrogative form.

The usefulness of assertions and assertion-containing questions in the process of writing is easy to demonstrate. Every writer, professional or amateur, begins, of course, from experience. The more fully digested the experience is, the easier will be the preliminary stages of writing. But no matter how completely the writer has assimilated the material he wishes to write about, and no matter how great his experience, he is bound to find that writing itself opens new possibilities of interpretation to him. When it does, he must explore those possibilities; that is, he must engage in the process of "inquiry" just as though he were entering new country. The adult amateur may have thought and felt as deeply as the professional, but he lacks the training in the solution of problems of expression that the professional utilizes when writing becomes difficult. The student writer lacks that training, too, and lacks also the kind and quality of experience that helps to provide quick and sound perceptions. For that reason, the student writer, and in some measure the adult amateur, can make asserting a practical instrument for dealing with difficulties at the beginning of, or anywhere in the course of, a piece of writing.

Assume that a student is preparing a paper on the federal Soil Bank Bill of 1956, a bill paying farmers a yearly fee for each acre, up to a specified number, taken out of production if that land was previously used for the growing of any one of several "surplus" crops (corn, wheat, and so on). The writer has read widely in preparation for his paper and has found sharply conflicting claims about the bill, not only from the politicians who framed it but from organizations of farmers, from economists, and even from sociologists. He is, in fact, almost submerged by what he has read, and his writing must be, first of all, an attempt to bring some order into the mental and written notes he has accumulated. It is precisely at this point that a conscious use of assertions is of most value to him.

Setting up general "topics" and "subtopics" (Causes, Purposes, Means) does little more than fence the field into sections, as does asking general questions: "What are the causes of the demand for a soil bank?" "What are its purposes?" "How does it operate?" Such topics and such questions provide only the subjects to be discussed; they scarcely hint at the predication, that is, the heart of the discussion. For that reason it is not until the writer is ready to frame tentative assertions that he can even come close to grappling with his subject matter. It does not matter particularly that the first assertions are very general or even that they are wrong. They provide the focus for fruitful activity. The assertion "The Soil Bank Bill was designed primarily to silence Democratic charges that the Republican administration was indifferent to the plight of the farmer" offers a limited and specific matter for consideration. As the writer marshals his knowledge and information around this assertion, he may come to the conclusion that what evidence he has does not warrant the expression "primarily" and change it to suit the data he has at hand. Having tested the value of this assertion, he proposes another, and so on until an order (in this instance, an order of purposes) begins to make itself apparent. In such a process, assertions become first the temporary scaffolding and eventually the permanent framework for the structure of the essay.

Moreover, when the writer alters a temporary assertion until it satisfies his evidence and his understanding, not only has he taken a major step in getting his paper under way, but he has also laid out for himself the responsibilities he must meet. Each final assertion is at the same time a demand. It demands that each of its parts be developed: the "subject" ("The Soil Bank Bill") must be *explained*, and the "predication" ("was designed primarily to give farmers immediate, though temporary, financial assistance in areas where surplus crops had seriously depressed prices") must be *defended*. The steps by which the writer thinks his way from other assertions to this one in the preliminary stage of his work become the steps by which he defends the predications at which he finally arrives.

Even if he works cautiously and slowly on the first draft of his paper, the student is likely to find, when he reads over what he has written, that for all his caution the first draft is as circuitous as a bird dog hunting pheasants in tall grass. It is at this point that skill in the framing of assertions can perform a second service for him.

What a first draft, even a very disorderly one, comprises is a series of coagulations of thought. By translating (through the use of notions like equivalence, inclusion, assumption, and implication) each of these coagulations into a single assertion, the student can distill the draft into a few statements—any number from a half dozen to a score. Thus distilled, the several steps of the paper become evident, and it will be easy to detect their individual inadequacies, as well as the relationships between them. Reduction of the sheer mass of the paper to a few statements also makes it possible for the student to see clearly what his obligations for explanation and defense are in each. In effect, he does nothing here that he was not doing earlier, as he wrote the first draft, but now he has the advantage of hindsight. He does not have to think about where the paper is going but may judge, more or less dispassionately, where it went. Through the medium of the abstracted assertions, he looks at it, so to speak, from outside, which is to say that he looks at it, in some measure, as his reader will do. As with the other matters which are discussed in this book, there is nothing automatic about the transfer of skill in analysis of assertions to skill in composition. Yet, if the development of skill in the making and understanding of assertions does no more than provide this partial perspective on what one has written, it is worth a great deal of study and effort indeed.

EXERCISES

1) Classify the following assertions as statements of convention, fact, opinion, or preference. When the classification is difficult to make, analyze the source of difficulty.

  a. Under a government which imprisons any unjustly, the true place for a just man is also a prison.
  b. Birds are as subject as men to the emotion of jealousy.

    c. No teetotaler drinks alcohol.

    d. No woman sits on the Supreme Court.

    e. No man is an island.

    f. No good poem plays on stock responses.

    g. The Spanish are a proud people.

    h. Chemistry is a hard subject.

    i. Pegasus was a winged horse.

    j. Haste makes waste.

    k. Inadequate discipline in the family causes juvenile delinquency.

2) What criticism(s) would you level against the following assertions? When possible, improve each through rewriting.

    a. It is not possible any longer to think anything out without a greater reality than one's self constantly pressing one's words in dramatic shape and unexpected meaning.

    b. The king had three cities taken.

    c. The atom bomb did some damage at Hiroshima.

    d. A veterinarian treats diseases.

    e. Hitler was responsible for the founding of Israel.

    f. American heavy industry was the creation of a few arrogant, ruthless, selfish men.

    g. Creativity is the handmaiden of art.

    h. Men differ from other species in having wide, flat fingernails.

    i. Some aspects of science militate against factors in education.

    j. All philosophy is footnotes to Plato.

    k. It took centuries for England to drive Ireland to rebellion, but it was worth it.

    l. The objective lies on the far side of the subjective.

    m. Disorders in the organism account for cancer.

3) What relationships hold between the following pairs of assertions?

    a. The theory of evolution is well substantiated.
        The theory of natural selection is probably false.

    b. Existence precedes essence.
        Essence precedes existence.

    c. A man cannot be both a liar and a good Christian.
        Either a man is honest, or he is not a good Christian.

    d. Jones is irascible, and no irascible person should be a social worker.
        Jones should not be a social worker.

    e. Every great advance in thought is the work of many minds.
        Einstein alone revolutionized our understanding of the physical world.

    f. Character is destiny.

       A man of Lincoln's integrity was bound to influence the course of human events.

    g. Conroy likes to play the horses.

       The Conroys are often in financial trouble.

4) What assumptions or implications do the following statements have?

    a. Students who cut classes and neglect their work throw away their chance to earn a good income after graduation.

    b. He smiled a lot, so he must have enjoyed the party.

    c. Because D. H. Lawrence was a man of feeling, he deplored Bertrand Russell's rationality.

    d. A fat paunch never breeds fine thoughts.

    e. If a country's economy is sound, its people are happy, and the Poles are not happy.

    f. The Lord protects drunkards, idiots, and Americans.

    g. *Tropic of Cancer* is pornography, and should never have been published.

5) Types of assertion can give structure to an essay.

    a. Plan a paper on a topic of your choice in which you move from statements of convention to statements of fact to statements of opinion, or from opinion to fact to preference.

    b. Plan a paper in which you begin with an assertion that you have heard in a lecture or recently read somewhere. After stating your belief that it is true or false, move to an examination of its assumptions (as evidence for its truth or falsity) and then to its implications, as evidence of the importance or triviality of the assertion.

    c. Begin from an oblique assertion (i.e.: "America has been a melting-pot so long that it has grown tired of its own stew") and develop a paper that progresses from clarification to definition to the matter of verification.

❋ *Proving*

An assertion can stand unsupported; many do. Consider "I'm hungry."
Or consider the assertion "An assertion can stand unsupported." When
the reader came upon it the first time he may have treated it in any one
of a number of ways: pondered it, thought about something else, repeated it quietly to himself, accepted it implicitly, forgotten it immediately, written it down in his notebook, rejected it out of hand,
analyzed its grammar, laughed aloud at it, translated it into German,
been reminded of a story by it, discovered in it the way out of his dilemma,
and so on. All of these responses, disagreeable though some would be to
the authors, were within the reader's rights. And if he responded in one of
these ways, the assertion was, for his purposes, sufficient in itself; he
required no sequel. But if his response was to challenge it, or doubt it,
or seek to test it for himself, then he raised issues that could only be
settled by further assertions, assertions that would either confirm or
refute the original one. That is, he was asking for proof: for although
an assertion may *stand* by itself, it can hardly *prove* itself. Loud and
repeated assertion may convince—witness the technique of the Big Lie—
but, in general, to assert is not to prove.

For the writer and the reader, proving has to do with relations
between statements, with the effort to certify one assertion by linking it
to another (or others) whose credentials are good. Another way of putting
it is to say that a proof, when it works right, uses one or more pieces
of certain, or familiar, or easily accessible information to get to a piece
of previously uncertain, or new, or inaccessible information. The case is
clearest in science, where much of our most valued knowledge—the
existence of protons and electrons, the laws of heredity, the causes of
disease—is such that investigators could not possibly have reached it by
observation, nor in any way other than through proof. As man and
scientist, Newton made a large number of observations, but he did not
observe the laws of thermodynamics, nor did Harvey observe the blood

circulating. Of course, the conclusion of a proof need not be new to the prover, but it had better be new to someone. A man who proves to you that you have two ears will, under normal circumstances, be wasting his and your time. Proving, then, is a matter of converting old knowledge into new, and, for the writer, of combining assertions so that one backs up another.

It need hardly be said that not every group of assertions will do, and not every arrangement of a proper group of assertions will do. That a woman swam the Bosporus last Tuesday does not prove that life exists on Venus, and it is fruitless to argue that because all states are made up of counties and San Bernardino County is a county, San Bernardino County is smaller than all states (though *something* follows about San Bernardino County). Clearly, one of the problems facing a writer is what criteria distinguish sound proofs from those arrays of information or statement which are either bad proofs or no proofs at all.

But first it is well to point out that, although proving reaches its peaks of elegance and rigor in mathematics, logic, science, history, jurisprudence, counterintelligence work, and the like, everyone spends some of his time proving, and not always badly at that. Proving has its roots in the utterly commonplace activity of backing up assertions with other assertions—giving reasons. Take the following as instances:

1) I know there's a mouse in the room, because I can see its tail under the couch.

2) You *were* driving recklessly: you were on the wrong side of the double line.

3) Only members are allowed at the club's bar on Sundays, so we'll have to have our drink somewhere else.

4) You never see rattlesnakes around here; probably the climate is too cold for them.

5) If the bank is a ten-minute drive from here, and if it closes at three, you will be too late.

6) Whenever there's ragweed around he sneezes continuously, so I suppose he suffers from hay fever.

7) Since he suffers from hay fever, he'll sneeze continuously whenever there's ragweed around.

8) Most Irishmen are Catholics, so Mr. MacNamara probably won't be able to eat meat tonight.

Not a single one of these arguments would pass muster as a formal proof, yet each is adequate to its job—each is in perfectly good order, given an appropriate context. It would be absurd, in ordinary conversation, to challenge the speaker in 8) by saying "You haven't stated all your premises," or "Your proof is neither deductive nor inductive." The kind of objection one would expect, if any, is "But MacNamara is a Scot," a claim, in other words, that the original speaker was mistaken about part of the context. For everyday purposes 8) is a strong argument as it stands, provided the facts are what the speaker implies.

Moreover, there is little danger of logical deception in arguments like these. Suppose 3) had run, "Only members are allowed at the club's bar on Sunday, so if we go to Leary's Tavern for our drink we won't run into anyone from the club." The speaker's companion, if he were on his toes, would immediately have sensed the flaw in reasoning (a flaw strictly in *logic,* as it happens). Most educated people reason well enough for most purposes most of the time.

Nor is it sensible to create a mystique about logic or scientific method. The ground rules followed by logicians and scientists have their source in the ground rules followed by all intelligent men in candid and serious argument. At the same time, it is essential to recognize that there is a great difference in complexity and rigor between the methods of the man in the laboratory and those of the man in Leary's Tavern, and that, while the expository writer need not adopt the standards of the theoretical physicist or those of the logician, he can rarely settle for the standards of Leary's Tavern. Arguments 1) through 8) are in the main too ephemeral or too trivial even to find their way into written prose, but if they were to appear in an essay the reader would have a right to complain about some. In 4), for instance, an observation about rattlesnakes is offered in support of a tentative hypothesis. In order for the hypothesis to carry much conviction, the listener would have to know how many observers have failed to see rattlesnakes, and for how long, and whether they were looking in the right places. A critical thinker would also ask whether rattlesnakes thrive in equally cold climates elsewhere, and whether there are other factors—such as too much or too little water, a shortage of rattlesnake food, an abundance of natural enemies, or the presence of geographical barriers—which could account as well as the cold climate for the absence of rattlesnakes. Good answers to all these questions would make the argument a strong one, but the investigator could tighten it up still more by discovering features of the rattlesnake's physiology which prevent it from living in the cold. The original hypothesis may be a plausible one (and that is all the speaker claimed for it), but it is a long way from certain on the basis of the reason put forth.[1] It seems clear, then, that linked assertions which serve adequately as proofs in casual talk may fail to pull their load in reasoned prose. This is one reason why a student, however fluent he is in offhand argument, does well to familiarize himself with the sanctions that govern more formal reasoned discourse before proving his point on paper.

[1] In point of fact, some rattlesnakes flourish in climates as cold as that of the Canadian great plains.

There is another reason, too. Notice that proofs 1) to 8) all have roughly the same shape. Sometimes, to be sure, the conclusion comes before its backing, and sometimes after; in some of the proofs the backing consists of two assertions rather than of one, and some lack of logical connective. But all eight have an elementary structure something like this.

Backing assertion; therefore ——→ concluding assertion.

This is, indeed, the standard form for a casual argument. Yet even a cursory inspection of the eight proofs is enough to show how misleading this similarity is. Consider these special characteristics:

Backing
> 1) offers, as backing for its conclusion, a single piece of conclusive evidence, but the backing in 6) sums up a number of past observations. The backing in 2) is not so much the evidence presented as an assumed partial *definition* of reckless driving. In 8) the backing is not evidence at all, but a general principle. In 5) the backing is not even stated as true.

Conclusion
> The conclusion of 6) is an explanatory hypothesis, that of 1) a particular fact, that of 7) a confident prediction, that of 8) a statement of probability.

The connection between backing and conclusion
> In 2) the conclusion follows inevitably from the backing, given the relevant traffic law, but in 4), as we have shown, a great deal more information is required before the backing will make the conclusion certain. Clearly 6) and 7) represent different types of proof; the conclusion of 6) is the backing of 7); and the observations of sneezing which constitute the backing of 6) turn up as predicted observations in the conclusion of 7).

The eight arguments also vary considerably in the number and kind of additional steps needed in order to make them formally complete. And of course the completed arguments would take a variety of forms.

In other words, beneath their simple external form, these proofs reveal a fair amount of complexity, and by no means the same kind of complexity in each case. And although this complexity need not emerge in casual talk—indeed, if it did, trivial worldly affairs would become both interminable and hopelessly dull—as soon as a *writer* undertakes to prove a point, the true shape of his argument becomes crucial. For, since the rules and conventions by which his argument will be judged sound or unsound depend on the submerged form of that argument, he can scarcely know whether he is talking sense or nonsense unless he has at least an intuitive grasp of the logic of his position. Now this is not to say that what he finally puts on paper must match up neatly with one or another fully expanded form of proof. On the contrary, he may well settle for the rudimentary form, Backing ⟶ Conclusion. But if so, he must know what steps he is doing without; he must know that these steps are legitimate; and he must know that his *reader* will be able to fill them in and sense their legitimacy. Otherwise, his proof will fail to convince, and both he and the reader will be shortchanged. So if a writer wishes to combine assertions to make proofs, it behooves him to know something about the formal properties of arguments—in short, about logic.

1) THE LIMITS OF LOGIC

Before we turn to the procedures of logic, however, two objections had better be anticipated. First, and most obviously, not all writing is argumentative. Granted. Description, narration, meditation, analysis, explanation, and many other types of prose can do their work flawlessly without a trace of overt argument. It would be difficult to find a proof in this piece of description:

> The bed-frame is not tall or at all ornate, as many iron frames are. Its former surface of hard white paint is worn almost entirely away to the bare, blue-brown iron. It is a three-quarter bed, which means a double bed so far as tenant usage is concerned.
>
> JAMES AGEE, *Let Us Now Praise Famous Men*

At the same time, even writers in these modes aim to *convince*, to capture the reader's assent; and when the reader's assent is at stake, the writer must always be concerned with the authority of his assertions. But the authority of his assertions depends upon the backing which might be adduced to support them, even if in fact it is not. And questions of backing are questions of proof. So it is wise to admit that argument lurks in more corners than might be suspected of harboring it, and that very little rational activity is altogether innocent of proof.

A passage written by the physiologist Walter B. Cannon will illustrate the point:

> Organisms, composed of material which is characterized by the utmost inconstancy and unsteadiness, have somehow learned the methods of maintaining constancy and keeping steady in the presence of conditions which might reasonably be expected to prove profoundly disturbing. Men may be exposed to dry heat at temperatures from 115 to 128 degrees Centigrade (239 to 257 degrees Fahrenheit) without an increase of their body temperature above normal. On the other hand arctic mammals, when exposed to cold as low as 35 degrees Centigrade below freezing (31 degrees below zero Fahrenheit) do not manifest any noteworthy fall of body temperature. Furthermore, in regions where the air is extremely dry the inhabitants have little difficulty in retaining their body fluids. And in

these days of high ventures in mountain climbing and in airplanes human beings may be surrounded by a greatly reduced pressure of oxygen in the air without showing serious effects of oxygen want.

The Wisdom of the Body

Although at first reading the passage looks to be simply a series of factual statements, clearly it is an argument: the last four sentences count as backing for the generalization of the first. Nor does the relevance of proving end there. Each of the supporting assertions is itself a generalization from, presumably, a large number of observations, and they will not have the impact they are intended to have unless the reader senses this. (Cannon's mention of precise temperatures assures the reader that the appropriate observations and experiments really have been made, as does his use of the verbs "manifest" and "showing.") Notice, too, that the four facts are chosen, not randomly, but for their argumentative force. The first shows that the body maintains constant temperature in extreme heat. But a reader might still wonder whether body temperature resists extreme cold, and the second fact stills that query. At this point, however, a reasonable hypothesis might be constructed to the effect that mammalian stability is merely *temperature-proof.* Cannon is pressing for a much more general hypothesis: he adds evidence about the body's independence of atmospheric dryness. Both dryness and temperature impinge mainly on the body's surface: wouldn't physiological steadiness be upset by a shortage of some essential substance that is taken *into* the body? The last fact dispels this conjecture. Not one of the four assertions is redundant; each one, in addition to supporting Cannon's generalization, reduces the number of competing hypotheses. Thus a passage presented as a bundle of information actually works for Cannon as a rather cleverly structured argument. If the submerged argument had been faulty, the passage would not have done its job. Hence, even when a writer describes, or states facts, or analyzes, he had better be aware that these activities are seldom hermetically sealed off from proving.

The second objection: not all efforts to convince depend on logic. Again, granted. The mystic's euphoria, the novelist's sense of pathos in daily existence, the poet's nostalgia for his childhood—these can be *transmitted,* and convincingly so, but hardly argued logically. And these are valuable things, central to richly human modes of life. Man is not inveterately, not even inherently, a logical creature: logic is his achievement rather than his inheritance. Beneath the subtle structure of logic which he has learned to erect lies a life of perceptions and emotions still largely uncharted. So to recommend logical procedures is not to ignore other valuable ways of knowing what is true ("The heart has its reasons," said Pascal); it is only to encourage the use of those procedures over which thoughtful men, in the course of two thousand years and more, have learned to exercise control and through which they have learned to reach useful conclusions and make viable judgments.

By and large it is not with the entirely unprovable that the writer has to deal. Twentieth-century discoveries in psychology, our philosophical love affair with "the absurd," and an increasing emphasis in the arts on irrational forces in human life have all conspired to produce a widespread suspicion of logic in our own day. However, to jettison logic altogether is to demean man's dignity and deprive him of the soundest way we know for him to comprehend his experience.

2) CLASSICAL DEDUCTIVE PROOFS

It will be convenient to begin by making things look simpler than they are. Logicians have commonly divided proofs into two types, *deductive* and *inductive*.[2] This traditional division will serve as an introduction to the subject, though the reader should keep in mind its artificiality when set against the profusion of forms taken by actual verbal arguments.

A deductive proof is one whose conclusion follows with absolute inevitability from its backing, provided that conclusion and backing are properly related, according to certain rules. Mathematical proofs and those of symbolic logic are deductive, as are many arguments in law and in virtually every field of human inquiry. Given this variety of users, it is not surprising that the rules of deduction have been framed in a number of different ways. Moreover, they have at times attained a tortuous complexity and a degree of abstraction that are of little concern to the writer who argues in words. So in our limited space we shall barely hint at the technical elaborations of deductive reasoning, but shall seek mainly to establish its nature and its place as an instrument of thought.

Classical deductive logic, as developed by Aristotle, and perfected in the late Middle Ages, is built around a linking of at least three assertions (not *two,* as in most everyday proving) in such a way that the first two could not be true without also making the third one true.[3]

9) All Frenchmen understand love.   Backing
   All Roquefort cheese makers are Frenchmen.

   All Roquefort cheese makers understand love.   Conclusion

---

[2] Arguments of *probability* are sometimes presented as a third type in no man's land between induction and deduction, and are sometimes assimilated to one or the other.

[3] Technically these arguments are called *syllogisms;* the backing assertions are *premises.*

10) Only Frenchmen have understood love.   Backing
    Don Juan was not a Frenchman.

    Don Juan did not understand love.   Conclusion

11) Every man is either an amorous bungler or a Frenchman.   Backing
    All Parisians are men.
    Some Parisians are amorous bunglers.

    Some Parisians are not Frenchmen.   Conclusion

However *silly* these proofs are, the reader can tell with a little scrutiny that if he is willing to concede the backing assertions, he can not, without contradiction, deny the conclusions. In other words, these are *valid* arguments, whatever their degree of soundness.

To see why they are valid, look at the matter in this way: each assertion can be thought of as saying something about the relationship between two *classes,* or between one or more individuals and a class. Thus the first assertion of (9) states that the class of Frenchmen is included in the class of people who understand love. A different way of putting it is to say that every member of the class of Frenchmen also belongs to the class of people who understand love. The relationship might be diagramed like this:

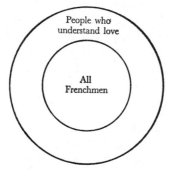

The second assertion has it that the class of Frenchmen includes the class of Roquefort cheese makers:

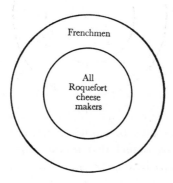

But if one class is part of a second class, which is in turn part of a third, then the first class must also be a part of the third; hence, the class of Roquefort cheese makers must also be included in the class of people who understand love:

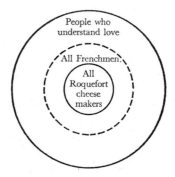

Class relationships being what they are, the argument is air-tight; just as, chronology being what it is, if Henry VIII antedates Cromwell, and Cromwell antedates Lloyd George, it follows inexorably that Henry VIII antedates Lloyd George.

Arguments 10) and 11) are a bit harder to translate into statements about classes. The first assertion of (10) might appear to have the same import as the first assertion of (9), but actually it reverses the class relationship. Rather than stating that the class "people who have understood love" *includes* the class "Frenchmen," it states that all people who have understood love *belong to* the class of Frenchmen. Clearly, if Don Juan did not belong to that class, he could not possibly have belonged to a *part* of that class:

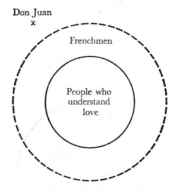

In 11), the first assertion states that the class of amorous bunglers and the class of Frenchmen include, between them, the entire class of men. So if the class of Parisians is included in the class of men, and if it has some members that also belong to the class of amorous bunglers, then

naturally the class of Parisians has at least some members (these same ones) that are not members of the class of Frenchmen:

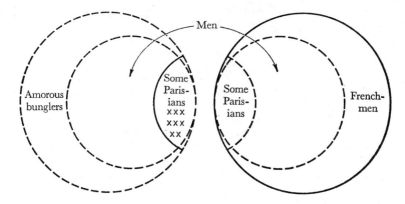

In like manner, any deductive argument of this sort can be converted into a group of statements about classes and their members.

Such analysis will also show, of course, when an argument is *invalid*. Take this one:

12) Only Frenchmen are good lovers.   Backing
    Every Roquefort cheese maker is a Frenchman.

    Every Roquefort cheese maker is a good lover.   Conclusion

The class of Roquefort cheese makers is contained in the class of Frenchmen, and so is the class of good lovers. But from this it does not follow that the cheese makers all belong to the class of good lovers, or even that a single cheese maker can court a woman skilfully. For the first assertion leaves open the possibility that a great many Frenchmen are *not* good lovers, and all the cheese makers might belong to that unhappy class of beings. So the following is a possible state of affairs, given the first two assertions:

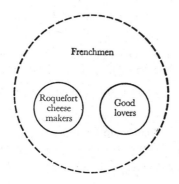

So, for that matter is this:

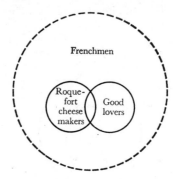

Or either of these:

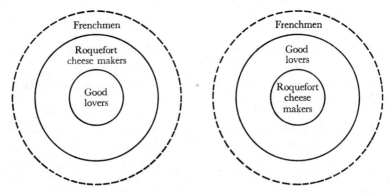

In short, the backing assertions prove nothing at all about the relationship between the two subclasses of Frenchmen, and so the argument fails.

Now the reader may have noticed that arguments 9) through 12), similar though they are in their general shape, contain assertions of various types. Such assertions can be positive or negative. They can speak of whole classes ("all," "only," "every"), of parts of classes ("some"), or of individuals ("Don Juan," "a," "the"). They can be unequivocal ("all men are") or equivocal ("all men are either *x* or *y*"). Moreover, they can be partly or wholly *hypothetical;* that is, 9) might be converted into

> 13) If any man is a Frenchman he understands love.
> All Roquefort cheese makers are Frenchmen.
>
> All Roquefort cheese makers understand love.

or

> 14) If any man is a Frenchman he understands love.
> If any man is a Roquefort cheese maker he is a Frenchman.
>
> If any man is a Roquefort cheese maker he understands love.

Since the conclusion one can draw from backing assertions varies with the form of those assertions, it is obvious both that the rules for classical deduction are fairly complex and that the legitimate manipulations are numerous. But there is no need for a writer who plans to *use* logic rather than *study* logic to learn all the rules and manipulations. He will have little difficulty with short arguments of this sort if he remembers that they can all be reduced to statements about class membership and class inclusion. His lifelong familiarity with the concept of classes will do the rest (aided, perhaps, by diagrams like those illustrated above). Perhaps it is possible to venture another definition at this point: a classical deductive argument is one in which two or more assertions about classes and members of classes precede an assertion which relates two of these classes, or one member and one class, in a new way.

3) DEDUCTION BASED ON THE TRUTH AND FALSITY OF STATEMENTS

Deductive logic has, in this century, assumed forms considerably more intricate and powerful than the one just described. They had their roots in the work of Gottlob Frege during the last quarter of the nineteenth century, but it was not until the publication (1910–1913) of *Principia Mathematica,* by Bertrand Russell and Alfred North Whitehead, that the study called "symbolic logic" or "mathematical logic" began to flourish, yielding techniques undreamt of by Aristotle (though some were anticipated by the medieval scholastic philosophers and later forgotten). This chapter will have little to do with such complex matters. Nor would a full treatment be of much use to the writer, since most theorems of modern logic are, like those of mathematics, far removed indeed from the give-and-take of verbal argument. But a few basic concepts, directly relevant to ordinary proving, merit a quick glance.

Many proofs which are plainly deductive according to the definition on page 78 do not fit any of the classical forms. As an example, consider the following:

15) Either there was a strong wind last night, or   Backing
     somebody stole our tent.
     But there was not a strong wind last night.
       [Edgar was here, and he says so.]

     Therefore somebody must have stolen our tent.   Conclusion

With considerable ingenuity one might phrase this argument in terms of classes, or picture it with circles, but doing so would not reveal why it works (try, and see for yourself). That is because the crucial elements in this argument are not classes and members of classes, but *statements.* The sense of the first assertion is that one of two statements must be

true, and since the other assertion tells us that the first of the two statements is false, we know that the second statement is true.

This proof is not puzzling, but a longer one of the same sort can be
very puzzling indeed:

> 16) If it is the case both that the cook had been drinking   Backing
> and that the scullery door was unlocked, or if it is false
> that no one was on duty at the switchboard in the vil-
> lage, then it must be true either that the butler killed
> Lord Winchester or that the weapon was a coal scuttle
> and Stubbs is lying, unless it is not true both that some-
> one left the house after dark and that Miss Hitchens got
> to work early that night. Now we know that the cook had
> been drinking, but the scullery door, we are assured, was
> never unlocked. Still, the switchboard in the village was
> quite certainly attended—we have overwhelming evidence
> of that. Moreover, someone did leave the house after
> dark, and Miss Hitchens did get to work early. As for
> Stubbs, he was unquestionably lying, from first to last.
> Well, then, what about the weapon? Our coroner's testi-
> mony shows us that it must have been something far
> heavier than a coal scuttle.

> And so, gentlemen, it is clear beyond a possibility of   Conclusion
> doubt that the murderer of Lord Winchester was his own
> butler. Arrest him, Carter.

Every reader of mysteries has encountered, usually on the last page or
so, demonstrations like this, though perhaps not quite so tortured. How
can one be sure that there is no sleight of hand in the inspector's
juggling of all these statements?

The task becomes infinitely simpler if some of our common knowledge
about statements is expressed in symbolic terms.[4] These symbols will suffice for most problems:

> a) Let "P," "Q," "R," etc., stand for individual statements (*propositions*,
> technically speaking) which must be true or false. Hence "P" means
> " 'P' is true." If "P" stands for "The cook had been drinking," then
> "P" is true if the cook had, in fact, been drinking.

> b) Let "−" stand for "not." "−P" means " 'P' is false."

> c) Let " • " stand for "and." "P • Q" means "both 'P' and 'Q' are true."

> d) Let "v" stand for "or." "PvQ" means "at least one of the two state-
> ments 'P' and 'Q' is true."[5]

[4] What follows is a specially adapted and abbreviated version of what logicians
call the "propositional calculus," or "truth functional logic."

[5] Note that this is a different sense of "or" than the one we used on page 79,
where "either _____ or _____ had the added proviso, "but not both." This sense
is captured in our symbolism by "P < Q."

e) Let "$<$" stand for "unless." "$P < Q$" means " 'P' is true unless 'Q' is true." "$<$" also means "either _____ or _____, but not both."

f) Let "$\longrightarrow$" stand for "if _____, then _____," or for "entails." Thus "$P \longrightarrow Q$" will mean "if 'P' is true, then 'Q' is also true," or " 'P' entails 'Q'." (A caution: when the original reads "P if Q," then the symbolic rendering must be "$Q \longrightarrow P$," for obviously the truth of "P" depends upon that of "Q," rather than vice versa.)[6]

g) Another useful symbol, which we shall not use until later, is "$\equiv$," meaning "if, and only if." "$P \equiv Q$" means " 'P' is true if, and only if, 'Q' is true." (It also means " 'Q' is true if, and only if, 'P' is true.")

At this point it should be easy to see that the truth or falsity of a combination of statements and logical connectives follows from the truth or falsity of the separate statements, plus the meanings of the terms that link them. Hence these rules of thumb are a matter of common sense coupled with a knowledge of English:

h) "$-P$" is true if "P" is false, false if "P" is true.

i) "$P \cdot Q$" is true when, and only when, both "P" and "Q" are true.

j) "PvQ" is true when "P" is true, when "Q" is true, and when both "P" and "Q" are true. Similarly, if we know that "PvQ" is true, we know that if either "P" or "Q" is false the other must be true.

k) If "$P < Q$" is true, then the truth of either statement implies the falsity of the other, and vice versa. Notice too that if "P" and "Q" are both true or both false, then "$P < Q$" is false.

The connective "$\longrightarrow$" is different. The truth or falsity of "$P \longrightarrow Q$" cannot be determined from the truth or falsity of "P" and "Q." But it is possible to reckon as follows:

l) If we know that "$P \longrightarrow Q$," we know that if "P" is true then "Q" must also be true. We also know that if "Q" is false, "P" is false (make sure you understand why). On the other hand, if "P" is false we do not know whether "Q" is true or false; likewise, if "Q" is true, "P" may be either true or false.[7]

Now one can deal with actual proofs like (15). If the statement "there was a strong wind last night" is called "P," and the statement "somebody

---

[6] " 'P' is true only if 'Q' is true" can be written "$(Q \longrightarrow P) \cdot (- Q \longrightarrow - P)$." Work this out to your own satisfaction.

[7] Students and instructors trained in logic will have noticed that we depart at a a number of points from the procedures and symbolism customary in most texts. This treatment of "if" deviates especially from standard usage. Our aim, of course is to present a simple system of definitions and rules which correpond as closely as possible to ordinary language and thought. Where formal logic fails to do justice to English argumentation, we have left formal logic behind, preferring usefulness and intuitive rightness to the greater elegance and power of formal techniques.

stole our tent," "Q," then the first backing assertion is of the form "PvQ." And of course it is given as true. So according to rule (j), if either "P" or "Q" is false, the other must be true, and since the second backing assertion tells us that "P" is false, "Q" is true. As this is what the conclusion states, the argument is valid.

But symbols are not needed to tell us this. The system may be useful for checking out such proofs as (15), but it will not be worth the trouble unless it can unravel (16) and the like. Two further procedures must be adopted: First, substitute "+" for true statements, and "O" for false ones. Second, group statements that belong together by using "( )," "[ ]," and "⌈ ⌉," to avoid confusion. (Consider the ambiguity in written English of "He will come Tuesday and she will come Thursday unless there is a storm," which could be either "P · (Q < R)" or "(P · Q) < R" —two quite different assertions.)

To begin, then, assign letters to the separate statements of 16):

> P—The cook had been drinking.
> Q—The scullery door was unlocked.
> R—No one was on duty at the switchboard in the village.
> S—The butler killed Lord Winchester.
> T—The weapon was a coal scuttle.
> U—Stubbs is lying.
> V—Someone left the house after dark.
> W—Miss Hitchens got to work early that night.

The first sentence of 16), which is true as a whole, may now be given a symbolic transcription:

$$[(P \cdot Q) \ v \ -R] \longrightarrow \big][S \ v \ (T \cdot U)] < [- \ (V \cdot W)]\big]$$

Next, substitute "+" or "O," according to the information provided by the inspector, for each statement except S, which is the one he is trying to prove:

	II	
I	IIa	IIb
$[(+\cdot O)v-O] \longrightarrow$	$[Sv(O\cdot+)]$	$< \ [-(+\cdot+)]$

Now solve for S like an equation, using rules (h) through (l). Begin inside parentheses and work outward. First, I:

	$(+\cdot O)$	becomes	O	rule (i)
leaving:	$O \ v - O$			
	$- O$	becomes	$+$	rule (h)
leaving:	$O \ v +$	which becomes	$+$	rule (j)

So I as a whole is true. Therefore II is also true.   rule (1)
Next, it is necessary to know the status of IIb:

| | $(+ \cdot +)$ | becomes | $+$ | rule (i) |
| leaving: | $- +$ | which becomes | O | rule (h) |

If IIb is false, then IIa is true.   rule (k)
Next:

| | $O \cdot +$ | becomes | O | rule (i) |
| leaving: | $S \vee O$ | | | |

Therefore S is true, the inspector is triumphantly justified, and the hapless butler is doomed.

The solution may at first glance appear as difficult in symbolic form as in words, but a very little practice at translating English into symbols and reducing complex expressions will lead to surprising proficiency. And the procedure makes a simple mechanical task out of checking arguments (one's own or those of another writer) which would fuddle or altogether elude one's unaided powers of reasoning—in much the same way as a few rules, plus pencil and paper, enable one to do problems in long division that would be impossible to do in one's head. Through these methods the writer can also *clarify* his argument for himself—for instance, by noticing ambiguities of grouping.

It is worth mentioning three other ways of using these rules and symbols, before leaving the subject. First, given complex true assertions like the first one of 16), it is possible to simplify the problem if one knows the truth or falsity of *any* component statement, sometimes to an astonishing degree. Thus, to stick with our example, if one knows only that someone was on duty at the switchboard, that Stubbs is telling the truth, and that someone left the house after dark, he knows that the butler murdered Lord Winchester unless Miss Hitchens got to work early. One more piece of information, and the problem is solved. (The student should work this out for himself.)

A second application of these methods follows from the fact that a *whole* complex assertion can be assessed if one knows which of its components are true and which false, unless the whole assertion contains " $\longrightarrow$." If it is true that Robinson won the race ("P") and false that Hemingway was a poet ("Q"), then "PvQ" is true. But so are "P $\cdot$ -Q" and "P < Q." In other words, the given information is *consistent* with a number of formulations, and back in the nonlogical world one still has a right to ask which formulation does most justice to the facts. But this very notion of consistency can be of great value when the complex assertion is not merely a string of factual statements, but a lawlike comment on connections between events or states of affairs. Then, even if it contains " $\longrightarrow$," one can check it for consistency with a given body of information, and find out whether, to that extent, it holds good.

Suppose that a political theorist has proposed this hypothesis: Whenever the President's party has not controlled Congress, most administration bills failed to pass and the President's popularity declined, unless either the country was at war, or all three of the following conditions held: average income rose, there was no split in the President's party, and crops were good. Assign these letters to the individual statements:

P—The President's party did not control Congress.
Q—Most administration bills failed to pass.
R—The President's popularity declined.
S—The country was at war.
T—Average income rose.
U—There was a split in the President's party.
V—Crops were good.

Then the hypothesis may be schematized like this:

$$P \longrightarrow \big[(Q \cdot R) < [S \vee (T \cdot -U \cdot V)]\big]$$

(Satisfy yourself that this is right, particularly that "$\longrightarrow$" is a good translation of "whenever.")

It will be possible now to test the hypothesis against known historical facts. Suppose that during two Eisenhower years the Democrats controlled Congress, most administration bills failed, Eisenhower became more popular, there was no war, average income rose, the Republicans stuck together, and crops did well. Substituting the appropriate values, one gets:

$$+ \longrightarrow \big[(+ \cdot O) < [O \vee (+ \cdot -O \cdot +)]\big]$$

By the usual rules, the scheme reduces as follows:

$$+ \longrightarrow \big[O < [O \vee (+ \cdot + \cdot +)]\big]$$
$$+ \longrightarrow [O < (O \vee +)]$$
$$+ \longrightarrow (O < +)$$
$$+ \longrightarrow +$$

Since "$+ \longrightarrow +$" is a valid sequence (see rule [1]), the facts during these two years *are* consistent with the hypothesis, and will therefore count in support of it, though of course it will not be *demonstrated* until it has been tested out for the whole of American history. The symbols earn their keep here, as in (16), by making manageable what would otherwise be extremely cumbersome.

In the previous chapter we spoke of "equivalent assertions." The third by-product of the present section is a method of checking logically complex assertions for equivalence. Two such assertions are equivalent if they have exactly the same logical force no matter what truth values are substituted for their P's and Q's. It is a simple task, thus, to find out that "Either television will prosper and the movies will not, or the movies will prosper and television will not," is equivalent to "Television will prosper unless the movies do." We can set up the equivalence this way:

$$(P \cdot -Q) \text{ v } (Q \cdot -P) \equiv P < Q \qquad \text{(see [g] for "} \equiv \text{")}$$

If P and Q are both true or both false, this expression reduces to "$O \equiv O$," and if one is true and the other false, it reduces to "$+ \equiv +$." Hence a writer might substitute one of the two original assertions for the other without changing the logical impact of what he is saying (though he should remember that *any* change in wording leads to at least minor changes in connotative or rhetorical meaning).

Even as hasty a tour of deductive logic as we have conducted in these pages[8] reveals some of its advantages as an instrument of thought and an aid to the writer. The clarity, the neatness, and the certainty of a well-made deductive proof should be attractive lures to anyone constructing an argument, whether he uses the notion of logical form as a model for his actual phrasing, or merely for putting his thoughts in order. A valid proof is not the noblest work of man, but it must always command respect, especially if it is somewhat intricate. And bear in mind that there is no such thing as a *fairly* valid proof (though there are many proofs whose validity is impossible to ascertain because their terms are unclear). Validity is an all-or-nothing affair. It is comforting, in the welter of charge and countercharge, confusion and deception, to have, even as an occasional sanctuary, the fixity of deductive argument.

4) *VALIDITY AND TRUTH*

Still, if the reader has read this section with occasional misgivings, his response is warranted; there are serious limitations on the value of deductive logic. For one thing, not all arguments lend themselves to the

---

[8] At this point we would like to acknowledge our indebtedness to several books, which we also recommend for further reading in the field of logic and critical thinking. As an introduction to formal logic we suggest Willard Van Orman Quine's *Methods of Logic.* P. F. Strawson's *Introduction to Logical Theory* and Stephen Toulmin's *The Uses of Argument* treat the subject more philosophically and less technically; both authors are concerned with the relationship between logic and ordinary language. Three works which deal with the whole field of proving are *An Introduction to Logic and Scientific Method,* by Morris R. Cohen and Ernest Nagel; *Critical Thinking,* by Max Black; and *Thinking Straight,* by Monroe C. Beardsley. The last two are more elementary than the first. Nelson Goodman's *Fact, Fiction, and Forecast* and S. F. Barker's *Induction and Hypothesis* focus on the theory of inductive logic. Finally, a useful and entertaining book on argumentative mishaps is *Fallacy— The Counterfeit of Argument,* by W. Ward Fearnside and William B. Holther. Any student who cares to pursue the subject of this chapter will find many other excellent books to help him.

modes of analysis explicated here. How can anyone judge the recalcitrant proofs? Surely they are not all faulty. Even more disturbing, deductive proofs can function convincingly only if a good deal has already been proven. That is, the backing assertions must have their credentials in order, or there is no point in going on to the conclusion.

In other words there is an important distinction between *validity* and *truth*. Even though an argument is valid, its conclusion may be false unless its backing assertions are true. Consider:

17) All smokers have tuberculosis.
    Everyone with tuberculosis is diseased.   Backing

    All smokers are diseased.   Conclusion

Valid, but perfectly useless, because the first backing assertion introduces a falsehood that gets deposited in the conclusion in a different form. More puzzling still, it is possible to arrive validly at a true conclusion from totally false backing:

18) If Griggs is a normal man, he
        has three legs.   Backing
    If Griggs has three legs, he
        has ten toes.

    If Griggs is a normal man, he   Conclusion
        has ten toes.

One might say that the end justifies the means, but no one is likely to be happy with this proof, notwithstanding its true conclusion and valid form.

The problem of truth is one that deduction cannot surmount by itself, yet deduction is inextricably bound up with truth in all practical matters, if not in all the examples of logicians. This difficulty has been so persistent that it has cast some philosophers into a state of disillusionment with formal deductions, even when those deductions are valid and true throughout. To be sure, they contend, it is easy to tell that since no American President before 1961 was a Catholic, and since Benjamin Harrison was President before 1961, Harrison was not a Catholic. But how was the truth of the backing generalization discovered? Presumably by knowing the religion of every President before 1961, Harrison among them. In that case, however, we already knew, and must have known, what the conclusion tells us. And why clutter up the argumentative scene with those other thirty-two Presidents? Here, as in most deductive proofs (including much less trivial ones), the more general, lawlike, and interesting assertions appear in the backing, not the conclusion. The proof simply *uses* them; they must have been *established* by other means.

It is best, therefore, to regard deductive forms as precisely that:

forms into which the raw materials of argument can be pressed, in order to give them maximum power and efficiency. Once they are there, the rest is mechanical. Deductive methods do not so much perform the labor of argument as reveal when that labor is done. Now this is an invaluable function; without it human reasoning would be crippled. But for the ultimate source of our knowledge about the world, other processes must be reviewed.

5) INDUCTIVE PROOFS

Of these processes, the most fundamental is of course perception. The child knows that his kitten's fur is soft by feeling it, and in similar ways he collects a vast amount of information about a large number of things. But even in moving from the single, momentary fragment of perceptual knowledge to a *collection* of *facts,* the child does something which has long baffled philosophers. For how can he know from having touched the cat five minutes ago that its fur is soft now? Well, probably he knows that physical things do not as a rule change their qualities abruptly and without cause. But how does he know *this?* Surely this rule is still farther from simple observation than the present softness of the cat's fur. So, too, the rules that all cat fur is soft, that if a dog frightens a cat the cat's fur will stand on end, and so on and on through the whole catalogue of what is considered knowledge. Almost none of the things people know at a given moment come from their sensory experience at that moment, and surprisingly few can even be said to come directly from memories of past sensory experience. Much of what people know, on the contrary, they know about things they could not possibly have come in sensory contact with (all cat fur, for instance, or what will happen tomorrow if a dog frightens a cat). Yet people do know these things. Indeed, such things and their ilk—generalizations, facts about the past, laws, certainties about the future—are absolutely crucial to our conduct and thinking. It is not surprising that the philosophical attempt to justify them has been massive and confusing, especially since the forceful attacks on the foundations of such knowledge by George Berkeley and David Hume in the eighteenth century.

This turbulent controversy is not of deep concern here. But since it bears directly on inductive argument—part of it is known as "the problem of induction"—a few remarks will be apposite, dogmatically though they must be offered. In the first place, even Hume at his most skeptical was well aware how foreign his philosophical doubts were to everyday experience. "I dine," he wrote,

> I play a game of back-gammon, I converse, and am merry with my friends; and when after three or four hours' amusement I wou'd return to these

speculations, they appear so cold, and strain'd, and ridiculous, that I cannot find in my heart to enter into them any further.

Treatise of Human Nature, book I, part iv

Life goes on, however suspect philosophically our knowledge of causes, laws, and generalities. For the dependence on such knowledge is profoundly natural to human beings, and even to lower animals. Somewhere between perception and thought there is an instinctive tendency to look for samenesses: this bundle of sensations and that one yesterday and that other one all mean "tomato," though of course no two tomatoes and no two sensings of the same tomato are exactly alike. And the word "tomato" is the same word each time we hear it, whether uttered fast or slow, soprano or bass—even printed on a page. To the very roots, men are categorizing animals. Moreover, we expect things of the same kind to behave alike, and to behave in the future as they have in the past. About these expectations not much can be said, except that human beings come with them as standard equipment, and that they pay off rather well on the whole. The findings of perception theorists in this matter are confirmed by the psychological study of learning. What a man or animal does once and is punished for, he will be less likely to do again; if he is rewarded he will be more likely to repeat. This process of "conditioning," in both elementary and more complex forms, accounts for much learning, though by no means for all. And its success compels the belief that organisms have an innate tendency to expect experience to repeat itself. Of course the fact that this expectation exists is no proof that the expectation is justified, but it does reduce to a certain hollowness the philosopher's cries of "no certainty."

If men must ask, in spite of the question's oddity, what justifies them in passing from limited experience to generalizations that go beyond it, and if "justify" is interpreted in a strict logical sense, the answer should probably be Hume's resounding "Nothing." But if the question is taken to mean, "How is it that some generalizations are reasonable and others not?" then the answer should be that a generalization is justifiable when it meets the standards by which generalizations are judged, exactly as a deduction is justified when it follows the rules for deduction. This answer may sound circular, as well as philosophically evasive, but it has the advantage of corresponding to the way people actually behave. Besides, it opens the door to a set of new questions far more relevant to the writer's problems of argumentation—questions about the several procedures of inductive proof and the requirements that such proofs must satisfy.

It is time to offer a definition: an inductive proof is one that moves either a) from a group of assertions about *some* events, things, or situations of a certain class to an assertion about *all* such events, things, or situations, or b) from assertions about miscellaneous things and events to an assertion which *explains* them in a relatively simple way. Types a) and b) belong together in the one definition because, logically speaking, type a) is a variety of type b), however different their conclusions may look. If one moves from "All the Hungarians I've met are intellectuals" to "All Hungarians are intellectuals," he does so precisely because the latter assertion (the generalization) seems the best explanation of the evidence described by the first. Notice that a different explanation may be better—if, for instance, the only Hungarians one has met were exchange professors at his university. In other words, the inference from some to all is justified only when the "some" are known to be a random selection. Thus inductions of Type a)—generalizations—are special cases of Type b)—explanations.

As will become increasingly clear later, this definition cuts some corners: the activities that go on under the heading of induction are too varied to submit to a description both neat and inclusive. But the main criteria are certainly the ones stated above: in an inductive argument the assertions are to the conclusion as parts to a whole or as facts to explanation.

Two examples should clarify the point:

19) Disease X is unknown in northern Canada and Greenland.

It occurs rarely in New York State.

Epidemics of disease X have occurred in the Mediterranean countries.   Backing

It is endemic to Central America.

It is fairly common in Burma.

Disease X thrives in all warm climates, and only in warm climates.   Conclusion

20) Disease X thrives only in warm climates.

It never strikes where the temperature drops below freezing in the summer.

It breaks out in seaports and passes to the interior from there.

Epidemics occur in large cities, especially.   Backing

The disease is uncommon where the water supply is carefully purified.

The city poor are especially susceptible.

Rats always die in large numbers when there is an epidemic.

Disease X is unknown in arid climates.

Disease X is caused by bacteria which flourish in water, but die from exposure to the sun or freezing. They are carried by rats, and spread through contaminated water supplies or from person to person.   Conclusion

Argument 19) takes several facts about the distribution of disease X and converts them into a general statement. This is the simplest type of induction, but even it presents some difficulties. Canada, Central America, Burma, and so on are not the only places in the world, yet the conclusion makes a claim about the whole world. From backing to conclusion the prover of 19) has taken the so-called *inductive leap,* a leap from partial evidence to a generalization that goes well beyond that evidence. It might turn out, of course, that the very next piece of evidence acquired —for instance, that disease X is unknown in the Congo—would upset the conclusion. And such things happen constantly: philologists who were familiar mainly with European languages drew a number of general conclusions about language which proved to be quite false when more of the world's 3000 languages were described. Certainly 19) makes too large an inductive leap to inspire much confidence. Besides, the conclusion of 19) looks as if it were intended to apply to the past and future, as well as to the present, so it poses in addition the old problem of projecting past experience into the future. Still, 19) has a perfectly legitimate *form,* and if the data were three or four times as bulky, and all favorable, few would be seriously disturbed by the proof.

Argument 20) differs in several important ways from 19). The conclusion, of course, does more than generalize from the backing assertions: it purports to explain them. Thus it is of a different type from them, in that it introduces the notion of cause. Moreover, it posits a factor, bacteria, which was nowhere mentioned in the backing. The same might seem to be true in 19), but actually the conclusion of 19) merely brings into the open a factor, climate, which was implicit in the backing. For these reasons it is harder to see the nature of the inductive leap in 20). The best way to do so is to ask what we would want to know in addition to the given information before we could feel relatively certain about the conclusion. Certainly it would be pertinent to know that a certain kind of bacteria were always found in the blood at some stage of disease X, that the same bacteria could be observed in the sick rats and in the water supply, that these bacteria attack the organism in a certain way to produce the symptoms of the disease, and so on. In other words, as it stands now, the conclusion of 20) is what we call an *hypothesis,* which needs further *confirmation.* The leap is from partial confirmation to all-inclusive hypothesis. Generalization and hypothesis shade into one another, but the distinction does have its usefulness in the classification of inductive arguments.

Another way to understand the nature of induction is by contrast with deduction. In a deductive proof the backing entails the conclusion; in an inductive proof the relationship is precisely the reverse: the conclusion entails the backing. Thus if disease X always thrives in warm climates and only in warm climates, it must necessarily be common in Central

America, rare in New York state, and so on. This fact offers another perspective on the inductive leap. Even if the conclusion does in fact entail all the backing assertions, it may not be the right conclusion, for other ones may entail the very same assertions. In 19), for example, the evidence is also consistent with the conclusion that disease X occurs only in very *sunny* climates, or only in Catholic, Buddhist, Jewish and Moslem countries. One of the main problems in induction is choosing the best hypothesis or generalization. For another thing, the conclusion will usually entail many facts other than the ones used in getting to it. Hence a vital way of determining whether an hypothesis is the best one is by checking its additional consequences (and those of alternative hypotheses). If disease X turns out to be common in Ireland, that fact would count against the conclusion of 19), and in favor of the rather ludicrous alternative which links disease X with religion. An hypothesis, though it is the best one for certain data, may still turn out to be false, given further data.

The subject of hypotheses (and of *theories,* which are relatively well-confirmed hypotheses) is one of the most controversial in all philosophy. We shall not enter the fray beyond suggesting a few useful standards for evaluating hypotheses. We have already said that a good hypothesis should account for all the evidence; this much is obvious. But the difficulty comes in weighing hypotheses against each other, for no "good" hypothesis will be good enough unless it can outlast its competitors. A few decades ago American crime statistics clearly showed that more crimes were committed, proportionately, by foreign-born citizens than by natives. From this, many freely concluded that foreigners were inherently less law-abiding than natives. This hypothesis, though plausible, will not stand up against more serious scrutiny of the evidence. For of the foreign born, an unusually high proportion were men, belonged to low economic groups, had had little education, and so on. Now men commit more crimes than women, the poor than the rich, the ignorant than the educated. Therefore, all of these factors must be eliminated in any study of the criminal tendencies of foreigners. As it happens, once foreigners were matched up with natives according to level of education, sex, and the rest of the factors, it became obvious that people of foreign birth actually commited *fewer* crimes than like groups of native Americans. Hasty formation of hypotheses, without adequate attention to other possibilities, is perhaps the most common and most grievous flaw in ordinary argument, one responsible for untold quantities of prejudice, superstition, and shoddy thinking.

An hypothesis does not stand or fall only on its power to handle the available evidence. Often a number of hypotheses will do this much. How to choose among them? Three principles are worth mentioning here:

A) Other things being equal, the simpler of two hypotheses is to be preferred. Why this is so is hard to say, but here is an example. Assume there is a traffic jam a mile long before a major intersection at 6:00 P.M. on the third day of a holiday weekend. Is it better to guess that the traffic-regulating system at the intersection proved inadequate to the unusually heavy traffic, or that the local police have been bribed by Republican officials to create a jam and thereby embarrass the Democrats in their attempt to block the highway bill before the legislature, so that in the next local election the Main Street vote will go Republican?

B) An hypothesis never stands in isolation from what we know of the world in general. Even if it fits the evidence it is designed to explain, it will not hold up unless it jibes with the sum total of human knowledge, fact and theory. Thus the hypothesis that disease X is distributed along religious lines, although consistent with the facts at hand, goes against very general and well-founded notions both about religion and about disease, and will have a lot more against it from the start than an hypothesis which links disease and climate. Likewise the hypothesis of the scientist who, according to an old story, said "Jump" to a flea, which eventually jumped; then he pulled the hind legs off the flea, and said again, "Jump," but the flea did nothing, and the scientist concluded that when you amputate a flea's legs its hearing is impaired. Of the same sort, but more puzzling, is the hypothesis that the world was created last Tuesday, complete with fossils, memories, pregnant women and history books (to what assumptions about the world would one have to appeal in order to refute *this* hypothesis?). An interesting actual example from recent years is the reluctance of scientists and people generally to accept extrasensory perception as an hypothesis, although it is consistent with a good deal of experimental evidence. Inductive arguments depend on all sorts of unobtrusive assumptions about the way the world works, much as a deductive argument presupposes the rules of logic, and multiplication presupposes the axioms of arithmetic. Still, even when an hypothesis upsets the most cherished of received truths, it may eventually gain acceptance if it is powerful and cogent enough. After all, men came finally to believe that Copernicus was right, and think what a difference *his* hypothesis made in the structure of human belief!

C) An hypothesis will be more credible to the extent that it explains not only the facts that elicit it, but seemingly unrelated facts as well. Dalton hypothesized the atom to account for a few simple characteristics of chemical compounds, but the notion illuminated the whole field of chemistry, and explained various phenomena of radiation and spectroscopy. Moreover, it led to the discovery of new elements, and eventually made possible quantum mechanics, nuclear physics, and a whole range of new hypotheses and experiments. The great hypotheses of science have had this capacity to connect the previously unconnected, proliferate new hypotheses and uncover new facts, thus enlarging human knowledge far more than was the intent of their originators.

What we have said about the conclusions of inductive proofs can be summed up in a rather simplified scheme. Roughly, these conclusions are of four types. Some are *generalizations,* whose function is to describe or arrange the data and project the description outward to cover possible new data. ("Disease X thrives only in warm climates.") Some are *particular hypotheses,* designed to explain a unique group of circumstances. ("Norsemen must have landed on Cape Cod in the tenth century.") The other two types have more general importance for discovery and understanding. One, the *law,* establishes a causal connection between events or situations and specifies precisely their relationship. ("Ontogeny recapitulates phylogeny"; "wars are always followed by brief periods of economic prosperity.") Notice, by the way, that laws always imply predictions; they speak of regularities in past experience which are supposed to hold for the future as well. Conclusions of the fourth type might best be labeled *principles.* They are like laws, but of such sweeping generality that they leave particular observations or experiments far behind. ("$E = mc^2$"; "human nature never changes.") To repeat a warning, so multiform are the processes of induction that no simple classification will do justice to them. But this breakdown according to type of conclusion at least gives some idea of their range and scope.

6) EVIDENCE

The discussion in the last several pages may have given the impression that induction is the preserve mainly of scientists. To be sure, the most full and rigorous uses of induction have been scientific, ever since Francis Bacon brushed away the cobwebs of *a priori* argument in the early seventeenth century. But of course induction is the servant of argument in every scholarly field, and in garden-variety proving too. The differences between scientific induction and more humble proving do not show so much in an analysis of conclusions as in an analysis of backing. Most of the backing for scientific conclusions derives either from experiment (as in chemistry) or from highly skilled observation (as in botany), often aided by instruments (as in astronomy). But most of the inductive argument practiced by students in expository writing depends upon evidence considerably more accessible to the layman. For the purposes of this book, then, it is important to mention at least briefly some of the major types of backing. It is also important to remember that not all good arguments need be conducted on scientific models, and that what counts as good evidence will vary greatly from field to field and context to context.

In the humanities, in the social sciences, and in casual talk (as in science), the central type of evidence, from which all others derive, is *observation*. "I know there's a mouse in the room because I can see it" is still the prototype of a powerful argument. Not much need be said about observation, except the truisms that a trained eye is better than an untrained one, that a random mass of data is worth less than a few carefully selected observations, that even the senses are fallible, not to mention the memory, and that, since an observer's bias may color his observation, observations that compensate for such bias are better than observations that don't. Once these qualifications are recorded, it remains unarguable that the evidence of the senses is the best we have.

The difficulties multiply when an argument relies for its backing (as most do), not on the prover's observations, but on evidence gathered from other sources. In history, economics, social criticism, and the like, that evidence is most likely to come from *reports,* either of other people's observations or of still further reports which have a more remote origin in observation. Evaluating such reports is a major responsibility of the scholar, one that can be hinted at by a list of questions which he might wish to ask of a given book, article, or document:

SOURCE •

> What is the nature of the source? Is it one from which other reports have come? If so, what is their known reliability? Is the source of a kind that is likely to provide accurate transmission of data? Is it subject to inadvertent error? to distortion because of prejudice, ignorance, the situation or time in which it occurs, necessity to avoid or provide opposition, intention to conceal or deceive?

AUTHOR OR TRANSMITTER •

> Is the authorship certainly known? If so, is the author's reliability known from any other documents? What are the author's or transmitter's qualifications as a reporter? Did he have opportunity to observe directly the data he uses? Does he display sound knowledge of his subject and general intelligence on other scores? Is there any ground for thinking him susceptible to bias or pressures likely to cause him to alter or suppress data?

DATA •

> Are the data such as can be observed directly? If so, were they observed directly? With what degree of accuracy can they be recorded? Are they verifiable by others? Have they been so verified? Do they stand in conflict with other data? Are they complete, or only "representative"? If "representative," what were the grounds of selection? Are the methods of

analysis used appropriate? Do the data actually support the conclusions drawn from them? Would they support alternative conclusions as well, or nearly as well?

A report that weathers such a line of questioning has a reasonable claim to reliability. Its solidity, even if all the questions are favorably answered, may never be beyond dispute, but in many fields of inquiry such a report counts as highly convincing evidence.

One step further removed from actual observation is evidence based on *authority*—that is, on opinions, judgments, generalizations, and principles voiced by people who should know. Since everyone lives in daily contact with complexities far beyond his comprehension, it is easy to understand why authority is such a popular ground for belief. As a shortcut to truth, the layman relies on the expert to tell him what happens to the economy after a tax cut, whether the text of *Macbeth* is corrupt, what effect a new drug has, or whether Moses was an actual historical figure. There is nothing wrong with this dependence; it is inevitable. But anyone conducting a serious argument should remember that some authorities are better than others, and that even the best authorities often disagree. Moreover, an authority in a particular field is not necessarily an authority in all matters that touch on that field: citizens listen to the general when he talks of military strategy, but his testimony on the social and political effects of military occupation is more vulnerable, and other authorities should be called in on these subjects. In the end, a certain skepticism about all authoritative judgments is warranted: it took a highly complicated study of radioactivity to prove the recency of the bones of Piltdown man, whose antiquity had been authenticated by many reputable scientists; but it took only an ingenious fanatic to fabricate them in the first place.

A similar type of backing consists of assertions whose credibility depends on *persistence*. If enough people believe something long enough it becomes part of a stock of "common knowledge" and will be used freely and uncritically in argument. Of course persistence by itself is usually a shaky foundation for belief. The history of knowledge is a drama in which hypotheses harden into received truth only to be altered or replaced by new hypotheses which themselves harden and are exploded. Everyone knew the world was flat, but that did not prevent Columbus from being right. Persistence does carry some weight when it represents a quantity of shared human experience—which is to say observation. Yet even farmers' rules of thumb are shot through with superstition, and it is an uncritical arguer who will rest his claims on persistence alone.

What, then, of *intuition*, the most ephemeral kind of evidence, the furthest removed from observation, and the most inaccessible to rigorous checking? The answer seems obvious, and yet we all rely on our intuitions

from time to time—though probably not with such confidence as
D. H. Lawrence, who told Aldous Huxley that he rejected the theory of
evolution because he "did not feel it *here*," meaning "here in the solar
plexus." The trouble with Lawrence's method of demonstration was that
the status quo in his solar plexus had rather little to do with the truth
about evolution. There are fields of inquiry (psychology, for one) in
which intuitions have some value as evidence: some powerful theories in
descriptive linguistics depend partly upon the intuitions of native
speakers. But in most fields the investigator had best regard his intuitions
as no more than hints on which to proceed in the labor of experiment
and rational argument. The intuition of an expert may incorporate a
good deal of condensed wisdom and observation, but it is not likely to
convince anyone else unless the wisdom and observation are made
explicit.

On a different footing from all these types of evidence is backing based
on *convention*. The speaker who concluded that his friend was driving
recklessly because he was over the double line rested his case partly on
a definition of reckless driving: one of the things *meant* by "reckless
driving" is crossing the double line. This sort of gambit belongs more
to deductive proving than to inductive, but it can and often should find
employment at some stage of an essentially inductive proof. When the
writer does call on convention (or stipulative definition) for support he
stands on ground as solid as that of observation, provided that he reads
the convention aright. And of course he must remember that convention
is strictly a verbal matter and cannot prove anything about the way the
world is. The fact that the sun "rises" does not prove that it orbits
around the earth, nor is the whale cold-blooded because it is a "fish."
In cases like these the conventions of ordinary usage must yield to the
discoveries of science and the conventions of scientific language. But the
authority of common usage is sufficient for most argumentative purposes.

7) FORMS AND STRATEGIES

So far, most of what we have said has encouraged a schematic view
of proving. We have divided proofs into two fundamental types, deductive and inductive. We have developed two systems of deduction, each
with its rules and conventions. We have classified inductive proofs
according to their conclusions and backing, and have suggested some
criteria for evaluating them. All of this apparatus has its use in the
practical business of writing argumentatively, which, without some fixed
points of reference or some ground rules, can too easily disintegrate into
impressionism, smoke screening, and high dudgeon. But the system, as
we have cautioned at intervals, is too neat; it is time to consider a some-

what looser approach, one capable of suggesting more richly the varieties of actual written argument.

That arguments can defy strict categorization is evident from such instances as this:

21) Both Napoleon's France and Hitler's Germany met defeat in attempting to expand eastward.

Therefore, if the Soviet Union tries to conquer the West, it will probably fall.

It is unclear, to begin with, whether the argument is primarily inductive or deductive. Conceivably, it rests on a general principle to the effect that all great powers fare alike in similar undertakings. If so, additional backing assertions linking these three countries as great powers and their undertakings as similar would make the proof a deductive one of sorts. But perhaps its force is rather to *establish,* inductively, the principle that great powers fare alike in similar undertakings. From this principle the conclusion follows simply. In either case the word "probably" poses extra problems, for neither strict induction nor strict deduction, as we have explained them, allows for a sudden intrusion of probability in the concluding assertion.

Now the nature of this argument is obscure partly because so much is missing. But another cause of confusion is the gap, always present, between the actual language of proving and abstract logical *forms*. Proofs that are basically inductive or deductive may stray far from their prototypes without losing their essential character; a great many proofs blend induction and deduction; others seem to lack the features of either major type. Moreover, as already indicated, the major types branch out into a number of subtypes (and there are many more), so that simply calling a proof inductive or deductive says relatively little about its structure or about the standards to be used in evaluating it.

This complexity may seem untidy, but it is real, and the writer should reconcile himself to it. There is no automatic way to pour all arguments into logical molds without distorting some of them beyond recognition, and although the writer owes deference to logic, he has a still stronger obligation to the precise and sometimes unique intricacies of his own argument. The major forms of proof remain available as standards of rigor and clarity, by which a writer may measure his own argument, and to which he may sometimes wish to reduce it. But to require every proof to satisfy this or that set of formal criteria would be as arbitrary as to require everyone to be exactly this or that many inches tall, with no unseemly fractions left over. People argue in words, after all, and combinations of words are infinitely various.

To compress into a few pages a survey of the full range of proofs would be impossible. Instead, what follows is a brief outline of forms and procedures to serve as points of reference in the framing of actual arguments. We need not cover again the ground that we have been over; we shall merely summarize such matters.

A) DEDUCTIVE ARGUMENTS •

   1) With classes:

      a) *Three-part arguments*
         The standard three-part proof of this type can take many, many forms; but these are amply suggested by proofs 9) to 14) above, excluding the invalid 12), of course. The precise shape of such an argument will depend upon whether its assertions contain "all _____" ("every _____,"), "only _____," "some _____," "no _____," "if," "either _____ or _____," or reference to an individual member of a class.

      b) *Chain arguments*

         22) All residents of Pine Street are laborers.
             All laborers voted for Gurski.
             Everyone who voted for Gurski was paid off in cash.
             No one paid off in cash is dissatisfied.
             No resident of Pine Street is dissatisfied.

         Clearly the rules for the shorter arguments apply here, with appropriate modifications. Notice that the backing assertions lead to other conclusions too, such as the conclusion that all laborers were paid off in cash, but if this were the point of the argument, there would be no sense in having so many backing assertions.

      c) *Abbreviated arguments*
         Both of the following are truncated versions of the same three-part proof; each makes do without one backing assertion:

         23) Every alchemist is a charlatan, so Bruno must be a charlatan.

         24) Bruno is an alchemist, so he must be a charlatan.

         These are extremely common forms, in writing as in speech. They escape the bulkiness of the full three-part proof and are perfectly adequate when the omitted assertion is a matter of universal knowledge, or has already been established. It remains in the background as an *assumption,* to use the language of the preceding chapter. The conclusion can also be left out:

         25) Bruno is an alchemist, and every alchemist is a charlatan.

         In this form, the argument may seem to work by insinuation, but it has a more honorable use in the hands of a writer who simply does not want to insult his reader by stating the thunderingly obvious.

d) *Proofs that depend on additional assumptions*

Given what we all know about relationships such as "taller than," "older than," "brother of," "similar to," "before," and "north of," it is possible to build arguments that are clearly deductive according to our definition, but that do not depend on relations between classes:

26) Diamond is harder than steel, so it must be harder than glass, which is not so hard as steel.

27) Oswald is George's only son, and he is a bachelor, so George has no daughters-in-law.

28) The congressman's future depends upon the vote upstate, and the weather on election day always affects the upstate vote, so the congressman's future hangs partly on the election day weather.

29) Since most ball games are nine innings long, and since most take under three hours, at least some nine-inning games take less than three hours.

Such arguments can be multiplied indefinitely, and the fact that they are not customarily treated in logic texts says nothing against their propriety, or their validity.

e) *Arguments of possibility*

Classical deduction has another offshoot in proofs which depend on the notion of "may" or "possible":

30) Some piano tuners have perfect pitch.
Mr. Canelli is a piano tuner.

Mr. Canelli may have perfect pitch.

Arguments like this one also have a firm place in ordinary usage, and must not be ruled out because they cannot be dealt with rigorously in the logic of classes.

f) *Arguments of assimilation*

The most notorious misuse of classical deductive logic is that represented by Argument 12). In recent years it has burst into new prominence in politics: we know it as "guilt by association," in forms like this:

31) Some (all) communists take part in the peace movement.
Some (all) world federalists take part in the peace movement.

Therefore some (all) world federalists are communists.

Alternatively,

32) All traitors praise the Soviet Union.
    Professor Stone praises the Soviet Union.

    Professor Stone is a traitor.

Such proofs are as contemptible intellectually as they are crude politically, and one would like to write a stop to their infamous history. But it bears mentioning here that arguments rather similar to these do sometimes make good sense. From the fact that New Zealanders speak English and the fact that Virginians speak English, one cannot, to be sure, conclude that Virginians are New Zealanders—or even that a single New Zealander is a Virginian. But one *can* argue as follows:

33) New Zealanders speak English.
    Virginians speak English.

    Virginians and New Zealanders are similar in their linguistic and cultural heritages.

And, in general, if two people or groups of people share one important characteristic, they are likely to share others. Two men who have the same opinion of the New Deal will probably agree about censorship as well; and two Mexicans will probably be closer to each other in their eating habits than either of them is to a Swede. But such matters take us out of the province of deductive logic.

2) Deductive proofs involving the truth or falsity of statements: Arguments that can be formalized in terms of P's and Q's also come in many varieties, but these can all be handled within the framework of rules elaborated earlier in this chapter.

B) INDUCTIVE ARGUMENTS •
   1) From particulars to a generalization:

   a) *With an inductive leap*
      This argumentative pattern in its simplest form can cause little trouble, beyond that of the inductive leap, which was discussed previously. But generalization is often more intellectually taxing than the argument that, because every crow sighted to date is black, all crows must be black. Sometimes it is difficult to tell which generalization, out of many possible ones, is the appropriate one to make. Thus it may seem to be true of freshmen who flunk out of college X that they live in dormitories, that they are enrolled in English 100, that they come from east of the

Mississippi, that they have domineering mothers, that they pledge fraternities, that they go away on weekends, and that they seldom enter the library. But some of these generalizations are obviously spurious (*all* freshmen take English 100), and others are of dubious relevance to the failure of the freshmen. In fact, it may be wrong in these circumstances to look for any single generalization to solve the dean's problem. Shoddy argument results as often from vacuous generalization as from faulty generalization or from excessive inductive leaping. In any case, this example makes it clear that generalization slips over into hypothesis, and that reaching useful generalizations is no trivial business.

b) *With no inductive leap*
Now and then it is worth while to generalize even when all the particulars are available. To prove that every one of Faulkner's novels contains Christian symbolism might well be valuable—more valuable, say, than knowing that most do and only suspecting that the others do. Such generalizations can often be incorporated, as backing assertions, in larger arguments. And they involve real problems: the problem, for instance, of deciding what is to count as an instance of Christian symbolism.

2) From facts to an hypothesis or theory

a) *From miscellaneous facts to a particular hypothesis*
The great eighteenth-century philologist Sir William Jones, basing his conclusion on a wealth of knowledge about many languages, argued that the major European languages, plus Sanskrit, Persian, and a few others, exhibited similarities of structure and vocabulary too great to be a matter of chance, and that all these languages must have sprung from a common ancestor. There was nothing lawlike or general about Jones' hypothesis (which has been richly confirmed); it did not posit a general rule of linguistic development, or make predictions, or talk about repeated causal connections. It merely set up a unique train of historical events which made sense of multitudinous facts whose interconnectedness had not previously been noticed. A large amount of scientific proving is of this type; in history and in literary criticism it is probably the dominant type. (A critic who analyzes a poem seeks to discover a single principle of construction, or a theme, or a set of biographical facts about the poet which account for all the words in the poem, and their arrangement.) In this absolutely vital procedure, which takes innumerable forms, the hypothesis must meet the usual tests: it must actually illuminate all the evidence;

it must do so as neatly as possible; and it must do so better than competing hypotheses.

b) *From facts to a law*

These arguments may be classified according to the relations stated in their conclusions.

JOINT-PRESENCE

34) Wherever there is poverty, there is disease.

SEQUENCE

35) After every war there is a period of moral laxity and experimentation.

EXCLUSION

36) No dictator can flourish where there is a free press.

CO-VARIATION

37) The larger the audience appealed to by a medium of communication, the lower the intellectual quality of its offerings.

CAUSATION

38) A deficiency of vitamin B causes beri-beri.

Observe that, as with most laws, these contain an element of *prediction;* in other words, they are timeless, approximating in this the model of scientific laws. As for *explanation,* some laws do more of it than others; but no law will be worth its salt unless the things it relates (whether causally or not) seem to have some *significant* connection with each other. Thus, although (34) as it stands does not explain disease, it does point to a condition importantly related to disease—a condition (for example) that any health-minded government should be concerned over. If (34) ran, "wherever there is architecture there is disease," its truth would be undeniable, but it could scarcely lay claim, as a law, to anyone's serious attention.

c) *From facts to a principle*

There is no clear line between laws and principles, but the difference is one of generality. A principle gathers in and accounts for a great range of data: the conduct of all men toward each other at all times, not just the conduct of soldiers in combat; the motions of all physical bodies, not just bodies in orbit. Needless to say, the successful establishing of principles is usually the work of learned and brilliant investigators, not of the apprentice researcher.

3) More complex procedures of induction:

a) *Choosing an hypothesis*

Often the facts are readily available, but not readily understood. Then the investigator's task may be one of eliminating inferior hypotheses and settling on the best one (or best combination). We all know there was a depression in the thirties; why did it happen? All normal children learn to talk: but how? An argument designed for such circumstances might be constructed like this:

39) Fact: American education proceeds at a slower pace than European education.

Possible Explanations:

i) Teachers' salaries are too low in America, and the most able young people go into other work.

ii) American education is dominated by the philosophy of John Dewey.

iii) American parents expect less of their children.

iv) Prosperity breeds slackness.

v) The American system rewards action rather than contemplation and knowledge.

vi) Administrators have too much power, teachers too little in the American school.

vii) American education is slowed down (but justifiably) by the democratic principle of equal education for all.

(And so on.)

Elimination of unsatisfactory hypotheses: They do not fit facts; they do not differentiate America from Europe; they do not get to the heart of the matter; and so forth.

Defense of the remaining hypothesis or combination of hypotheses.

The writer who pursues this path will, of course, be looking at his facts in new ways as he treats the various hypotheses; he may also find it necessary to look at some new facts. Hence this type of proof shares some features with another common one:

b) *Moving from facts to a tentative hypothesis, to new facts, to a final hypothesis*

40) Facts: In factories A, B, C the workers were discontent and production was low. Teams of industrial sociologists studied working conditions and interviewed the employees, after which they recommended the institution of longer and more frequent rest periods. Their advice was taken, the workers were happier, and in spite of the shortened working day, production went up.

Tentative hypothesis: Efficiency and morale in industrial plants depend on adequate rest periods.

Search for new facts to confirm or disprove the hypothesis: If the hypothesis is true, the workers in plants A, B, and C should stay happy and productive as long as the system of rest periods is in effect. In other factories with similar problems there should be no similar improvement without increases in work breaks. But actually, production fell off and morale declined in plants A, B, and C within months after the reform. In other plants similar surveys were undertaken, and other reforms instituted: more coke machines, better lighting, more attractive lunch rooms, more recreation facilities, and so on. In each factory production and morale improved at first, but fell off later. Moreover, in some factories there were interviews and investigations, but no reforms. Even in those plants morale and production improved for a while.

Final hypothesis: *Any* attention to workers' complaints and needs will lead to more efficiency and better morale, but the effect is temporary.[9]

In inductive arguments the heaviest going often comes after the original data are in and the early hypotheses posed. Some ways of proceeding from this point are worth mentioning as arguments in themselves:

c) *Assuming that a favored hypothesis is right, determining what facts should follow from it, and checking it against these facts (as in 40)*

d) *Assuming the truth of a competing hypothesis, and showing that it does not suit the facts*

41) Facts: Prices of rare antiques, rare coins and stamps, rare paintings, and so on, increased fivefold to a hundredfold from 1950 to 1960, a period of general prosperity in the United States. The rise in prices was steady. There were many new collectors from low and middle income brackets.

Hypothesis: People with a lot of extra money, much of it new money, forced the prices up by competing for rarities.

Competing hypothesis: The large numbers of new collectors forced prices up by increasing the relative scarcity of sought-after items.

Refutation of the competing hypothesis: If the price rise had been caused primarily by the new collectors, it would have been interrupted by the recessions of the decade, since people in low income brackets are hurt most by such economic setbacks. But the rise was steady; hence the hypothesis does not hold up.[10]

---

[9] This case is imaginary, but it bears a close resemblance to actual cases.

[10] Of course *both* hypotheses may be wrong, but this procedure at least leads to a decision between these two.

e) *Assuming that the favored hypothesis is* false, *and showing that such an assumption is incompatible with the facts, or leads to conceptual or logical absurdity*

42) Facts: Authorship of some of the Federalist papers is disputed, the two possibilities being Hamilton and Madison. Recent statistical analyses show that the incidence in these papers of many unimportant words and locutions ("upon," for instance, instead of "on") is very close to their frequency in writing known to be Madison's, and quite different from their frequency in Hamilton's prose.

Hypothesis: Madison wrote the disputed papers.

Supposition: If Madison did not write the papers, one of two things must be true: either Hamilton imitated Madison's style, or the statistical correlations are chance. But in order to imitate Madison's style with this degree of success, Hamilton would have to have known as much about the incidence of unimportant words as the statisticians have uncovered with the aid of computers. For a man without computers to get this data would take at least several lifetimes (not to mention the difficulty of approximating someone else's style after the data are in). And that the correlations are chance is almost unthinkable, for the odds against any single correlation occurring by chance are thousands to one, and the total odds astronomical.

Conclusion: Madison wrote the disputed papers.

A final word about induction: clearly some of these arguments incorporate deductive methods. To decide what should *follow* from an hypothesis is to make deductions from it (remember the suggestion that induction is the inverse of deduction). It should also be clear by now that actual arguments can amalgamate the "pure" types and subtypes in an infinity of ways barely hinted at by our outline. At some point in the classification of proofs it becomes senseless to maintain the artificially simple distinction between induction and deduction. Be that as it may, in bringing our outline to a close, we shall purposely abandon the distinction, and consider briefly two species of proof which either straddle it or lie outside it.

C) ARGUMENTS OF PROBABILITY ·

Often the context of an argument neither warrants a firm deduction nor allows the passage, through induction, to a general hypothesis. Yet there are still conclusions to be drawn. Just as in ordinary talk, people hedge their bets by inserting "probably," "it is likely that," and so on, in more formal argument it is possible to retain soundness in the face of uncertainty, simply by building the uncertainty into the proof. Indeed, an important principle in the ethics of proving is that the writer should acknowledge, both to himself and to his audience, the loopholes in his argument. Sometimes he can do so only by the tentativeness of his presentation. But when he is dealing with relatively fixed uncertainties, with regular likelihoods, he can pay his respects to uncertainty and still achieve a measure of rigor. Such are the advantages that make arguments of probability attractive—so much so that a whole scientific field, that of statistics, has grown up around them. For the complexities of that discipline there is no place in this book; we can only list a few of the common-sense methods from which it springs.

1) From the whole to an individual

   43) Most Democrats favor a tax cut.
       Burns is a Democrat.

       Therefore Burns probably favors a tax cut.

   44) Since the suicide of a famous person generally leads to a rash of imitative suicides, and since Nola Roberts killed herself yesterday, there will probably be a number of suicide attempts soon.

2) From the whole to a precise estimate

   45) Twins occur once in every 87 births. Therefore, the likelihood that any given pregnancy will result in twins is 1/87.

3) From an individual to a whole

   46) The chances of rolling three with two dice are one in eighteen, so out of any ninety throws, about five will probably result in three.

4) From a sample to the whole

   47) Out of a random sample of 10,000 citizens, 5621 disapprove of the present administration. It is probable, therefore, that about 56% of the whole population is against the administration.

The uncertainty contained in this conclusion by the word "probable" can be made quite precise by statistical methods. That is, statisticians could say how likely the figure 56 per cent is, given the size of the sample and the size of the whole population. They could also specify the likelihood that the figure is 51 per cent or 58 per cent, and so on. But calculations are based on ideal circumstances, and every observer of the pollsters knows how often events belie their predictions. One reason is the extreme difficulty of obtaining a truly random sample. It will not do simply to knock on every seventh door: the neighborhood may be unusually proadministration because it is wealthy or poor, because most of the people there work in the oil industry, because a large government project has brought money into the area, and so on. The same problems beset anyone who tries to weigh the chances of this or that occurrence, or attempts to generalize about the composition of a whole group on the basis of limited past experience or a limited sample. But for all that, the assessment of probabilities goes on, and goes on well enough on the whole to justify the risk of error.

D) ARGUMENTS BY ANALOGY •

As everyone knows, the fact that there are waves of water and waves of light does not prove that if you stand in the sun you will get wet. The analogy does not stretch that far. Still, it was useful to physicists in developing a theory of light, and, later, in explaining that theory to novices. Perhaps these are the two principal uses of analogy—to assist in the initial groping for an hypothesis, and to clarify an argument or a description. In the service of these causes, an analogy can be more graphic and economical than a direct attack on the problem. Unfortunately, these virtues do not guarantee equal success to analogy in actual proofs. The fact that two things (situations, sets of events, and so forth) are alike in some respects does not logically entail their similarity in any further characteristics. Thus analogical proofs are not valid, in the strict sense of the word. Yet they have their cogency, particularly when the two things compared are of the same general sort. At least three argumentative uses of analogy are worth mention here.

1) To predict further similarities:

> 48) In many ways the social, economic, and political organization of human settlements resembles the plant and animal ecology of natural environments; the resemblance is especially close in the delicate interdependencies of people, in the one case, and of plants and animals in the other. Therefore, just as the influx of a new species of insects is certain to have a profound impact on the ecology of a river basin, so a large and sudden immigration of a new race or class is bound to destroy the social equilibrium of a city and lead to a new system of balances.

Notice that the proof lacks final conviction: people are not insects. Certainly an investigator interested in the hypothesis would hope that he could finally rest his case on a thorough study of historical immigrations (that is, on induction). But the analogical proof does more than simply open up an avenue of research. So alike are ecology and social organization *in principle* (not just in a fanciful, metaphorical way), that what disrupts the one seems almost certain to disrupt the other. Analogy is most useful to an argument founded on likenesses of this sort.

2) To expose a fallacy:

> 49) Arguing that we should abolish surgery because some patients die on the operating table is like arguing that we should all stop eating because some people die of food poisoning. The two lines of reasoning are equally absurd.

Of course they are not *quite* equally absurd: without surgery the
the species would survive, but not without food. Yet the arguments
are close enough in structure so that the analogy is telling, in spite
of its rhetorical overstatement. This use of analogy depends, obviously, on similarities between arguments themselves, as well as
between events, situations, and so forth.

3) To establish a classification:

A British pathologist has argued that the symptoms which
Thucydides describes in victims of the famous plague of Athens
(430 B.C.) are so like those of typhoid patients today that the
Athenian pestilence must also have been typhoid fever. Similarly,
students of myth classify the protagonist of a traditional story as a
mythic hero if his life resembles the lives of other mythic
heroes. Such characteristics as divine or semi-divine birth and
a period of early obscurity determine the classification, even
though the particular circumstances of birth and childhood vary
greatly. The mythologists assume that the hero-myth, in its most
general outlines, issues from universal patterns of human need
and human imagination, and this assumption warrants classification by analogy even when the analogy might seem remote to a
layman. Categories are essential to all thought; classification is
usually necessary before induction or deduction can even begin.
For this reason alone, the process of analogy, in spite of its abuses,
deserves a place among the methods of argument.

It may be wise to conclude this survey with a reminder of what should
by now be abundantly clear—that our outline is arbitrarily simplified,
that the types of argument shade into one another, that they may be
compounded in almost every conceivable way, and that there is no automatic way either of choosing the appropriate form, of translating logic
into English, or of insuring soundness. None of this means that the
writer concerned with argument (or for that matter, with truth) can
afford to ignore the structures of formal and informal proof; for those
structures represent a codification of sound thinking itself and constitute
one of the signal achievements of rational man.

8) REFUTATION

When a writer rejects a competing hypothesis, as in 41), or discards
a tentative hypothesis, as in 40), or assumes that his own hypothesis
is false and demonstrates that such an assumption leads to absurdity, as
in 42), he is engaged in *refutation*. As the preceding section shows, refutation can be a useful step in a proof, especially in an inductive proof.
An inductive hypothesis is seldom absolutely certain, and one way to

increase its relative credibility is to prove that others which have been proposed will not hold up, at least not so well as the one in question. When there are seemingly two or more hypotheses that can account for the data, refutation becomes a firm responsibility for the writer, since merely to show that *his* hypothesis accounts for the data is not to establish its superiority. And almost any essay that tries to prove something will have competing positions to deal with.

Moreover, it is often appropriate to refute an argument or an assertion even when the writer has nothing to offer in its place. No one knows for sure the identity of that "Junius" whose letters, during the reign of George III, revealed so many British state secrets and scandals, but it was of considerable importance to Edmund Burke and others accused of authorship to be able to refute the charges. Likewise, although neither Darwin nor anyone else has established the precise date of the earth's origin, Darwin's researches showed conclusively that the earth could *not* have been created in 4004 B.C., and that knowledge has its own value. The fact that refutation is a negative activity does not mean that it is a useless one: considering the amount of nonsense at large in the world, every successful refutation is a service to the cause of truth.

In treating the various forms of argument, we have already implied a good deal about refutation; to show that a proof deviates from acceptable form is to refute it. And the section on fallacies at the end of this chapter adds more information on the subject. But since refutation is often a separate activity with problems of its own, it will be well to state a few general principles here.

Most important is the distinction, often ignored, between refuting an argument and refuting an assertion. The validity of an argument depends upon its adherence to the standards of good form—deductive, inductive, or other—which govern it. In order to refute an argument, therefore, one must show that its procedure is somehow illegitimate. An attack on its *conclusion* is simply not to the point, for the argument may be valid though the conclusion is false, as in 17). Conversely, the writer who wishes to refute a conclusion must do so by attacking that assertion (as false, self-contradictory, and so on); to refute the argument that led to it is not sufficient, since there may be other arguments, sound ones, that legitimately support it. When Kant refuted St. Anselm's ontological proof of the existence of God, he did not intend to refute the conclusion, and in fact Kant himself believed in a divine being, though not in a conventional way. The writer must keep in mind the two types of refutation or risk irrelevance and confusion.

How, then, may an argument be refuted? By pointing to a fallacy in it. By exhibiting a flaw in its deductive logic. By showing its inductive leap to be unwarranted. By showing that it begs the question. By proving it inconclusive (showing, that is, that other conclusions follow equally well from its backing assertions). And so on. All of these methods are ways of attacking the move from backing assertions to conclusion. One may also attack the backing assertions themselves. To show that at least one of them is false or uncertain is to prove the argument *unsound,* though not invalid.

Refuting an assertion (whether or not it is the conclusion of an argument) calls for quite different stratagems. If the assertion is one of simple fact (Mrs. Jones has blue eyes), it may be refuted by direct appeal to experience or to reliable reports. But if it is a generalization, a law, or a principle, such an appeal will rarely suffice. Take the hypothesis, "Every child of blue-eyed parents has blue eyes." No one can examine the eyes of *all* such children; but notice that if the statement is intended literally, and not just as a rough approximation, the discovery of one brown-eyed child of blue-eyed parents refutes it. A single *counterexample,* that is to say, is enough to refute a rigid hypothesis, no matter how many supporting examples there are.

Even when no counterexample is available, it is often possible to refute a generalization or law. The most useful technique for doing so is known as *reductio ad absurdum:* the refuter assumes that the hypothesis he wants to defeat is true, and shows that intolerable consequences follow from such an assumption. In 42) there is an example of this procedure, when it is assumed that Madison did *not* write the disputed Federalist papers, in order to prove, eventually, that he *did.* Or consider the old puzzle of the three wise men, each with either a white or a black spot on his forehead, who are placed together in a mirrorless room, forbidden to talk to each other, and told that if any of them guesses the color of his spot he will be richly rewarded, that if he guesses wrong he will be executed, and that not all three spots are black. Wise man A solves the problem, after a time. He sees that both B and C have white spots. He suspects that his own spot is also white, but he assumes it to be black, and argues as follows: "B, then, would see a white spot and a black spot. But if so, it would be obvious to him that his own spot must be white, for otherwise C would see two black spots and know immediately that his own must be white. Since neither B nor C, wise as they both are, has hit upon this solution, my own spot must be white." Wise man A not only employs *reductio ad absurdum,* but imagines B as using it too. The example is fanciful, but the technique is invaluable for refutation.

Finally, one may challenge an assertion by showing it to fail through vagueness, meaninglessness, self-contradiction, and so on—the various shortcomings dealt with in the last chapter. In brief, an assertion, like a proof, must measure up to certain standards. Refutation is the invoking of those standards to point to inadequacies, and as such it is an essential technique, both of proving and of rational thought in general.

9) MORAL AND ESTHETIC ARGUMENTS

Perhaps this is the best place for an aside about what happens to logic when it encounters the good and the beautiful, as well as the true. Philosophers, especially in this century, have been concerned with the rather special status of evaluative assertions (some of their conclusions are reflected in the previous chapter). It is not necessary to go into the controversies; it is enough simply to state our belief that, contrary to the positions of some philosophers, moral and esthetic judgments have as much claim to truth (or falsity) as other assertions, although the claim is based on complex sanctions. This being the case, there is no reason that a proof cannot legitimately arrive at the conclusion that such and such a course of action is good, or that this or that painting is beautiful. Indeed, moral issues probably give rise to more argument than issues of any other sort. And since people care as much about what is right as they do about what is true, sound moral conclusions are indispensable—to political and social thought, to philosophy, and to ordinary conduct. Thus it is comforting to know that moral arguments can be pursued logically, and that in general the same methods lead to soundness in both moral and esthetic proofs as in other types. But there is one additional requirement, which for moral arguments runs like this: no moral precept can be well grounded in argument unless the backing itself includes one or more assertions with ethical weight, or contains ethical assumptions. It might seem at first glance that the following reasonable argument violates this rule.

50) Slums usually breed disease, crime, and unhappiness.

It is a duty of the moral society, therefore, to solve the problem of slums.

But clearly the proof *assumes* that disease, crime, and unhappiness are social evils, and that it is the duty of a moral society to attack social evils. The prover had best make such moral assumptions explicit, unless they are completely apparent and universally acceptable, for no field is more controverted than ethics.

Esthetic judgments, too, depend upon critical assumptions with evaluative content. That is why esthetic arguments about this or that artistic creation tend to open out into much larger arguments, which leave the particular work far behind. Suppose that two critics disagree about the value of Stravinsky's "Rite of Spring." One considers it a frightful blare

of sheer noise, and the other finds in it a stirring evocation of primitive
emotions. This conflict will probably not be resolved by examining the
data—the piece of music itself—for both critics are already acquainted
with it at the outset. Rather, the argument will move to a higher level
of generality: "Only traditional harmonies and consistent tempos can
produce great music," claims the anti-Stravinskian, and his opponent
counters vociferously. Finally the discussion is likely to reach a still more
general level, that of ultimate esthetic values such as form, discipline,
and power. If the two critics can agree at this level, perhaps they can
work back down the scale to the music itself and achieve some measure
of concord. If not, the argument is irresolvable—not, notice, a trivial
difference in *taste,* but a significant difference in esthetic *principles.*
Since critical assumptions vary widely, the writer should state his explicitly, or make them clear in other ways, to avoid fruitless confusion
between disagreements on principle and disagreements about facts. Moreover, he will gain insight into his own deepest beliefs if, rather than
contenting himself with particular judgments like "This novel fails
because the hero is not lifelike," he seeks to discover the assumptions
that lie beneath.

10) SETTING UP THE ARGUMENT

Because even a highly abbreviated discussion of the procedures of
proof is bound to be more or less technical, the relevance of those procedures to the actual processes of thinking and writing sometimes becomes
obscured. Traveling from a problem, to a formalization of that problem,
to a solution, and finally to a coherent essay is not always easy. But the
passage becomes smoother with the aid of a few general rules.

First, it is important to frame the question properly in the beginning.
To be sure, an argument sometimes germinates in a writer's mind, not
with a question, but with evidence or backing assertions deductively
linked. Most of the time, however, in science as in ordinary proving, the
point of origin is a muddle, a problem, a paradox, a failure of understanding, an error. When it is, the investigator can simplify his task
enormously by asking the right question, thereby making it clear to
himself and his audience what procedures will lead most economically
to an answer. He thus avoids both waste motion and further confusion.
If he asks "What are the causes of unemployment?" instead of "What is
the cause of unemployment?" he may escape a failure through oversimplification. On the other hand, he may be wise to limit the question
more narrowly still, by asking "Is foreign competition a cause of the
present unemployment?" In this way, he reduces the problem to manageable proportions in the hope of salvaging at least a small measure of

certainty from the prevailing confusion. Or perhaps the prudent course is to begin by asking whether the present unemployment is even abnormally high—whether, that is, the analyst should look for a new and special cause, or try to find his answer in more permanent features of the economy. A move in the right direction at this point will not only save trouble later, but may well determine the very form of the proof.

Once the writer has posed his problem satisfactorily, he should assess it in order to decide what kind or kinds of proof are most pertinent, and which sections of the proof are likely to cause the most trouble. Some things he can assume without proof; others will require painstaking demonstration. To speak figuratively, each assertion lays an obligation on the writer: he must calculate the kind and amount of expansion necessary to make that assertion comprehensible and believable to his reader. To say that he must "calculate" the kind and amount is not to say that all his calculation is conscious. If he has a feeling for argument he will know without reflection how much explanation or proof an assertion requires and whether he has provided the right kind and amount. Lacking such an intuition, he should guard against disproportion by remembering the distinctions among assertions and kinds of proof suitable to each. He must keep alive his sensitivity to the difference between common knowledge and startling novelty, between the obvious and the paradoxical, between assertions that can stand by themselves and assertions that need backing up.

When he comes to the point of lining up his arguments, the writer should consider that not all backing assertions have equal weight or relevance. Since it is difficult to cast out one's hard-won knowledge, most students have a natural tendency to include all the evidence that they have uncovered, all the backing assertions that have passed across their minds; but the tendency must be resisted. In any proof some kinds of backing are crucial, others are trivial, and others are irrelevant. The writer will weaken his argument (logically and rhetorically) by giving undue emphasis to the trivial, or including the irrelevant. The danger is especially great in literary analysis. One word does not set the theme of a poem, nor one incident the theme of a novel. Tone, structure, and context are likely to be more important than isolated images or connotations, and it takes a keen sense of the work as a whole to prevent grotesque distortions of interpretation. The fact that Hamlet goes on a sea voyage is not enough to prove that Shakespeare's play is patterned after the *Odyssey*. In other kinds of argument, as in criticism, the value of any piece of evidence depends upon the shape of the entire problem, and slavish enumeration of "the facts" can only blur the lines of proof and destroy economy and elegance.

To put the matter more affirmatively, there is room for a good deal of ingenuity in the marshaling of data. Are campus riots and peace marches both evidence of undergraduate alienation from the status quo? Perhaps, but it will take perceptiveness and care to demonstrate the likeness (or the *absence* of likeness, for that matter). The process of sorting out backing assertions almost always goes beyond mechanical drudgery.

Much the same thing is true of the writer's handling of troublesome evidence. He can sometimes convert a seeming exception into a particularly compelling argument in favor of his case if he is alert to all the implications of his hypothesis. Nightmares seem, on the face of it, damaging to the hypothesis that all dreams are wish-fulfilment; but if the horror of the dreamer can be interpreted as a device for excusing him from the guilt that should accompany the wish, say, to murder his father, then the apparent exception actually strengthens the hypothesis. On the other hand, a law or generalization may be worth preserving even if it does have some exceptions—provided that the exceptions are relatively minor, and that the hypothesis simplifies most of the data so sweepingly that a few exceptions will barely tell against its usefulness. A Minneapolis bird watcher may sight a robin in December, but that in itself is not sufficient to make ornithologists give up the hypothesis of seasonal migration. Even if the writer cannot explain away the exceptions or relegate them to a minor role, he owes it to integrity and completeness to deal with them. They may force him to adopt a tone of respectful tentativeness, but sometimes it is better to have a doubtful conclusion than no conclusion at all. And any proof will inspire more respect if the prover has faced all the difficulties openly.

As for the writing itself, no amount of logic can make cogent prose flow copiously from the pen. But more often than not the writer can use the patterns of proof as an aid to organization. The whole essay may fall into shape if he conceives it on the model of, say, facts to tentative hypothesis to new facts to final hypothesis, or of a deductive chain argument, whatever course he has followed to his conclusion in the prewriting stage. Paragraphs, too, can be made to cohere neatly around logical forms, and transitions become much less a problem. The literal transfer of logical procedures to expository discourse will, to be sure, produce nothing very lively or personal, and it is not recommended here as anything except a way of learning to manage what one has to say in an orderly and lucid manner. One must have something to say in the first place. But as with most things, genuine freedom in writing is greatest when the writer accepts firm boundaries. The power of invention is increased and the path to discovery shortened by the necessity to work within form, and not even the most imaginative writer can always afford to be liberated from the structures of argument, formal and informal. Rightly used, they will almost always enlarge a writer's powers, not constrict him.

11) POSTSCRIPT: FALLACIES

A fallacy is a flaw in an argument, or a bogus argument, or an argument gone astray. Since the ethics of exposition and the writer's responsibility toward his assertions have been discussed in all three chapters, a number of fallacies have been mentioned already: persuasive definition, circularity, irrelevance, illicit use of authority, hasty generalization, and so on. There is no need to repeat here. Nor is it necessary to pursue the strictly logical fallacies, since the logical rules set forth in this chapter are sufficient guard against invalidity. The writer can spot a logical fallacy by noticing that this or that proof does not proceed according to the rules, and it matters little here what the various names are by which logicians have designated these fallacies. But there remains a residue of miscellaneous common fallacies, to be listed here with examples.

1) *Equivocation,* or shifting the sense of a word.

51) "Through the past decade our various states have drawn together into one great political unit: Pomposia. Hence Pomposia stands united, ready to fight against foreign aggression."

("Pomposia" means a union of political districts the first time it occurs, but a cooperative union of people the second time. What is true of the first need not be true of the second.)

2) *Accident,* or treating as permanent a quality that may be only temporary.

52) "Ten years ago Hubert Lutz was definitely shown to be a hopeless alcoholic. Today that same Hubert Lutz stands before us as a candidate for sheriff. Are we to have an alcoholic for our protector?"

(Some people overcome alcoholism.)

3) *Smuggled connotation.*

53) "We have overwhelming evidence that Lutz drinks wine daily and in large quantities. Shall we, by naming him sheriff, commit our safety to a wino?"

(A wino is not simply a person who drinks wine voluminously; the word has extra connotations of dereliction and depravity, and the speaker has not shown that Lutz's case deserves those connotations.)

4) *Misuse of etymology.*

54) " 'Education' comes from the Latin roots 'e—' = (out) plus 'ducere' (lead, bring). Thus education is literally a bringing out of what is in the student, and the institution that attempts to impose knowledge from outside is perverting the aims of education."

("Education" means education, whatever the roots may have meant, and in any case, it is not possible to prove that practices in the non-verbal world are good or bad by analyzing the meanings of words. This fallacy is a special case of persuasive definition and is all too frequently used by writers who should know better.)

5) *Reification:* treating an abstract concept as a real entity.

55) "America became a great power because it was her destiny to do so." (Is everything that ever happens caused by destiny? If so, destiny seems a superfluous concept, no different from the concept of *happening.* If not, what is this mysterious entity, destiny, that it should be able to cause large and significant events? This fallacy is closely related to circularity.)

The fallacies mentioned so far all involve, in one way or another, trickery with words. The next group, by contrast, achieve whatever plausibility they possess by perverting legitimate argumentative methods, mainly inductive.

6) *Post hoc, ergo propter hoc* (after the fact, therefore because of it).

56) "Both the French and the Russian revolutions were followed by periods of literary rebellion. Clearly political revolt causes revolt in the arts."

(And, by the same logic, the repeal of prohibition must have caused the Second World War. Perhaps literary and political rebellion are both caused by a third factor; perhaps there is no relationship other than chance. The facts presented do not in themselves allow any interesting conclusion at all.)

7) *Large numbers.*

57) "Fifteen million people suffer from mental illness in the United States. This is our main social problem."

(In a country of 170,000,000, still more people may suffer from other kinds of distress. And by what rule is the seriousness of social problems measured in sheer numbers? Almost everyone suffers from tooth decay, but tooth decay is not our main medical problem. Large numbers impress us too much; they should not be allowed to rout logic.)

8) *Composition:* assuming that what holds for each member of a class will hold for the class as a whole.

58) "This must be a biased committee, since all of its members are biased."

(Perhaps the individual biases cancel each other out.)

9) *Division:* the opposite fallacy.

59) "If we increase our outlay for salaries by twenty per cent, everyone will have twenty per cent more to spend."

(That depends on how the money is apportioned.)

10) *Genetic fallacy:* assuming that the present form of a thing reveals its origins, or vice versa.

> 60) "The law is one of our most complex institutions; hence it must have arisen long after simple institutions like the family."
>
> (Societies don't always move from simple to complex. But more important, the only way to find out for sure whether the law or the family came first is to *find out*—through history, archaeology, and so on. Such things cannot be proven by rational speculation in an arm chair.)
>
> 61) "*Kubla Khan* came to Coleridge in a dream, so it must lack rational structure."
>
> (No, it doesn't.)

11) *The call for perfection:* taking one objection (or a few) as decisive.

> 62) "The automation of industry throws people out of work; therefore it is economically inadvisable."
>
> (The advantages may outweigh this disadvantage; or any alternative plan may have worse disadvantages. Objections exist to every plan, but that is no reason for leaving things as they are.)

12) *Begging the question,* or arguing in a circle.

> 63) "Lawyers are honest. Their integrity is vouched for by *Men and the Law,* a book praised unreservedly for its reliability by Professor Ryan; Professor Ryan is unquestionably trustworthy, for he is himself a prominent barrister."
>
> (The value of Professor Ryan's testimony, upon which the backing depends, is itself contingent upon the conclusion of the argument, namely that lawyers are honest. Such arguments can be highly deceptive when they are complex, and when their language subtly shifts— as from "lawyer" to "barrister.")

These fallacies twist arguments into invalid shapes. The ones that remain to be discussed detour arguments from their proper courses by evading issues, intruding red herrings, and so on. They would be beneath notice except that they are, alas, so common and often so effective.

13) *Proving the wrong conclusion.*

> 64) A writer sets out to show that the German people were responsible for the extermination of the Jews. He rests his case in a demonstration that most Germans disliked Jews, and that they were at least roughly aware of what was happening to the Jews. These are relevant points, but not *the* point.

14) *Two wrongs make a right.*

> 65) "Harding is not to be blamed for Teapot Dome; other presidents have allowed worse scandals."
>
> (What the other presidents did has no bearing on the issue, unless the prover can show that they were not to be blamed either.)

15) *Diversion:* introducing an anecdote for humorous or rhetorical effect.

> 66) "The arguments of the American Medical Association against socialized medicine remind me of the fat wolf who proved with a great show of logic that it was in the nature of sheep to be eaten."
>
> (Very well; now let's get back to the arguments. Such diversions are harmless enough, to be sure, so long as they do not masquerade as proofs.)

16) *Damning the source,* or discrediting an argument because of its origin.

> 67) "Let anyone who is tempted to believe in the efficacy of propaganda remember that Adolf Hitler was its first great spokesman."
>
> (If the devil himself first made the claim, it may still be true.)

17) *Ad hominem:* discrediting one's opponent.

> 68) "You say that most policemen don't take bribes, but after all you're a policeman yourself—what else could you say?"
>
> (!)

One reminder: a fallacious argument may arrive at a true conclusion, but it will not have *proved* that conclusion. In proving, the end never justifies the means.

EXERCISES

1) Expand and rework proofs 2) to 8) in such a way as to bring out their logical structures and make them qualify for relatively formal discourse.

2) According to the rules of classical deductive logic, what conclusion (if any) follows from each of the following pairs of backing assertions?

> a. Some professional golfers are rich.
>   No rich man goes hungry.
> c. Every man is either a liberal or a conservative.
>   Some conservatives are Democrats.
> b. No car costs over $20,000 unless it is a Rolls Royce.
>   All the cars in my garage cost over $20,000.

d. If any book came out before 1400, it was not printed.
Some printed books are prayer books.

e. No monk is married.
Time waits for no bachelor.

f. Some poets are fascists.
Only fascists scorn personal liberty.

g. A coin collector is a numismatist.
Many students collect coins.

h. A man who seeks fame is a fool.
If any man is a fool, he does not deserve fame.

i. Keats was no philosopher.
No philosopher has solved the riddle of life.

j. Where there's life there's hope.
There is no hope in Mexico today.

(Notice that the only problem in most of these examples is getting the assertions into proper form—that is, expressing them in terms of classes. As we have said previously, deductive proving is mechanical once the argument is set up.)

3) Analyze the following proofs for truth and validity:

a. Cats are animals, and all animals need food; therefore cats need food.

b. Dogs are reptiles, and reptiles are warm-blooded; therefore dogs are warm-blooded.

c. Fish are vegetarians and vegetarians eat nothing but bread; therefore fish eat nothing but bread.

d. Birds build nests and sparrows build nests; therefore sparrows are birds.

e. Snakes are harmful and snakes are popular; therefore harmful things are popular.

f. Horses are becoming stronger, and anything that is becoming stronger needs more to eat; therefore horses need more to eat.

g. Whales are mammals and mammals lay eggs; therefore whales' eggs are mammalian.

4) Solve 16) for S (the butler murdered Lord Winchester) if
a. $P = O, Q = O, R = +$, and T, U, V, and W all $= +$
b. $R = O, T = O, U = O$, and $V = O$.
c. P, Q, R, T, U, V, and W all $= +$.

5) Construct an argument in English on this model, drawing the appropriate conclusion about Q:

$$(P \cdot Q) \longrightarrow \big[[(RvS) \cdot T] < U \big];$$
$P = +, R = O, S = O, T = +$, and $U = O$;
therefore, $Q = ?$

6) Translate the following into logical symbols, produce an *equivalent*

logical expression for each, and then translate the equivalent expression back into English. In what ways are the resulting pairs of English expressions "the same" in meaning?

  a. I will take my umbrella if and only if it rains.
  b. Either Jones was a pickpocket or my wallet fell out, unless I forgot to bring the wallet in the first place.
  c. Where there's smoke, there's fire.
  d. It is not true that professors are infallible and that students are infallible.

7) Take the following hypothesis: if a novel comes out during the summer, it will fail commercially unless it either treats sex in detail or is by a famous author. Suppose that a certain novel, published in July, written by a nonentity, and full of sex, fails commercially. Does this instance support the hypothesis?

8) How would you account for the following facts? In most American cities downtown areas have been declining for some years. Public transportation has diminished in scope and volume. Industry has increasingly settled in nearby rural areas. Highway building has proceeded at a great rate, but traffic problems continue to worsen. Suburban shopping centers flourish.

What alternative hypotheses would you have to consider? What addititional evidence would you need before settling for certain on an explanation? What additional facts will your hypothesis explain?

9) Consider the hypothesis that the poet Yeats was a mystic, and suppose that the following evidence is available:

  a. There are well-documented reports that he was a disciple of Madame Blavatsky, the theosophist.
  b. He was seen at seances.
  c. In his book *A Vision,* he developed a mystical system, but said at one point that perhaps his symbols were just "metaphors for poetry."
  d. People often say that Yeats was a mystic.
  e. Professor X, a specialist in modern poetry, says that Yeats was a mystic.
  f. Some of his poems are impossible to understand without knowing the system of *A Vision.*
  g. Reading Yeats's poetry gives you a feeling that he was a mystic.
  h. He was active in Irish political affairs.
  i. You know a mystic who likes Yeats's poetry.
  j. A number of great poets are known to have been mystics.
  k. Yeats expressed in print belief in a "great soul" with which we are all in touch from time to time.

How would you evaluate each of these pieces of evidence? Apply tests for reliability, and assess the relevance or persuasiveness of each fact. (The point of this exercise is not to decide the issue, but to judge the evidence.)

10) From a *World Almanac,* get statistics on the growth in population of major American cities during the last fifty years. What generalization can you make about the correlation between geographical location and increase in size? Do any other generalizations suggest themselves?

11) Problem for investigation: what kind of college or university is most likely to produce famous graduates? Consult *Who's Who in America* and find out systematically (e.g., by covering the letters "B" and "C" or by taking every tenth name) where the people listed got their education. Then work out some schemes for classifying colleges—by type of institution, by location, by date of founding, by sex or sexes of students, and so on. Other relevant classifications should suggest themselves. Remember to allow for differences in size. When you have drawn your conclusions make sure to indicate the places at which your analysis may be weak.

12) What steps would you take to test the truth of the following propositions?

    a. that women are superior to men
    b. that fluorine prevents tooth decay
    c. that God exists
    d. that international socialism is inevitable
    e. that air power was decisive in World War II
    f. that a religious revival is taking place in the colleges
    g. that smoking causes cancer
    h. that College Board scores have no predictive value
    i. that eighteen-year-olds should be allowed to vote
    j. that Caesar suffered from diabetes
    k. that Western civilization is dying
    l. that no man is an island
    m. that economic pressures were responsible for the American Revolution
    n. that Homer was a woman
    o. that the German character is militaristic
       What form or forms of proof would recommend themselves in each case? Why?

13) Produce three examples each of hypotheses, laws, and principles.

14) This selection is from a speech by a leading English philosopher of the nineteenth century to an American audience. A comparison has

already been made between the "spasmodic" energy of the savage and the "persistent industry" of the American.

What I have seen and heard during my stay among you has forced on me the belief that this slow change from habitual inertness to persistent activity has reached an extreme from which there must begin a counter-change—a reaction. Everywhere I have been struck with the number of faces which told in strong lines of the burdens that had to be borne. I have been struck, too, with the large proportion of gray-haired men; and inquiries have brought out the fact, that with you the hair commonly begins to turn some ten years earlier than with us. Moreover, in every circle I have met men who had themselves suffered from nervous collapse due to stress of business, or named friends who had either killed themselves by overwork, or had been permanently incapacitated, or had wasted long periods in endeavours to recover health. I do but echo the opinion of all the observant persons I have spoken to, that immense injury is being done by this high-pressure life—the physique is being undermined. That subtle thinker and poet whom you have lately had to mourn, Emerson, says, in his essay on the Gentleman, that the first requisite is that he shall be a good animal. The requisite is a general one—it extends to the man, to the father, to the citizen. We hear a great deal about "the vile body"; and many are encouraged by the phrase to transgress the laws of health. But Nature quietly suppresses those who treat thus disrespectfully one of her highest products, and leaves the world to be peopled by the descendants of those who are not so foolish.

HERBERT SPENCER, *Essays Scientific, Political and Speculative*

Discuss the passage with regard to sources of evidence, reliability of the sources, types of reasoning, and correctness of procedure.

❈ *Persuading*

MATHEMATICS is often spoken of as a "pure language," and in this century those who have greatest need for precision and stability in their assertions have learned to make mathematical symbols serve where once no one would have thought of using anything but words. "Mathematical logic," for example, is not just the logic of mathematics, but the use of mathematical procedures to extend the power of logic far beyond what is practical in ordinary human discourse. This interesting development is the direct result of frustration with language, and the frustration rises from the fact that words are, from one point of view, unreliable as a means of reference.

There are two principal ways in which words commonly display their shortcomings as reliable means of reference. (1) A word frequently refers to more than one thing; this characteristic is called "ambiguity." (2) A word may refer to one thing and, at the same time, indicate an attitude to be taken toward it; such words—"home" and "mother" are examples used earlier—have a strong connotative aura. Using mathematical symbols in place of words controls both conditions effectively and at the same time allows great economy of statement.

Still, it is clear that few of us are going to conduct our conversations and do our writing in mathematical symbols, so it becomes necessary to deal with the vagaries—if that is what they are—of words. And it may even be asked how we come to have so much unreliability in language if that unreliability serves no good purpose.

It may be useful to point out at this point that it is not words only that have connotations. Sentence structures have them, too, and even punctuation. The syntax of much eighteenth-century prose is often described as "stately," because its balanced phrases and clauses have a certain architectural grandeur that affects the reader. The dashes and spattered commas and interspersed exclamation points of *Tristram*

127

Shandy, on the other hand, by themselves evoke the adjectives "impulsive," "erratic," and "flippant."

If words do more than refer, and if sentences do more than communicate information, what else is it that they do? They move; they persuade.

1) THE UBIQUITY OF PERSUASION

In a broad sense of the term, all communication is persuasive, a fact which Kenneth Burke has compressed into the effective statement, "Style is ingratiation." The generalization does not mean, of course, that a writer is always consciously intent on cajoling or swaying the reader. Yet the fact that a writer must choose among words and combinations of words does mean that there must be a ground of choice, and that ground is essentially their capacity to "persuade." Although a communication may be apparently only explanatory or descriptive in purpose, it is at the same time an attempt to lead others to see or understand something as the writer sees or understands it. Strictly speaking, there is no such thing as "objective" writing. A writer's words refer to events, ideas, things, and their qualities, true enough, but it is to events, ideas, things, and qualities as they are known to the writer. His use is always one man's use (though not necessarily different from every man's use, for all that), and his communication is the act of getting others to accept that use, even if only temporarily.

The fundamental persuasiveness of the act of communicating is enhanced by the nature of words themselves, and since it is with words (with words-in-order, to be precise) that a writer conducts his communication, a treatment of persuasion may well begin from them.

2) THE SOURCES OF CONNOTATIVE MEANING

The discussions of defining and asserting have already required that some attention be given to the expressive or emotive effect of words, to their connotations. Now it is necessary to examine closely the properties of words and the conditions of their use which combine to make such a phenomenon as connotation occur.

First, it is important to remember that words are arbitrary, that— to use the words of John Locke—there is no "natural connection . . . between particular articulate sounds and certain ideas, for then there would be but one language amongst all men." Yet, though words are arbitrary, they are not all alike in their referential character, and since it is partly with the character of words that persuasion is concerned, some way must be found of distinguishing among words on that basis.

In the first place, it is clear that the concepts to which some words refer are much broader than those to which others refer. The referent of "pay," for instance, is large enough to *include* the referents of "salary," "wages," and "stipend." It is the work of the definer to sort these referents into categories and subcategories even though, in ordinary discourse, one word is often used rather than another without very careful attention to the distinctions at which a good definer would arrive.

There is more to the matter than getting the definitions straight, however. A person may be able to make absolutely airtight distinctions between the words "fat," "stout," and "obese" and still hesitate about which word to use in referring to a person who is overweight. The point of interest here is the ground on which a choice among those adjectives might be made. To speak of a "fat" bank roll is certainly to say nothing in dispraise of it, but to refer to a woman as "fat" may be very uncomplimentary indeed. In part, the difference is that fatness is generally thought, in our culture, to be a good characteristic of bank rolls and a bad one of persons. But if the fatness of the woman is a fact, and if the fact must be mentioned, a writer still may choose to avoid using the word "fat" about a woman and decide to substitute for it the word "stout," "plump," "large," or "sizable."

In rhetoric, such words are sometimes referred to as "euphemisms," but to call them "euphemisms" is not to explain their character or to explain our choice. What is it that makes one word more or less palatable than another?

Now, for a few words in the English language, there does appear actually to be something in the character of the word itself that affects its meaning. Those words take on distinct coloration because they contain sounds which, for reasons not fully understood, generally occur in words of a particular connotative tendency. Thus, when William Faulkner named one of his fictional families "Snopes," he helped to establish its unsavory character, even before he depicted it, by using the sound "sn-" in its name. The English language has a remarkably large number of sn- words having unpleasant associations—*snoop, sneak, snide, snort, snare, snag, snarl, snob, snout, snap, snitch*—and "Snopes" catches some of the unpleasantness by aural association.

The number of words that have such indigenous bias is not great, but its smallness should not obscure the fact that the *sound* of a word may be a part of its persuasive capacity. Indeed, those words which we call "onomatopœic" because they are attempts to reproduce "natural" sounds—"crunch," "murmur," "buzz," and so on—are effective largely because of their sound. Advertisers constantly play upon our responsiveness to the sound of words, and poets, of course, do so, too. But, except in single words or brief phrases, neither can rely primarily on sound to convey meaning, or even to stimulate feeling. Not until idea joins sound, as it soon comes to do even in onomatopœic words, is the persuasive capacity of the word fully realized.

A much more important source of the persuasive effect of words is the context in which they are habitually used. A word that is "borrowed" from one situation and applied to another carries over to the new situation some of the associations of the one it has left. Thus, the word "scientific" is frequently employed to provide the stamp of approval even though nothing that remotely resembles scientific study may be involved. Hotels advertise themselves as "homey." A dress design is said to have a "Fifth Avenue" or "Nob Hill" look. Much of this borrowing is metaphorical, as in "rosy complexion." All of it seeks to extend meaning by multiplying the notions called to mind when the word or phrase is uttered.

There are, of course, no rules by which one can determine the connotative aura of a particular word; one must simply know. Such knowing is chiefly the result of a broad experience with words, and wide reading is perhaps the surest avenue to such experience. It takes more than wide reading, however, to make a person aware of still another way in which single words may persuade, a way that is often summed up in the word "metaphor." For an appreciation of the power of metaphor, the reading must be not only wide but perceptive and thoughtful.

3) THE METAPHORICAL GROUND

Metaphor is one of the most fundamental of linguistic activities; some have even suggested that most language is, at bottom, metaphorical. However that may be, it is certainly true that all developed language is deeply indebted to metaphor and that all good writing reflects the writer's consciousness of the metaphorical vitality of the words he uses.

A metaphor is a locution in which the context demands that one or more words not be taken literally. In Shakespeare's famous line, "All the world's a stage," the word "stage" is used metaphorically; the assertion would be false and silly if "stage" were meant literally. To put it another way, in metaphor the attributes of one thing are imputed to a different thing. To take an example close at hand, the previous paragraph speaks of developed language as "deeply indebted to metaphor." A debt is something owed by one person to another; to say that language owes a debt to metaphor is to personify language and to speak metaphorically. More obvious metaphors (a child's observation, for instance, that the sun is "smily") are easy to detect and fairly easy to use. Submerged metaphors like the one just examined are likely to conceal their very real persuasive effect under the bland façade of ordinariness.

The way in which overt and submerged metaphors do their work becomes apparent if we consider carefully a passage of prose which is written with both kinds in mind.

> "The style is the man"; but the social and rhetorical influences adulterate and debase it, until not one man in a thousand achieves his birthright, or claims his second self. The fire of the soul burns all too feeble, and warms itself by the reflected heat from the society around it. We give back words of tepid greeting, without improvement. We talk to our fellows in the phrases we learn from them, which come to mean less and less as they grow worn with use. Then we exaggerate and distort, heaping epithet upon epithet in the endeavour to get a little warmth out of the smouldering pile. The quiet cynicism of our everyday demeanour is open and shameless, we callously anticipate objections founded on the well-known vacuity of our seeming emotions, and assure our friends that we are "truly" grieved or "sincerely" rejoiced at their hap—as if joy or grief that really exists were some rare and precious brand of joy or grief. In its trivial conversational uses so simple and pure a thing as joy becomes a sandwich-man—humanity degraded to an advertisement. The poor dejected word shuffles along through the mud in the services of the sleek trader who employs it, and not until it meets with a poet is it rehabilitated and restored to dignity.
>
> WALTER RALEIGH, "Social and Rhetorical Corruptions," in *Style*

This passage is so heavily metaphorical that meaning is as often obscured as revealed in it, but its dense figurativeness provides ample illustration of the ways in which metaphors work to persuade, and for that reason it is valuable for our purposes here. The *statement* of the passage is approximately this: "Conventional and unconsidered use of language destroys the capacity of words to express a man's thoughts and feelings." The expression of that statement is developed, in large part, by two metaphorical procedures: 1) *reification,* the treatment of abstractions as though they were things ("influences adulterate and debase"), and 2) *personification,* the treatment of things as though they were persons ("the poor dejected word shuffles along"). Two strong metaphors dominate: men's thoughts and feelings as "the fire of soul" which "burns . . . and warms," and joy as a "sandwich-man." Of these two, the first is continuously elaborated in other metaphorical expressions of slightly reduced intensity, the "smouldering pile" of epithets, the "tepid" greeting, and so on. Still further down on the scale of intensity, or of obviousness, other metaphors continue the transformation of abstract into concrete, of inanimate into animate: the "heaping" of epithets, the way in which we "callously" anticipate objections which are "founded" on the "vacuity" of our emotions, the progressive meaninglessness of words "worn" with use, the eventual "rehabilitation" and "restoration" of a word when it "meets with" a poet.

The overt metaphors strike eye and ear at once and, if they are fresh and apt, persuade us to consider their subject in a particular light. The submerged metaphors, though they make less noticeable impression, affect our consideration fully as much for the reason that the reader assents to them without thought or examination. An overt metaphor may induce us to accept a new way of looking at a matter, but it does so over a certain amount of resistance simply because the new way runs counter to habit. A good writer is likely, therefore, to be sparing in his use of strong figures of speech. And, because he knows that submerged metaphors have a persuasive effect out of proportion to their quiet presence, he will treat them with a great deal of respect.

Metaphor is, then, a very important instrument for directing the persuasive energy of language, probably the most effective single instrument when it comes to controlling the connotations of a particular word. It may seem that the associative aura of words is being treated here too much as though it had a demonic capacity to make effective communication almost impossible. Therefore it may be wise to point out that, in addition to the connotative spread already noted, there is another with which the writer must deal. Besides the indigenous bias of a few words (the sn- words mentioned above) and the general connotative aura of most words, there are "meanings" for words which are either entirely private or limited to a small number of people. Such specialized meanings (or "subjective intensions," as they are sometimes called) no writer can completely predict. The adjective "fat" annoys a large number of people; used as a verb, the word "contact" may arouse only a few beleaguered purists; and the noun "asparagus" may revolt only a neurotic John Doe, who once became violently ill after eating asparagus and cannot forget the experience. Even could he predict such connotations, the writer can do nothing directly about them. Indirectly, however, he can still manage to control such random associations by the way in which he makes sure that this word, and no other, is the one that serves his purpose at the moment. If the word, or the image, is exactly right for his purpose, its context will in large measure protect it from taking on associations other than those he desires it to evoke.

4) THE ART OF RHETORIC

Our earliest commentaries and analyses of rhetoric come from Greece and from a time in which the spoken was more common than the written word. Even among literate men, it was assumed that affairs of public character would be managed largely through conversation and oratory. For that reason, early studies of rhetoric are primarily concerned with speech and the means of making speech effective. The best of them—Aristotle's—is useful as a starting-point for further discussion, both because it is so good and because it will provide a means of making important distinctions between the rhetoric of speech and the rhetoric of written composition.

Aristotle begins his commentaries on rhetoric by distinguishing the elements that demand attention: *speaker, subject,* and *person addressed.* Rhetoric—persuasion—has to do with all three. The speaker persuades partly by the character he presents to his hearers. Insofar as it makes itself apparent in his words (by generosity of sentiment, for example, or—conversely—by belligerence or cynicism), his character becomes part of his rhetoric. He persuades also by his success in working up the emotions of his hearers; and, finally, by the kinds of arguments he develops in support of his propositions and by the manner in which he arranges and expresses those arguments. The distinctions are simple and obvious, once they have been stated.

What does the speaker have to work with? Words, of course, and words-in-order. A place and time, shared with his listeners. His own physical presence and what he can do with it in the way of clothing, manner, gestures, facial expression. His voice and all the meanings it can convey by stress, pitch, intonation, and pause. He has also the immediate responses of his listeners to guide him as he speaks. If he is sensitive to those responses and familiar with the resources of language, he can summon scores of rhetorical turns at need.

For the writer, rhetoric is a somewhat different matter. The three elements remain: writer, subject, reader—the one speaking, the matter spoken of, the one spoken to. But the resources are considerably changed. The writer must make words and syntax do all the speaker makes them do, and more. He must use them to accomplish what the speaker conveys by his presence and his voice. And, more often than not, he must write in ignorance of his reader and nearly always without any immediate or direct response from him. To offset these disadvantages, the writer has one advantage. Because he presents an enduring text, he can expect his reader to look back as necessary, to compare one part with another, and to respond to lengthy and subtle lines of argument by virtue of the fact that he can pore over them as much as he needs to do.

Here is the point: a writer has to make unaided language do more for him than a speaker does, but he can also expect his reader to absorb more matter, and more difficult matter, than a listener does. One may outweigh the other, or the two may balance out, but it is certain that the rhetoric of written composition and the rhetoric of speech are not identical. In the discussion that follows, terms relevant to the rhetoric of speech will occasionally appear simply because they are now current and vivid (the writer's "voice," for example, and the reader as "audience"). The discussion, itself, however, has to do only with writing.

5) *THE WRITER: CHARACTER, PERSONA, VOICE*

Consider, first, the writer himself. The minute he pulls the cover off his typewriter, he begins to assert himself; that is, he begins to assert *a* self, one of his several selves, or a part of his whole self. It's not so much that the writer isn't all there (take the expression however you will) as that, for the time being, he allows one part of himself to soak up all the rest. For the sake of what he has to say and in order to win the game he has decided to play, he gives up irrelevant parts of himself and concentrates his strength in the part that will best further his strategy. In doing so, the writer not only presents a coherent character to the scrutiny of his reader but offers one as well for his own contemplation. The final form he takes in any piece of writing may be the result of a long process in which the writer has tried out and discarded several other forms, like an actor putting on one mask after another until he finds the one that best represents not only what he has to say but the impression he would like to make while saying it. This "play" is, then, not something capricious. Rather, it is the outcome of continuing assessment of self, an external manifestation of self-knowledge.

In modern psychology this tactic, half-instinctive and half-conscious, is called "role playing"; in literary criticism of the past few decades it has been customary to speak of the writer's various "personae" (another word for "masks"). In both, the metaphor of play is implicit. For present purposes, a simpler term than "persona" will suffice. Let us say that, in every writing situation, the writer uses a "voice" to indicate the (dramatic) relationship he intends to establish between himself and his readers. No reader of sensibility is unaware of the writer's voice; therefore no writer can afford to be indifferent to it, and no good writer is. How *openly* the writer announces his special identity is another matter. Here, for example, are sections of an address Mark Twain wrote for delivery to members of the Associated Press on September 18, 1906. As you read them, identify as precisely as you can the rôle Mark Twain is playing, the voice he has assumed for the nonce.

The address begins:

> I am here to make an appeal to the nations in behalf of the simplified spelling. I have come here because they cannot all be reached except through you. There are only two forces that can carry light to all the corners of the globe—only two—the sun in the heavens and the Associated Press down here. I may seem to be flattering the sun, but I do not mean it so; I am meaning only to be just and fair all around. You speak with a million voices; no one can reach so many races, so many hearts and intellects, as you—except Rudyard Kipling, and he cannot do it without your help. If the Associated Press will adopt and use our simplified forms,

and thus spread them to the ends of the earth, covering the whole spacious planet with them as with a garden of flowers, our difficulties are at an end.

Every day of the three hundred and sixty-five the only pages of the world's countless newspapers that are read by all the human beings and angels and devils that can read, are these pages that are built out of Associated Press despatches. And so I beg you, I beseech you—oh, I implore you to spell them in our simplified forms. Do this daily, constantly, persistently, for three months—only three months—is all I ask. The infallible result?—victory, victory all down the line. For by that time all eyes here and above and below will have become adjusted to the change and in love with it, and the present clumsy and ragged forms will be grotesque to the eye and revolting to the soul. And we shall be rid of phthisis and phthisic and pneumonia and pneumatics, and diphtheria and pterodactyl, and all those other insane words which no man addicted to the simple Christian life can try to spell and not lose some of the bloom of his piety in the demoralizing attempt. Do not doubt it. We are chameleons, and our partialities and prejudices change places with an easy and blessed facility, and we are soon wonted to the change and happy in it.

Do I seem to be seeking the good of the world? That is the idea. It is my public attitude; privately I am merely seeking my own profit. We all do it, but it is sound and it is virtuous, for no public interest is anything other or nobler than a massed accumulation of private interests.

Several pages later, this passage occurs:

Now I wish to say just one entirely serious word:

I have reached a time of life, seventy years and a half, where none of the concerns of this world have much interest for me personally. I think I can speak dispassionately upon this matter, because in the little while that I have got to remain here I can get along very well with these old-fashioned forms, and I don't propose to make any trouble about it at all. I shall soon be where they won't care how I spell so long as I keep the Sabbath.

There are eighty-two millions of us people that use this orthography, and it ought to be simplified in our behalf, but it is kept in its present condition to satisfy one million people who like to have their literature in the old form. That looks to me to be rather selfish, and we keep the forms as they are while we have got one million people coming in here from foreign countries every year and they have got to struggle with this orthography of ours, and it keeps them back and damages their citizenship for years until they learn to spell the language, if they ever do learn. This is merely sentimental argument.

And the address closes in this fashion:

Now, you see before you the wreck and ruin of what was once a young person like yourselves. I am exhausted by the heat of the day. I must take what is left of this wreck and run out of your presence and carry it away to my home and spread it out there and sleep the sleep of the righteous. There is nothing much left of me but my age and my righteousness, but I leave with you my love and my blessing, and may you always keep your youth.

A shifting "voice" usually indicates multiple purposes or an unclear purpose. A reading of the full text of this address will reveal both, unless one can accept as the main purpose Mark Twain's desire to have a pleasant time with some people he liked and consider the cause of simplified spelling simply a convenient vehicle.

Although Mark Twain's address was written, and therefore assumes a reader, it was written with a listening audience in mind. Its enunciations of the writer's presence are stronger and more direct than one ordinarily finds in written prose. Yet voice continues to be heard, even when it is silent. Consider next an excerpt of a letter from father to son. The intimacy of relationship suggests that the writer need make no especial effort to make his reader aware of what he represents. Even so, we can swiftly detect the particular rôle the writer assumes as well as the seriousness with which he assumes it.

Dear Boy,

The art of pleasing is a very necessary one to possess; but a very difficult one to acquire. It can hardly be reduced to rules; and your own good sense and observation will teach you more of it than I can. Do as you would be done by is the surest method that I know of pleasing. Observe carefully what pleases you in others, and probably the same things in you will please others. If you are pleased with the complaisance and attention of others to your humours, your tastes, or your weaknesses, depend upon it the same complaisance and attention on your part to theirs will equally please them. Take the tone of the company that you are in, and do not pretend to give it; be serious, gay, or even trifling, as you find the present humour of the company; this is an attention due from every individual to the majority. Do not tell stories in company; there is nothing more tedious and disagreeable; if by chance you know a very short story, and exceedingly applicable to the present subject of conversation, tell it in as few words as possible; and even then throw out that you do not love to tell stories, but that the shortness of it tempted you. Of all things, banish the egotism out of your conversation, and never think of entertaining people with your own personal concerns or private affairs; though they are interesting to you, they are tedious and impertinent to everybody else; besides that, one cannot keep one's own private affairs too secret. . . .

If you would particularly gain the affection and friendship of particular people, whether men or women, endeavour to find out their predominant excellency, if they have one, and their prevailing weakness, which everybody has; and do justice to the one and something more than justice to the other. Men have various objects in which they may excel, or at least would be thought to excel; and, though they love to hear justice done to them where they know that they excel, yet they are most and best flattered upon those points where they wish to excel and yet are doubtful whether they do or not. As, for example: Cardinal Richelieu, who was undoubtedly the ablest statesman of his time or perhaps of any other, had the idle vanity of being thought the best poet too: he envied the great Corneille his reputation, and ordered a criticism to be written upon the *Cid*. Those, therefore, who flattered skilfully said little to him of his abilities in state affairs, or at least but *en passant,* and as it might naturally occur. But the incense which they gave him, the smoke of which they knew would turn his head in their favour, was as a *bel esprit* and a poet. Why? Because he was sure of one excellency and distrustful as to the other. . . .

Women have, in general, but one object, which is their beauty; upon which, scarce any flattery is too gross for them to swallow. Nature has hardly formed a woman ugly enough to be insensible to flattery upon her person; if her face is so shocking that she must in some degree be conscious of it, her figure and air, she trusts, make ample amends for it. If her figure is deformed, her face, she thinks, counterbalances it. If they are both bad, she comforts herself that she has graces; a certain manner, a *je ne sais quoi,* still more engaging than beauty. This truth is evident from the studied and elaborate dress of the ugliest women in the world. An undoubted, uncontested, conscious beauty is, of all women, the least sensible of flattery upon that head; she knows that it is her due and is therefore obliged to nobody for giving it her. She must be flattered upon her understanding, which, though she may possibly not doubt of herself, yet she suspects that men may distrust.

Do not mistake me and think that I mean to recommend to you abject and criminal flattery: no, flatter nobody's vices or crimes: on the contrary, abhor and discourage them. But there is no living in the world without a complaisant indulgence for people's weaknesses and innocent, though ridiculous, vanities. If a man has a mind to be thought wiser, and a woman handsomer, than they really are, their error is a comfortable one to themselves and an innocent one with regard to other people; and I would rather make them my friends by indulging them in it than my enemies by endeavouring (and that to no purpose) to undeceive them. . . .

These are some of the *arcana* necessary for your initiation in the great society of the world. I wish I had known them better at your age; I have paid the price of three-and-fifty years for them, and shall not grudge it if you reap the advantage. Adieu.

(from *Letters of Lord Chesterfield,* London, October 16, O.S. 1747)

These extended examples show how a writer may initiate the process of persuasion by so defining his own presence that he establishes, between himself and his reader, a relationship that will further his purpose.

As readers people are likely to associate the "voice" of anything they read with the man who wrote it. There is no harm in that so long as they do not expect the writer to be limited in real life (or in another piece of writing) to the voice with which he speaks in what they have just read. He may be, of course, but it is not sound to expect that he will be. For example, Dylan Thomas describing his efforts to light a cigarette out-doors in a December wind would scarcely use the nostalgic sing-song of this passage from his *Child's Christmas in Wales:*

> One Christmas was so much like another, in those years around the sea-corner now and out of all sound except the distant speaking of the voices I sometimes hear a moment before sleep, that I can never remember whether it snowed for six days and six nights when I was twelve or whether it snowed for twelve days and twelve nights when I was six.

Nor is it likely that Bernard DeVoto would have expressed his comments on the subject of marigold-culture with the same asperity as these on invasion of privacy:

> I like a country where it's nobody's damned business what magazines anyone reads, what he thinks, whom he had cocktails with. I like a country where we do not have to stuff the chimneys against listening ears and where what we say does not go into the FBI files along with a note from S-17 that I may have another wife in California.
>
> "Due Notice to the FBI"

To return to the figure of speech with which this discussion began: writing is a kind of play, even when it is entirely serious. One part of that play is the donning of a mask, the assuming of a voice. The reader's obligation is to recognize the voice for what it is—to recognize that it is one of the legitimate devices of a speaker or writer, one of his ways of persuading. Once he is aware of that fact, the reader is adequately warned against taking it at face value. He is an independent being, after all, and has the responsibility of weighing and considering before he judges or acts. The writer's voice is simply one of the many matters which the reader must summon wit to measure.

What, then, of the *writer's* obligation, since it is to writers that this book is addressed—to students-as-writers, more precisely; what are the concerns about voice to which the writer should attend? An answer will only recapitulate what has been said or suggested above, but recapitulation may clarify as well as emphasize.

A writer's voice depends on three things: his knowledge of himself, his awareness of the character of his audience, his understanding of the matter he wants to discuss. Unless he knows his subject, he will not be able to strike a clear attitude toward it; unless he knows his audience, he will not be able to choose means of persuasion likely to be effective with it; unless he knows himself, he will not understand his purposes clearly enough to appreciate which voice or voices he can honestly assume in making his appeal.

Since the only means a writer has are verbal means, it is proper to ask now by what verbal means he achieves a voice. No catalogue will list them all, but a short list will be suggestive and useful.

1) SELF-DESCRIPTION •   Mark Twain speaks of having "reached a time of life, seventy years and a half, where none of the concerns of this world have much interest for me personally"; he says he is "the wreck and ruin of what was once a young person like yourselves," a man "exhausted by the heat of the day." The voice emerging from this self-description is the one related to his subterranean appeal for good fellow-feeling, kindliness, tolerance, a bit of fun before the light goes out.

2) TERMS OF ADDRESS •   The language in which the writer lets his readers know he is aware of them even when that language is little more than a formula, may be highly persuasive. Lord Chesterfield begins his letter with an affectionate "Dear Boy." His "Do not mistake me and think that I mean to recommend to you abject and criminal flattery" is at once paternal and respectful of the son's intelligence. Mark Twain's broad flattery ("you" of the Associated Press as one of the two forces that "can carry light to all the corners of the globe") establishes the jocular relationship of men intimate enough to be able to poke fun at each other without fear of being misunderstood.

3) EMPHASIS ON THE WRITER'S PRESENCE •   A very different Bernard DeVoto would emerge from sentences in which the "I" lost its dominance. "What would be more pleasing to me would be a country where . . ." or "It would seem to me preferable that the country of one's residence be. . . ." In nothing is the inexperienced writer more awkward than in managing his own presence in what he writes, and unfortunately nothing but experience will be very helpful to him. It can be said, however, that the dominating "I" is often the mark of the writer who does not judge accurately the relative merit of what he has to say and of the fact that it is he who is saying it. ("I have come to the conclusion that every new country should be given one atomic reactor when it joins the U.N.") The less strident "we"—writer-and-reader-having-common-concern (as in textbooks), or the corporate, committee point of view (as in editorials)—often serves where "I" might offend, though its use is so ceremonial that it sometimes sounds absurdly pompous (as in the thesis written by a single person: "From these data, we conclude that. . . ."). Parenthetical appearances ("The plain fact, it seems to me . . ."; "Absolutely no-one, in our opinion, should waste . . .") may quite effectively disguise dogmatic language and lend a tone of moderateness and even modesty to positions that are very positive or even inflexible. But they may also have the effect of blunting force or even of giving statements an air of evasiveness.

4) STRICTNESS OF ORDER •   Mark Twain's procedures are as disjointed and casual as his purposes, but Lord Chesterfield's letter has all the neatness and concision of the mind without large and persistent purpose which is nonetheless scrupulous about orderliness and detail.

5) SUCCINCTNESS •   The distinction between the man of few words and the man of many probably has less to do with power of mind than with

tendency of character, and succinctness (or verbosity) is therefore properly a matter of voice. DeVoto's downright "I like" is as indicative of blunt honesty as Thomas' roundabout "I can never remember . . ." is of gentle and whimsical good humor.

6) DICTION •   Whatever voice is chosen must, of course, be supported throughout by language appropriate to it. Transpose the vocabulary, the images and figures, of Mark Twain and Lord Chesterfield and the game is up at once. Appropriateness is more than appropriate here; it is essential.

7) SYNTAX •   Like a starched shirt or a polo jersey, formality and informality of syntax swiftly represent the user's chosen manner. In the austere and formal parallelisms of Bacon's style, for instance, a reader meets the precise and disciplined analyst:

> Revenge is a kind of wild justice, which the more man's nature runs to, the more ought law to weed it out: for as for the first wrong, it doth but offend the law, but the revenge of that wrong putteth the law out of office. . . .
>
> The most tolerable sort of revenge is for those wrongs which there is no law to remedy; but then, let a man take heed the revenge be such as there is no law to punish, else a man's enemy is still beforehand, and it is two for one. . . .
>
> Public revenges are for the most part fortunate; as that for the death of Caesar; for the death of Pertinax; for the death of Henry the Third of France; and many more. But in private revenges it is not so; nay, rather vindicative persons live the life of witches, who, as they are mischievous, so end they infortunate.
>
> "Of Revenge"

By contrast, from the irregular and informal syntactic patterns that characterize D. H. Lawrence's prose in *Studies in Classic American Literature* emerges the image of a writer whose primary concern is to express himself without constraint. Lawrence obviously hopes to engage his reader's attention by representing in his syntax the disjointed processes of impulsive speculation.

> Benjamin Franklin had a specious little equation in providential mathematics:
>
> $$Rum + Savage = 0$$
>
> Awfully nice! You might add up the universe to nought, if you kept on. Rum plus Savage may equal a dead savage. But is a dead savage nought? Can you make a land virgin by killing off its aborigines?
>
> The Aztec is gone, and the Incas. The Red Indian, the Esquimo, the Patagonian are reduced to negligible numbers.
>
> *Où sont les neiges d'antan?*
>
> My dear, wherever they are, they will come down again next winter, sure as houses.

Not that the Red Indian will ever possess the broad lands of America. At least I presume not. But his ghost will. The Red Man dies hating the white man. What remnant of him lives, lives hating the white man. Go near the Indians, and you just feel it. As far as we are concerned, the Red Man is subtly and unremittingly diabolic. Even when he doesn't know it. He is dispossessed in life, and unforgiving. He doesn't believe in us and our civilization, and so is our mystic enemy, for we push him off the face of the earth.

8) ARGUMENTS AND EXAMPLES · Since the number of arguments that may be marshalled to support a proposition is often large, the choice, ordering, and emphasis of them will be an indirect indication of the rôle the writer is playing. Examples being even greater in number, the choice among relevant ones will be almost as significant as the diction adopted.

Whatever the strategies he devises, whatever the voices he assumes, the writer ultimately persuades not by his strategy or voice but by what the reader senses they stand for. If he is at all alert, the reader penetrates the artifice and discovers the artificer. He sees through the mask to the man, and he responds to the man in the degree that he finds him an embodiment of "good sense, good moral character, and good will" (Aristotle again, *Rhetoric,* Book II). The intelligent writer is too well aware of his readers' capacity to discern the false from the true to risk a voice that is patently inconsistent with his character. He should not want to, of course; but if tempted he should remember that deceit seldom deceives for long. A pose need not be an imposition.

6) THE READER: IDENTITY, SUSCEPTIBILITY, RESISTANCE

The speaker, as we have noted, can see his audience and be seen by it. (Paradoxically, modern communication by radio and television often gives the speaker an audience he cannot see and thus strips him of one of the classic advantages of the orator over the writer.) The writer commonly has not one reader but many, and even if they are of the same age, the same class in society, have had similar educations and no very different experiences, they remain different and therefore harder to reach by special appeal than is a single person. Very often, the writer has no way of knowing who will read what he has written; he pours his words into the sea of anonymity. And sometimes, he is in the most peculiar position of all, that of knowing he writes for one person to read but of being enjoined to write as though to a part of the world in general: that is very much the position of the college student when he prepares a term paper or a weekly essay.

Much of the unevenness and stuffiness in contemporary American writ-

ing is due directly to uncertainty about the reader. Tabloid newspapers
and highly specialized journals are almost the only publishing media
today that can assume a particular kind of reader and develop their
rhetorical strategy with him in mind. For everything else, the readers
vary so much in kind that a writer cannot simply fix his mind on a
definable reader and appeal only to him. He must instead either *create*
a group of readers to whom he can appeal, or find a substitute for
audience altogether.

One way of creating a group of readers is to appeal to the simplest
feelings only, those universally shared by men: fear of death or displace-
ment, love of self and of one's own, curiosity about the privacies of others,
suspicion of outsiders. The difficulty is that such appeals, in the gross
form they must take to be generally effective, are not relevant to many
things a writer may want to say.

A professional writer may in time so establish himself that he can be
fairly sure of his readers. The most obvious example is that of the
specialist who writes for his colleagues everywhere. What would be jargon
in a paper addressed to the general public is permissible diction in the
specialized paper, precisely because the writer knows that his readers not
only will fully expect to encounter, but will respond to, the special
terminology of their calling. Other than specialists, the number of writers
who can count on a "following" is not great. Some newspaper columnists
can do so, certainly—Walter Lippman, for instance; and a score or so of
those who have learned to popularize their specialty or to use their
reputations as specialists as the means of speaking out on subjects somewhat peripheral to their specialties—writers like Erich Fromm, Bertrand
Russell, and Reinhold Niebuhr. Most writers solve this problem of
identifying their audience indirectly, either by suiting their prose to a
particular vehicle (a family magazine, a sophisticated monthly journal, a
serious symposium, a politically oriented weekly, and the like), or by
abolishing special considerations of audience altogether and substituting
for them sole consideration of the work itself, the work as a work of art.

It is clearly not reasonable to expect the student-writer to "create" an
audience, in the sense described above. He is, in fact, all too well aware
that he already has one—the teacher who reads his paper or fellow
students before whom he will be expected to read it himself. His difficulties are less those of identifying an audience than of knowing how to
deal with the one he is given. On that score, his problems are the same
as every other writer's: assuming a reader of this or that kind, what
rhetorical appeals are available?

1) DIRECT APPEAL •

No matter who one's reader is, it is safe to assume that he has other
concerns in this world than reading, and especially than reading what any

particular writer has to say. He has to be attracted; and, once attracted, he has to be persuaded to give up his other concerns for the time being, and devote himself wholeheartedly to a single one. What we have here is the other half of the game in which the writer's first strategy is voice. The reader-as-player is, however, less eager than the writer-as-player; he has to be persuaded into playing in the first place, and persuaded to keep on playing until he is so caught up in the game that he needs no more coaxing. From that point on, the writer's moves are all calculated to win; before it, some must be designed specifically to overcome inertia, engage attention, and promote active participation.

The most obvious way to promote active participation is to invent it. Three devices present themselves—direct address, identification of writer with reader, identification of writer and reader with a common cause. The first is the most personal, therefore best suited to face-to-face encounters or to writing that imitates such encounters.

> Imagine, *if you can,* a small room, hexagonal in shape, like the cell of a bee.
>
> E. M. FORSTER, opening sentence of "The Machine Stops"

> You have seen a Hamlet, perhaps, who, on the first appearance of his father's spirit, has thrown himself into all the straining vociferation requisite to express rage and fury, and the house has thunder'd with applause . . . .
>
> COLLEY CIBBER, *An Apology for His Life by Colley Cibber*

This direct approach has another, somewhat less noticeable form, achieved by the ambiguity of our second-person pronoun.

> Once in a while you find yourself in an odd situation. You get into it by degrees and in the most natural way but, when you are right in the midst of it, you are suddenly astonished and ask yourself how in the world it all came about.
>
> THOR HEYERDAHL, *Kon-Tiki: Across the Pacific by Raft*

The same pronoun, this time subsumed in the imperative mode, provides an equally inconspicuous form of direct address to the reader:

> Take five-and-twenty heaps of cinders dumped here and there in an outside city lot; imagine some of them magnified into mountains, and the vacant lot the sea; and you will have a fit idea of the general aspect of the Encantadas, or Enchanted Isles.
>
> HERMAN MELVILLE, opening sentence of "The Encantadas:
> or, Enchanted Isles"

The "you" of Thor Heyerdahl's narrative is clearly both reader and writer; in using the grammatical form for the person-spoken-to, he is able to draw on the idiomatic meaning of "you" as "everyone"— including "me," the writer. This is only a step from the flattest and most presumptive of these obvious personal appeals, that of open identification of reader and writer. The approach is again pronominal, but—despite the pronoun—rather impersonal.

> We will now pass to *Hamlet,* in order to obviate some of the general prejudices against the author, in reference to the character of the hero. . . . The first question we should ask ourselves is—What did Shakespeare mean when he drew the character of Hamlet? He never wrote anything without design, and what was his design when he sat down to produce this tragedy? My belief is, that he always regarded his story, before he began to write, much in the same light as a painter regards his canvas, before he begins to paint—as a mere vehicle for his thoughts—as the ground upon which he was to work.
>
> SAMUEL TAYLOR COLERIDGE, Lecture XII of the Lectures of 1811–12

The initial "we" is, for Coleridge, little more than a convenience; he makes no attempt to identify his reader, simply uses him as company. The second use ("The first question we should ask ourselves") is more active, though it is, of course, a fiction. And as soon as the fiction has served its purpose, Coleridge drops it and begins to speak for himself ("My belief is . . .").

Both of the modes so far examined call on the reader to play a rôle. A third, that in which reader and writer are identified through a common cause, must have more than such a fiction as its ground. The appeal through it is both substantive and rhetorical: there really must be some cause, and the reader must recognize his relationship to it, or the appeal will fall flat from the beginning.

> Workers of the world, unite!
>
> (last sentence of *The Communist Manifesto*)

Could any appeal be simpler? In one phrase, the world is divided into those who "work" and those who don't. The common cause of the first group is implicit in the exhortation—"Unite!" Though less succinct, the approach in Thomas Paine's *Common Sense* is equally deft in identifying the reader and in suggesting that his cause is one with the writer's:

> These are the times that try men's souls. The summer soldier and the sunshine patriot [i.e., all those other than you and me]. . . .

The bond here is something larger than either writer or reader, something in which they can merge their individualities and become as one, and such a bond adds the emotional power of the cause (revolution, patriotic zeal) to the appeal for a hearing.

In general, these three kinds of direct appeal are more important at the beginning and end of a piece of writing than in its interior. They solicit the reader's participation at the outset and, at the end, recall to him the rôle he has played and must now convert from observation and instruction into action.

2) OBLIQUE APPEAL •

Oblique rhetorical appeal in writing of any kind uses the attractiveness of one object or activity to draw attention to another. The bond it creates with a reader is achieved in several ways, as examination of a series of oblique opening gambits will show. The ones that follow come from a single issue of *The New York Times Magazine* for Sunday, September 9, 1962. This newspaper addresses itself to an educated reading public and is generally recognized to be conservative in its prose style. At the same time, it is not a "scholarly" magazine and must therefore assume the need to make an overture to its readers, particularly since it asks them to shift attention, as one story succeeds another, to concerns as diverse as cock-fighting, urban renewal, resurgent militarism, and the condition of New York City's parks.

Let the exemplification begin with an example of direct appeal, to serve as foil for others:

> Many of us who have enthusiastically made plans for abolishing hunger in the under-developed countries began by basing these plans on our own conception of the ideal diet. Only gradually did we learn that it is nonsense to speak of the ideal diet—that these exist by the million.
>
> (from an article on the dietary habits of people other than ourselves)

The next is still direct, but less sharply so:

> More Americans pay a sales tax, and pay it more often than any other kind of tax. Yet because so much of it is in pennies, the take from sales taxes is relatively modest. It does not begin to compare with the massive sums that some 40,000,000 income-tax payers annually turn over to the tax collector.
>
> (from an article entitled "For Fastest Growth—What Kind of Tax?")

The easiest oblique appeal to manage is that beginning from an anecdote or from reference to some recent, well-publicized event. Note how, in the first of the two examples that follow, the writer has capitalized on the figure of a popular hero in Russia to reinforce a device already oblique in itself, that of looking at a situation "from the outside," as though one were a foreigner.

> When Maj. Gherman S. Titov, the Russian astronaut, visited New York last spring, he was asked by the reporters what he thought of the city after the first day of his visit. His answer was quick and disconcertingly accurate. "There are too many cars here," he said, "and there is very little green in the town."
> (from an article on the difference between parks in London and in New York City)

> When a party of peaceful English villagers is provoked into breaking up a political gathering with shotguns, pitchforks, and bare fists, it is reasonable

to suppose that something unusually offensive has come to their attention. And indeed, in the little Gloucestershire village of Guiting Power, the other day, there was a rank offense.

(from an article on mob action against "neo-Nazi meetings" in England)

Close to the anecdote is the biographical summary. In the one below, the writer has increased the appeal by a series of parenthetical asides. The closing sentence of the paragraph is, of course, an old joke, but it is given force here by placement: it becomes the focus for the statements that precede it.

O. Henry first laid eyes on New York in the spring of 1902; he spent most of the remaining eight years of his life in Manhattan (he was lucky enough to live for a time at that magnificent old Hotel Chelsea); he died in Polyclinic Hospital (nobody really knows whether he *was* afraid to go home in the dark); and his funeral was held in The Little Church Around the Corner. (There was even an O. Henry trick ending to it: a wedding scheduled for the same hour was held up by the services for him.) He was born a hundred years ago Tuesday; this was in Greensboro, N.C., and he was, therefore, a typical New Yorker.

(from an article entitled "O. Henry's New Yorkers—and Today's")

The rather flippant tone of that paragraph is appropriate to the memorial piece it introduces. In like manner, the pun with which another story is introduced, though it really has no bearing on the story itself, draws the reader in by making him collaborator in a witticism.

Cockfighting, a sport designed to discover who is really chicken, has become so prevalent in New York City this past year that nearly every month or so the police have raided somebody's basement and proceeded to turn the spectators into jailbirds and the roosters into soup. Recently, a janitor was arrested for operating a "cockpit," or cockfighting arena, in his Manhattan basement, and not long ago eighty-two men were caught watching a feathered brawl in a Brooklyn basement and were hauled in—over the screeching protests of thirty-eight angry gamecocks.

(from an article on a popular indoor sport)

One of the most frequently used of oblique appeals is the quotation. The three examples given below use, in this order, (a) an invented but believable sentence, (b) a series of widely heard phrases, and (c) an actual quotation which has now become part of American lore.

"They are here; but where are they?" This is the disquieting thought in the minds of the South Vietnamese Government troops who are engaged in the grinding, exhausting task of hunting down the Communist-led guerrillas (called the Viet Cong) who infest the vast, swampy southwestern part of the country. . . .

(from a picture-article on the "grim war in Vietnam")

"Land reform," "the plight of the peasants," "village-improvement ten year plans," "the population explosion in the rural areas"—such are the issues that continue to preoccupy today's foreign aid experts. But while these things are real, they are fast becoming secondary. Urban problems, not rural issues, increasingly constitute the challenge in under-developed countries.

(from an article on growing urban problems)

In Latin America, as elsewhere, old soldiers never die. But there, only too often, they decide that the good of their country requires them to take power—or to decide which civilians will rule in their name. During the past twelve months alone, military leaders have intervened in Brazil, Argentina, Ecuador, and Peru.

(from an article on the "wave of militarism sweeping" Latin America)

A combination of the biographical summary and the allusion (in this case to a legendary wanderer) is used in the next example both to make a rhetorical appeal and to define the subject matter itself: the artist whose work, like his life, is distinctly independent.

Mark Tobey, an American painter who will receive the latest of many accolades when the Museum of Modern Art opens a large retrospective exhibition of his work this Wednesday, may be accurately, if not completely, described, as a wanderer upon the face of the earth. His steadiest companion is his suitcase, and the only safe answer to questions about where he is likely to be at such and such a date is, "who knows?"

(from an article on a painter little known to the general public)

A final example, still from the same issue of the *Times Magazine,* will bridge to the next section, that in which the rhetorical appeal is concealed behind what appears to be an indifference to everything but the subject itself.

Charles de Gaulle's quarrels with the United States and Britain have formed a basic undertone of international affairs ever since he returned to power in 1958. The differences are not superficial. De Gaulle is, in fact, out to transform—some would say disrupt—the Atlantic alliance.

(from an article on De Gaulle and "his allies")

3) DELIBERATE AVOIDANCE OF APPEAL •

These direct and oblique appeals to the reader may seem to some beneath the dignity of the serious prose expositor. He may, in fact, feel that any conscious kowtowing to the reader is an admission of motives less than honorable. It is true enough that the approaches just illustrated are attractive to hucksters and confidence men; that is proof that they work. And it is also true that, unless a writer is very careful, the smudge from cheap use may rub off on his more high-minded one. Such choices, are a matter of discrimination and of personal integrity. The two criteria

of tastefulness and appropriateness should suffice to protect a writer insofar as he needs, and deserves, protection.

For much sober expository writing, especially if it can assume a serious
reader, these rhetorical appeals may be entirely supplanted by careful
stylistic control over straightforward statement. Let us say that for his
comments on the nature of humor a writer has some reason to assume
that whatever reader he has does not need to be beguiled into reading
what he has to say. He can begin at the beginning, omit both direct and
oblique appeals, relying on the subject matter itself. At least, that is
how it looks in print:

> Man is the only animal that laughs and weeps; for he is the only animal
> that is struck with the difference between what things are, and what they
> ought to be.
>
> WILLIAM HAZLITT, *Lectures on the English Poets and*
> *the English Comic Writers*

The subject of this essay in "wit and humour," and the opening sentence
wastes no time in fencing the field: the matter is a purely human one,
Hazlitt says, and it is fundamentally a matter of the difference between
the actual and the ideal. Yet for all its strict limitation to substance,
the opening sentence has a rhetorical strategy. It does not introduce the
reader gently to the subject; it does not ease his way in. Instead it requires
an immediate tautness of attention, a readiness to resist. How much is
demanded in it will appear from a rewriting, in which the way is made
easy.

> "Laugh and the world laughs with you" Why? Because a sense of humor
> is the universal solvent, the sovereign cure, the one tie that binds. It
> knows neither age nor condition; it disregards nationality, religion, race.
> It binds man to man because it is the sense—perhaps the only one—that
> none but men can know. Dogs may show grief or joy; we even read that
> Patroclus' horse wept at his master's death. Montaigne somewhere re-
> marks that as he played with his cat he was suddenly moved to ask himself
> if perhaps it was the cat who played with him. But since there is no
> evidence that a cat has ever entertained such a witty notion, Montaigne's
> query answers itself. No, man is the only animal that laughs and weeps,
> and the reason is obvious enough. He is the only one who has the power
> to imagine the world different from what it is, to conceive perfection
> though all he knows is imperfection. That is the heart and soul of humor
> —the ability to see how far apart are things-as-they-are from things-as-
> they-should-be. . . .

The purpose of the contrast is not to distinguish good writing from bad.
Both passages have their merit, and both have an appeal. But the appeal
is clearly different in the demand made on the reader.

Definition and division are not, of course, the only means of making
the reader begin his wrestle with meaning at the opening word. An

equally demanding device is that in which manifold discriminations are insisted on, and the reader must choose at the outset to abandon his reading or to sharpen his wits enough to follow the writer like a bloodhound. Here, for example, is the opening paragraph of Dr. Samuel Johnson's preface to his Dictionary of 1755:

> It is the fate of those who toil at the lower employments of life, to be rather driven by the fear of evil, than attracted by the prospect of good; to be exposed to censure, without hope of praise; to be disgraced by miscarriage, or punished for neglect, where success would have been without applause, and diligence without reward.

This stately and exacting text, which requires the reader to accept its pace and poise, may be converted into prose for those who read on the run or with only one eye open:

> Men and women of the laboring class work at their jobs because they have to, not because they want to. They work to keep from being hungry and cold and not to increase their stock of experience. They don't expect to be praised for their work and generally consider themselves lucky if what they do goes uncriticized. The jobs they do, no matter how hard they work or how skillfully they perform, bring neither fame nor praise. And, more often than not, a single slip or a slight inattention will put an end even to the little comfort they can take in simply managing to hold on to a job.

The same paragraph from Dr. Johnson's *Dictionary* will serve to recapitulate this section. The rewriting above relies entirely on style. An *oblique* appeal might be achieved by rewriting in this fashion:

> Men and women of the laboring classes, as Thoreau remarked of his neighbors in Concord a hundred years ago, lead lives of quiet desperation.

> (allusion)

or in this:

> "Nothing to look backward to with pride,/And nothing to look forward to with hope." In these memorable words Robert Frost sketches the barren life of his "hired man." The description is one that applies as well to all those who. . . .

> (quotation)

Finally, the statement might be given a *direct* rhetorical appeal in such fashion as this:

> The reading class in America is, by and large, the white-collar class, and few members of it have much sense of what life as a laborer means, simply in terms of elementary feelings about existence. . . .

or an even more direct appeal in this:

If you are one of the twenty million Americans who live in Suburbia, tend a blanket-size patch of lawn, shovel a fifty-foot walk in winter, and keep weeds out of the cracks in a macadamized driveway, you are undoubtedly also one who feels he qualifies as understanding critic of the working-man.

The range of these examples is admittedly great. Dr. Johnson's prose is directed to the cultivated reader, familiar with Ciceronian cadences; the final example is composed in the chummy prose of the family newspaper or magazine. Each serves a respectable purpose by employing the rhetoric suited to its audience.

From distinctiveness of style to the most obvious inclusion of reader by identification, the devices of appeal make provision for the reader to participate, to join the game. Like the writer, he retains his separate identity, of course. If he is a skilled reader, he is even able to observe his own reactions as he reads. But that is not the writer's concern. He will have done his part if he first succeeds in engaging the reader's attention, then creates a climate in which the reader can be persuaded to listen sympathetically to what he has to say.

7) THE SUBJECT: INVENTION, ARRANGEMENT, STYLE

Two rhetorical considerations have been discussed and illustrated to this point. By making clear what particular role he is playing at the moment, and by making sure that that role does not misrepresent his genuine convictions, the writer persuades through his own person, or "character," as Aristotle calls it. By judging the nature of his reader, or by deciding what kinds of readers he wants, the writer develops a strategy of appeal that will induce his putative readers to read. Both are considerations of importance, but both are hollow without a third. (To say they are hollow is not to say they are ineffective. More than one campaign has flourished on the appeal of character and the appeal to the special character of the listener alone.)

This third matter is, like the other two, not a matter of what but a matter of how, not of the proposition-and-proof but of the guise in which propositions-and-proof appear. A valid argument is not necessarily a persuasive one, nor a persuasive one necessarily valid. The duty of an honest expositor is, by definition, to make his argument both valid and persuasive. In the act of communication, logic and rhetoric are two sides of the same coin.

Now it is true that, in one sense, an argument that we find valid convinces us—persuades us—by its sheer validity. So, the tidy manipulations of the chapter on Proving in this book satisfy because the mind consents to the resolutions, the order, they develop at their end. But this consenting and agreeing are not always enough, simply because something more than intellect is involved. For decades a great number of intelligent people found the doctrine of evolution, even in its broad outlines, quite unacceptable, though they could only assent to the data and the line of reasoning from data on which it was posited. It ran counter to other doctrines to which they had so deep an attachment that, though shown, they were unconvinced. The same is true of the scores of notions which every generation has to shed as new knowledge or refinements of old knowledge invalidate them. The man with an argument to advance must reckon, then, with the fact that, where belief and will are engaged, proof needs the reinforcement of art, logic needs rhetoric.

What, precisely, can rhetoric provide that argument does not itself offer or does not offer in a form so powerful? First, invention; second, arrangement; third, style.

1) INVENTION ·

If a writer has a sound argument to advance, what else need be "invented"? There is, to be sure, the matter of clarity. Simply putting an argument in such a way that it can be understood is no small accomplishment. But that, too, may be assumed at this point. The question is rather of devising, or "inventing," the supplementary means needed to make the material not only clear but persuasive as well.

A first consideration is that of quantity. How fully is the argument to be developed? In what degree of particularity? With what ampleness of illustration and evidence? An old argument, remade, may need little in the way of elaboration. A new one may require not only detailed development and extensive illustration but studious limitation to specific issues. The argument for woman suffrage, for example, needs no extensive rehearsal today; that for the suffrage of eighteen-year-olds might require a good deal. For the first, swift recapitulation would suffice—and, having provided that, a writer might turn to discussion of the effect of such suffrage, to the plans for extension of it to nations where it does not exist, and so on. But, since suffrage of those under twenty-one is still moot, the arguments for and against it have a freshness and urgency that may warrant the writer's undivided attention.

The proper quantity of elaboration is easier to gauge than the proper quality. Almost any argument may be made simple; almost any description may be reduced to outline. The problem of quality is that of deciding what level of sophistication is suitable for the situation. For example, the simple injunction, often found in writing handbooks, to choose the word of Anglo-Saxon origin over the one of Latin origin is enough for rule-of-thumb instruction. If it had to be defended, an argument for the injunction might limit itself to the canon of brevity—Saxon words are usually shorter, therefore preferable; or extend itself to a proposition about residual metaphor—Saxon words retain a stronger sense of action-in-process, therefore produce more vigorous prose; or go beyond both of these extensions to a more philosophical hypothesis about the link between language and mode of thought. As it does for quantity, the general situation—voice, audience, subject—will dictate the appropriate measure of intricacy and refinement in the development.

Whatever the quantity or the quality of expansion and argument, the writer must invent a manner suitable to the general strategy he plans to use. If he is the master explaining something obvious to his pupil, his manner will be of one kind; if he is the man with an unpopular cause attempting to persuade a hostile reader to change his point of view, his manner will be of another. The range runs from belaboring by repetition and extensive illustration to appealing by use of subtlest insertion of controversial material into matter that is likely to be palatable.

2) ARRANGEMENT •

The traditional patterns of arrangement for prose exposition and argument—by chronology, process, cause-to-effect, classification, comparison and contrast, logic of argument—are a matter of the ordering of substance for greatest effect. They are, then, rhetorical in the sense that they persuade the reader to accept one, rather than another, possible way of looking at the matter in hand. But there is a rhetoric that goes beyond this rhetoric of substantive order.

Take a simple example of order by classification: the evidence for and against hiring students as extra mail carriers at rush seasons. "For" and "against" make an initial classification. Within it others are possible: economic, political, social, biological, perhaps even moral. The rhetorical consideration becomes, then, one not only of which classifications to use for the purpose at hand but, a decision having been made, of arranging the successive classifications and the items within each. The order may be climactic or anti-climactic; it may force emphasis on one by minimizing others; it may defer in order to gain suspense. As for rhetorical matters in general, no particular effect can be posited abstractly for any order, but there is no gainsaying the fact that order will have some effect. If a writer is conscious that it will, he can soon enough find his way, by observant reading and practice, to rhetorical patterns of order appropriate to his characteristic voice and to the matter and audience with which he customarily deals.

3) STYLE •

The grand rhetorical consideration is style, a term often used to cover everything that is not raw matter. "The style is the man himself"—what definition has been more quoted? And quoted because, whether it is helpful or not, it is patently true. Here, in a chapter on persuasion, additional attention to style may seem entirely redundant. What, after all, have all the preceding pages been about, if not about style? True enough, those pages are about style, about style as a matter of conscious contrivance. But there is something more to be said about style that is not simply more of the same.

In the sense that the style is the man, we have to recognize that a writer develops a characteristic manner which becomes his hallmark. It may or may not be natural, but it certainly becomes habitual, that is, becomes part of his acquired nature. That habitual style is the ground for all the special styles of stylistic maneuvers he may adopt; it is like the persistent and identifying one-two-three of waltz time underneath doublets, triplets, and various kinds of syncopation. The particular situation that calls forth a piece of writing may require the writer's fullest ingenuity in style, but underneath that ingenuity a careful reader will observe, and a careful writer will rely on, the patterns of syntax, diction, imagery, and order that represent his fundamental way of looking at the world.

Two passages of nineteenth-century prose by John Stuart Mill show how the established sobriety of a distinctive expository style can become the basis for narrative style of muted, but real, excitement.

> The abuses of endowments are flagrant, monstrous, and wholly inexcusable. But what funds, public or private, would not be a prey to malversation if the law took no notice of it; or if, though the law was what it ought to be, there was no individual whose interest and no public officer whose duty it was to put the law in force? There is surely nothing visionary in imagining these things remedied. It cannot be impossible, where there is the will, to prevent public funds from being diverted to private pockets. Nor can it be doubted that the variety of endowed institutions, and the influence of the State exerted within its proper limits, would ensure adequate provision for including in the course of education (either everywhere or only somewhere, according to the necessities of the case) whatever has any just claim to form a part of it. . . .

> "Endowments," 1869

In this essay, Mill develops his statement through a series of pairings, something we might expect from one disciplined from his childhood in rigorous logic. The focal pair of terms is public-private, and the two-term pattern makes itself felt throughout: public funds-private funds, public funds-private pockets, individual-public officer, endowed institutions-state, even in everywhere-somewhere. This is the style of a sorting and two-valued mind, one that inclines to make sharp separations of the unlike rather than to seek gradations between them.

Though at first glance the narrative style of Mill's *Autobiography* seems utterly different—much more direct, much more varied, close attention to it will reveal that it has a great deal in common with the expository piece above.

> From the winter of 1821, when I first read Bentham, and especially from the commencement of the *Westminster Review,* I had what might truly be called an object in life; to be a reformer of the world. My conception of my own happiness was entirely identified with this object. The personal sympathies I wished for were those of fellow labourers in this enterprise. I endeavoured to pick up as many flowers as I could by the way; but as a serious and permanent personal satisfaction to rest upon, my whole reliance was placed on this; and I was accustomed to felicitate myself on the certainty of a happy life which I enjoyed, through placing my happiness in something durable and distant, in which some progress might be always making, while it could never be exhausted by complete attainment. This did very well for several years, during which the general improvement going on in the world and the idea of myself as engaged with others in struggling to promote it, seemed enough to fill up an interesting and animated existence. But the time came when I awakened from this as from a dream. It was in the autumn of 1826. I was in a dull state of nerves, such as everybody is occasionally liable to; unsusceptible to enjoyment or pleasurable excitement; one of those moods when what is pleasure at other times, becomes insipid or indifferent; the state, I should think, in which converts to Methodism usually are, when smitten by their first "conviction of sin." In this frame of mind it occurred to me to put the question directly to myself: "Suppose that all your objects in life were realized; that all the changes in institutions and opinions which you are looking forward to, could be completely effected at this very instant: would this be a great joy and happiness to you?" And an irrepressible self-consciousness distinctly answered, "No!" At this my heart sank within me: the whole foundation on which my life was constructed fell down. All my happiness was to have been found in the continual pursuit of this end. The end had ceased to charm, and how could there ever again be any interest in the means? I seemed to have nothing left to live for.

> *Autobiography,* 1873

The whole passage, though narrative, is built on a contrast, the contrast between cheerful purposefulness and melancholy aimlessness. Notice that Mill places much emphasis on these two states, relatively little on the transition between them. His two-valued habit of mind persists, even when his subject is the unfolding succession of events over a period of five years. Within the major opposition (purposefulness-aimlessness) he builds his prose on a series of lesser ones: personal happiness-public reform, flowers by the way-serious and permanent satisfaction, constant progress-no complete attainment, animated existence-dull indifference, end-means. Yet the contrasts are much less obtrusive here: Mill does not seem to be making any particular effort to capitalize on a peculiarity of style. He simply alters his habitual patterns enough to suit the immediate situation. He makes use of the style-that-is-the-man as a basis for the style of this voice on this subject to this audience.

A larger consideration of style has to do not with the sentence-by-sentence expression of one's turn of mind and habit of speech but with larger structures, with the frame in which a writer chooses to mold whatever he has to say. It is obvious that expository writing is a compound of many activities. By definition, it "exposes" or puts forward, but even so limited a notion of exposition is rather complex. It will include description and explanation, certainly, and may make use of narration as well. It must make place for paraphrase and summary, analysis or synthesis, qualification, concession, elaboration, exemplification, rebuttal. These we assume to be proper expository activities or strategies.

All of these activities may be enhanced by the form into which they are cast. Their power to persuade may be immensely heightened by a writer's decision to use one or another of the special perspectives available to him. Because it is primarily a matter not of his presence, or character, or of an assessment of the reader he wishes to reach, it is proper to discuss this matter of perspective, and the structures relevant to it, under the heading of "Subject."

The simplest perspective is probably that of *direct confrontation.* The writer stands before his subject, walks around it, studies it. The tone he adopts when he is using such a perspective may be cordial and comradely, that of "Come and look with me" or perhaps rather distant or even patronizing, that of "Stay there and I'll tell you what there is to be seen." In unskilled writing, the first tone is likely to take the form of exhortation ("Let us look now at . . .") and the second, the form of passive and impersonal constructions ("The matter can be considered . . ."). Yet neither is a necessary consequence of the perspective and tone; the same effects can be achieved without awkwardness by the skilled writer simply through careful choice of language and careful management of structure.

Instead of looking at the subject directly and in the round, the author may choose to take an oblique view of it, as though he were standing to one side with an eye (and perhaps a mind) half closed. By this means he sees the subject, as it were, in relief, and perhaps in profile. Angularities which seemed a part of the general harmony when the object was viewed in the round now are stark and even incongruous. The purpose of such perspective, of course, is emphasis, and its ground is a conscious bias, in the radical sense of that word. The writer views the subject from an announced or implied vantage point in sensation or emotion or thought. By that oblique viewing he brings clearly into view some aspect of the object which has heretofore been hidden. It is clear that this procedure has to do with something more than the manipulation of words, though it is through words that it will necessarily achieve its end. What actually happens is that a writer transforms the properties of whatever he is discussing, either by actually misrepresenting them or by misrepresenting their relationship with each other: an idiosyncrasy is exaggerated, something detestable is praised or something praise-worthy is condemned, the inconsequential is made important and the important inconsequential. Through these deliberate distortions the writer realizes his purpose of persuading the reader to re-examine a subject under his direction.

To speak of a writer's "perspective" as partly make-believe may be somewhat misleading. A better way to describe what is meant by those terms is perhaps to say that they are conscious and artful means of conveying insight and feeling. To "distort" an object is therefore, not falsification but revelation.

The actual means by which perspective is accomplished are several, and each is different from the other not only in nature but in purpose. One very effective way of persuading a reader to disapprove of something is to make a parody of it. In essence, a *parody* is simply an exaggeration, though not all exaggerations are by any means parodies. Underneath this device there is the assumption that almost any human proceeding has a certain amount of absurdity at its core. By seizing upon distinctive characteristics of the proceeding and stretching them, the parodist attempts to make that absurdity evident, and through it, to discredit the proceeding itself. The schoolboy who entertains his fellows with an artful imitation of the manner and speech of his teacher is a parodist; so, too, in a hackneyed fashion, is the after-dinner speaker at the suburban country club who begins with the phrase, "Friends, Roamers, and Country Gentlemen. . . ." These examples suggest another requirement of parody: it must have as its subject something that is well known, or the exaggeration will not be apparent. In fiction, parody is common; in expository writing, its use is less frequent but not for that reason ineffective. It may, in fact, be the most economical means of presenting a criticism, as in this excerpt from a book review.

> The new book which Mr. ——— has written about the Constitution is a very different kind of book. You can read it without thinking. If you have got tired trying to read the other kind of books, you will be glad of the nice restful book that Mr. ——— has written. It runs along like a story in a very interesting way. Most of the story is about how the Constitution got made. This is really history, but it is written in a very lively way like a novel, with a great many characters, almost all male, and plenty of conversation and a very exciting plot. Many of the chapters have names like those in a novel such as "The Opening of the Battle," "The Crisis," "The Dawn," "Nearing the End," "The Curtain Falls," and others. Besides the story there are many quotations from Shakespeare, Beethoven, Horace, Isaiah, Euripides, Beard, and other famous men. Many of these

quotations are quite old, but some of them seem fairly new. They help to make the book a real high-class book. There is not much more to say about the part of the book that tells how the Constitution got made, except that it is fun and easy to read and seems pretty true to life.

THOMAS REED POWELL, "Constitutional Metaphors"

Although the writer has not announced his intention to make fun of the style and content of the book he is reviewing, it is quickly apparent that he is doing so. The repetition of excessively simple sentences, the patronizing colloquialisms, the patent emptiness of much that is said— all of these are criticisms conveyed by parody.

A more elaborate device of persuasion than parody is *satire*. Where parody is largely concerned with the manner of an action (and, of course, with whatever that manner implies about the actor), satire deals with the action itself. Through selection, exaggeration, and meaningful juxtaposition, it attempts to expose and to bring into ridicule whatever is unnatural or unwise or evil. It plays primarily upon the difference between the actual state of something and its ideal condition and is therefore commonly employed to lay bare the hypocrisy of human action, as when it shows the claim of service for the common good to be subterfuge for the satisfaction of private interest, or the assertion of righteous indignation to be a public disguise for wounded vanity.

The satirist, of course, may himself be a literal hypocrite, in the sense that he may pretend to approve what he actually detests. When he gives such approval, however, he does it in such a way that his detestation is apparent to all but the most obtuse. One of his favorite devices is to shift the apparent time or place of the action; another, to rename characters and places; a third, to analogize from one action to another. Thus, George Orwell's novel *1984* is really concerned with the political tendencies he discerned as threatening in 1948; and Aldous Huxley's *Brave New World,* another anti-Utopia, is really an account of a coming world "brave" only in its disregard of human values. Another way to develop a satire is to create a series of situations parallel to the ones to be criticized and then to present the created situations in such a fashion as to make their absurdity, or their wrongness, obvious. When, in *A Modest Proposal,* Swift advocated that babies be fattened for human consumption as a means of alleviating the twin problems of overpopulation and poverty in Ireland, he did so in most solemn and reasonable vein, and some actually took him to mean what he said. Here the satiric device is to treat matter-of-factly that which is horrible beyond imagining. Swift uses an oblique way of presenting the callous attitude of the English Parliament of the time toward the oppressed and famine-stricken Irish people who were subject to its authority. Still another way is to pretend ignorance about the premises on which certain actions are based, a procedure much more effective than might at first be imagined. If a bird, for instance, were endowed with a highly developed power to reason but were completely ignorant of human behavior, what would it make of a tennis game? or of a church service? It would note the actions as well as any other intelligent being, but it would have to guess at or reach the meaningfulness and the relatedness of the actions by continued observation and a laborious inductive process. Either means is certain to be full of errors and false leads, and it is such errors and false leads that the satirist relies on to reveal the oddities of those things with which the reader has always thought himself perfectly well acquainted. And, finally, the most obvious means of the satirist is direct contradiction: a character contradicts the precepts he preaches by what he does; a situation belies what is predicted or postulated of it.

The writer of expository prose will find the devices of satire most useful when his general intent is to encourage change, for satire is essentially the vehicle of reform. By making faults ridiculous, it seeks to provide enlightenment, to stimulate disapproval, and to make correction mandatory. In its commitment to reform, it is more clearly an instrument of social action than parody, which mocks as much in fun as in hope of improvement. Because reform is the goal of satire, the subject matter must be, either directly or by implication, the behavior of human beings. La Fontaine's fables, for instance, have animals as their evident subject matter, but the correspondence of the animals' actions and speech in the fables to the actions and speech of human beings is so patent that every adult reader knows that the fables are really criticisms of human behavior.

The peculiar power of satire to persuade lies in its manipulation of different, and often contradictory, emotions. Though the faults which it attacks may be, and generally are, faults which the reader commits or has committed, the fact that he is brought to laugh at them, and thus at himself, destroys some of his power to resist the attack and to refute the demand for reform. As with all rhetorical devices, miscalculation in the use of satire—too gross an exaggeration, too obvious a contradiction, too blatant an absurdity—destroys effectiveness. Such miscalculation, it might be noted, is not always simply an awkwardness in the handling of the device but often a symptom of some intellectual dishonesty—of an attempt to misrepresent the reality as well as the appearance of the object.

Both parody and satire are formal structures; or, to use the metaphor of perspective, they are distortions which result from presenting the object obliquely so that details become magnified or dislocated. *Irony* is not so much an arrangement of situations as an attitude toward them and a device for conveying meaning by saying the opposite of what is meant. There is another difference. Satire and parody work on materials which are well enough known so that the falsification of them is apparent to nearly everyone. Irony, on the other hand, is an exclusive practice: it assumes a fairly large audience which may take words to mean only what they say and a small audience, the one it is addressing, which will understand them to be only a façade for another meaning. Irony is subtle and often delicate; it compares with satire as the sting of a whiplash compares with the pain of a thorough drubbing. Moreover, its purpose is often less clearly therapeutic than is that of satire. Irony notes the discrepancy between what things are and what they appear to be, or between what they are and what they ought to be, and it displays the writer's acuity and his amusement or contempt, but it does not always make a demand for reform. There is a kind of Olympian irony which affects to look on most human action with an indulgent smile, and a tragic irony which has no smile at all but a degree of compassion for the futility of the human condition. Whatever the kind, the ironist must in a sense look down on his subject, see it in a broader relationship than that available to most men, and then communicate what he has seen by such slight alterations in his language as will lead the initiated reader to know that the words he reads are to be understood as though they were preceded by "not."

The master ironist of the English language is probably the historian Edward Gibbon, and it is fitting that this discussion of irony close with a few illustrations from his *Decline and Fall of the Roman Empire*. A thoroughgoing eighteenth-century rationalist, Gibbon found religious controversy especially distasteful, referring to it as "the exquisite rancour of theological hatred," just as he both hated and feared the claims of supernatural intervention in the affairs of man, to which he gave the name "holy romances." Of the miraculous acts of St. James, the apostle, he writes:

> The gravest historians have celebrated his exploits; the miraculous shrine of Compostella displayed his power; and the sword of a military order, assisted by the terrors of the Inquisition, was sufficient to remove every objection of profane criticism.

Though much of his irony is directed against religion, and against Christianity in particular, Gibbon hated what he believed to be fraud or base servility wherever he found it. He speaks, for instance, of Herod and his sycophants in these words:

> . . . the greatest part of his life was spent in philosophic retirement at Athens and his adjacent villas, perpetually surrounded by sophists, who acknowledged without reluctance the superiority of a rich and generous rival.

As these examples show, irony is a devastating instrument of persuasion, for its agreeable surface deflects the expostulations even of

those whom its implications have wounded. It thus invites the reader
to participation with the writer by guaranteeing him safety even as it
offers him the flattery of being among the elect who discern the real intent of what is said.

8) *THE ETHICS OF PERSUASION*

To insist on the persuasiveness of language is to raise an ethical
problem which has always engaged the attention of writers and which
has been one of the main preoccupations of modern semanticists, or
students of the meaning of words. Although what has been said in this
chapter may often seem to imply that words have an autonomous life,
wielding power independent of their users, that proposition is itself
more metaphorical than not. *People* use words, and it is their way of
using them that is largely responsible for their persuasiveness.

The traditional term for the use of language to persuade is "rhetoric," and the fact that an ethical problem is associated with that use is
apparent in the disrepute into which the term has often fallen. In the
sixteenth century, Montaigne decried persuasive practices in these words:

> . . . Aristo wisely defines rhetoric as "a science to persuade the people";
> Socrates and Plato as "the art of deceiving and flattering." And they who
> deny the general definition verify it throughout in their precepts.
>
> The Mohammedans forbade their children to be instructed in the art,
> on account of its uselessness.
>
> And the Athenians, having perceived how pernicious was the practice
> of it, though it was held in high esteem in their city, ordained that the
> principal part, the appeal to the passions, should be abolished, together
> with the exordiums and perorations.
>
> It is a tool invented for handling and stirring up a mob and an unruly
> community; and it is a tool that is only employed for sick states, like
> medicine. . . .

Of the Vanity of Words

Montaigne, of course, is speaking here of the abuse of language, of
the deliberate attempt to use words so that they will stifle the reason
rather than encourage it to exert itself. It is against rhetoric of that kind
that popular books on semantics wage their chief battles, and nothing
said so far in this book should lead the reader to think that the act of
persuasion is automatically a good act or, conversely, that it is automatically a bad act, either. At the bottom of most popular semanticists'
worry about "loaded words," "slanting," and "prejudicial language" there
would seem to be a serious misconception. It is not words that are bad
or good but the intentions and methods of those who use them. Once
stated, the objection seems so obvious as not to need statement at all,

but the misconception is too common to be entirely ignored. The ethical problem is a serious one, of course, but it should not be confused with description of language itself.

9) CONCLUSION

To include all literary devices, all figurative forms of speech, and even the accidental encrustations on words as elements of persuasion may be to stretch the category until it is an omnium-gatherum in which all leftovers may find a resting place. Yet such catholicity has one virtue, and it is a virtue especially important to the concept of persuasion: to realize that all use of language is persuasive is to recognize that no user can safely be indifferent to his choice of words, his syntax, or his literary demeanor. Even as expositor of the slightest matter, he employs an instrument which has effects, produces reactions. Though he cannot predict reactions with certainty, he can in large measure control them if he is aware of the many ways in which language moves readers and if he then trains himself to use language wisely and well.

EXERCISES

1) Select the word or phrase in each passage whose connotations are inappropriate in this context and provide an appropriate substitute.

   a. The whole statement has the ring of truth. She has spoken precisely and firmly throughout; there is even a kind of radical zeal in what she says.
   b. Great men are often models for our action, and we do well to mimic them.
   c. She was singularly fair of aspect, her face charming and entirely regular save for a slight bump on the left brow.
   d. A good critic does not belabor his point but rams it home with the skill of a fencing master.
   e. Gore spurted from the artery like water from a fountain.

2) Examine a series of advertisement to discover how persuasion is effected by appeals to prestige, pity, money, popularity, prejudice, and so on. Reduce each advertisement to its informational content.

3) Compare two newspaper accounts of the same incident (one from a tabloid, one from a newspaper like *The New York Times*). Do the contents of the two reports differ? How is emphasis achieved? Can you find specific instances in which the selection of words casts different light on the topic?

4) Compare these two accounts of an episode in the French Revolution.

Early in October it began to be feared that the king was yielding again to the influences at the court which were hostile to reform, and a great mob from Paris invaded the gardens and palace at Versailles. The king was saved from the mob by the National Guard, but he was obliged to follow the advice of La Fayette and take up his residence, with his family, in Paris.

GEORGE BURTON ADAMS, *The Growth of the French Nation*

The dull dawn of a new morning, drizzly and chill, had but broken over Versailles, when it pleased destiny that a bodyguard should look out of the window, on the right wing of the chateau, to see what prospect there was in heaven and in earth. Rascality male and female is prowling in view of him. His fasting stomach is, with good cause, sour; he perhaps cannot forbear a passing malison on them; least of all can he forbear answering such.

Ill words breed worse: till the worst word come; and then the ill deed. Did the maledicent bodyguard, getting (as was too inevitable) better malediction than he gave, load his musketoon, and threaten to fire; nay actually fire? Were wise who wist! It stands asserted; to us not credibly. But be this as it may, menaced rascality, in whinnying scorn, is shaking at all grates; the fastening of one (some write, it was a chain merely) gives way; rascality is in the grand court, whinnying louder still.

The maledicent bodyguard, more bodyguards than he do now give fire; a man's arm is shattered. Lecointre will depose that "the Sieur Cardine, a national guard without arms, was stabbed." But see, sure enough poor Jerôme l'Héritier, an unarmed national guard he too, "cabinet-maker a saddler's son, of Paris," with the down of youthhood still on his chin, he reels deathstricken; rushes to the pavement, scattering it with his blood and brains! Alleleu! Wilder than Irish wakes rises the howl; of pity, of infinite revenge. In few moments, the grate of the inner and inmost court, which they name Court of Marble, this too is forced, or surprised, and bursts open: the court of marble too is overflowed; up the grand staircase, up all stairs and entrances rushes the living deluge! Deshuttes and Varigny, the two sentry bodyguards, are trodden down, are massacred with a hundred pikes. Women snatch their cutlasses, or any weapon, and storm in, Menadic; other women lift the corpse of shot Jerôme; lay it down in the marble steps; there shall the livid face and smashed head, dumb forever, *speak.*

THOMAS CARLYLE, *The French Revolution,* Chapter 10

What rhetorical figure is employed in each of these expressions?

rascality   living deluge
down of youthhood   Menadic

What is the precise descriptive achievement of the term "rascality" as it is coupled with verbs and reused in the passage?

5) Without making any direct reference to the relationship between writer and reader, write separate versions, as indicated, of the following:

    a. a letter of protest (to a close friend, to a subordinate, to a superior)

    b. an introduction to a talk to be given (before a high school audience, before a group of businessmen, before a group whom you suspect to hold an opinion of the subject quite different from yours)

    c. an announcement for the attention (of subway riders, of resort dwellers, of bed patients in a hospital)

    d. the opening paragraph of an essay on the poetry of a modern poet to be published (in the Sunday supplement of a good newspaper, in a scholarly journal, in a popular magazine)

6) Write an ironic sentence which will convey

    a. disapproval of the motives which led the city council to grant permission for pari-mutuel betting at the local race track

    b. disapproval of the principles on which a group of citizens based their argument against that permission

    c. doubt about the salubriousness of a much-publicized climate

    d. dissatisfaction with the outcome of a recent election

    e. displeasure at the fashion among college students of growing beards

7) The first passage below is an excerpt from a novel; the second is a parody of it. After examining both with care discuss the stylistic characteristics which the parodist chooses to ridicule.

> The fact that she "knew"—knew and yet neither chaffed him nor betrayed him—had in a short time begun to constitute between them a goodly bond, which became more marked when, within the year that followed their afternoon at Weatherend, the opportunities for meeting multiplied. The event that thus promoted these occasions was the death of the ancient lady her great-aunt, under whose wing, since losing her mother, she had to such an extent found shelter, and who, though but the widowed mother of the new successor to the property, had succeeded —thanks to a high tone and a high temper—in not forfeiting the supreme position at the great house.

> It was with the sense of a, for him, very memorable something that he peered now into the immediate future, and tried, not without compunction, to take that period up where he had, prospectively, left it. . . . The consciousness of dubiety was, for our friend, not, this morning, quite yet clean-cut enough to outline the figures on what she had called his "horizon," between which and himself the twilight was indeed of a quality somewhat intimidating.

8) Make a parody of your own on the style of the following excerpt.

> Toward evening the rain ceased; and rising up I went out a short distance to the neighboring stream, where I sat on a stone, and casting off my sandals, laved my bruised feet in the cool running water. The western half of the sky was blue again with that tender lucid blue seen after rain, but the leaves still glittered with water, and the wet trunks looked almost black under the green foliage. The rare loveliness of the scene touched and lightened my heart.

9) The following comic oration is a piece of satire written in August, 1825, by the Reverend Sydney Smith, vigorous contributor to the *Edinburgh Review*. Examine it, first, to identify the character of the speaker ("voice"), then to identify the audience, and finally to sort out and label the varieties of appeal made in the discourse. Outline the general argument and, after you have done that, examine the logic of the subordinate arguments that are meant to bolster it. Select any three successive sentences and classify them by one of the patterns discussed in the chapter on assertions.

NOODLE'S ORATION

"What would our ancestors say to this, sir? How does this measure tally with their institutions? How does it agree with their experience? Are we to put the wisdom of yesterday in competition with the wisdom of centuries? (*Hear, Hear!*) Is beardless youth to show no respect for the decisions of mature age? (*Loud cries of hear! hear!*) If this measure be right, would it have escaped the wisdom of those Saxon progenitors to whom we are indebted for so many of our best political institutions? Would the Dane have passed it over? Would the Norman have rejected it? Would such a notable discovery have been reserved for these modern and degenerate times? Besides, sir, if the measure itself is good, I ask the honourable gentlemen if this is the time for carrying it into execution—whether, in fact, a more unfortunate period could have been selected than that which he has chosen? If this were an ordinary measure, I should not oppose it with so much vehemence; but, sir, it calls in question the wisdom of an irrevocable law—of a law passed at the memorable period of the Revolution. What right have we, sir, to break down this firm column, on which the great men of that age stamped a character of eternity? Are not all authorities against this measure, Pitt, Fox, Cicero, and the Attorney and Solicitor General? The proposition is new, sir; it is the first time it was ever heard in this house. I am not prepared sir—this house is not prepared—to receive it. The measure implies a distrust of his majesty's government; their disapproval is sufficient to warrant opposition. Precaution only is requisite where danger is apprehended. Here the high character of the individuals in question is a sufficient guarantee against any ground of alarm. Give not, then, your sanction to this measure; for whatever be its character, if you do give your sanction to it, the same man by whom this is proposed, will propose to you others to which it will be impossible to give your consent. I care very little, sir, for the ostensible measure; but what is there behind? What are the honourable gentleman's future schemes? If we pass this bill, what fresh concessions may he not require? What further degradation is he planning for his country? Talk of evil and inconvenience, sir! look to other countries—study other aggregations and societies of men, and then see whether the laws of this country demand a remedy, or deserve a panegyric. Was the honourable gentleman (let me ask him) always of this way of thinking? Do I not remember when he was the advocate in this house of very opposite opinions? I not only quarrel with his present sentiments, sir, but I declare very frankly I do not like the party with which he acts. If his own motives were as pure as possible, they cannot but suffer contamination from those with whom he is politically associated. This measure may be a boon to the constitution, but I will accept no favour to the constitution from such hands (*Loud cries of hear! hear!*). I profess myself, sir, an honest and upright member of the British Parliament, and I am not afraid to profess myself an enemy to all change, and all innovation. I am satisfied with things as they are; and it will be my pride and pleasure to hand down this country to my children as I received it from those who preceded me. The honourable gentleman pretends to justify the severity with which he has attacked the noble lord who presides in the Court of Chancery. But I say such attacks are pregnant with mischief to government itself. Oppose ministers, you oppose government; disgrace ministers, you disgrace government; bring ministers into contempt, you bring government into contempt; and anarchy and civil war are the consequences. Besides, sir, the measure is unnecessary. Nobody complains of disorder in that shape in which it is the aim of your measure to propose a remedy to it. The business is one of the greatest importance; there is need of the greatest caution and circumspection. Do not let us be precipitate, sir; it is impossible to foresee all consequences. Everything should be gradual; the example of a neighbouring nation should fill us with alarm! The honourable gentleman has taxed me with illiberality, sir. I deny the charge. I hate innovation, but I love improvement. I am an enemy to the corruption of government, but I defend its influence. I dread reform, but I dread it only when it is intemperate. I consider the liberty of the press as the great palladium of the constitution; but at the same time, I hold the licentiousness of the press in the greatest abhorrence. Nobody is more conscious than I am of the splendid abilities of the honourable mover, but I tell him at once, his scheme is too good to be practicable. It savours of Utopia. It looks well in theory, but it won't do in practice. It will not do, I repeat, sir, in practice; and so the advocates of the measure will find, if, unfortunately, it should find its way through Parliament. (*Cheers.*) The source of that corruption to which the honourable member alludes is in the minds of the people; so rank and extensive is that corruption, that no political reform can have any effect in removing it. Instead of reforming others—instead of reforming the state, the constitution, and everything that is most excellent, let each man reform himself! let him look at home, he will find there enough to do, without looking abroad, and aiming at what is out of his power. (*Loud cheers.*) And now, sir, as it is frequently the custom in this house to end with a quotation, and as the gentleman who preceded me in the debate has anticipated me in my favourite quotation of the 'Strong pull and the long pull,' I shall end with the memorable words of the assembled Barons—*Nolumus leges Angliae mutari.*"

The first four chapters of this book provide a discussion of as many characteristic uses to which words and word-structures are frequently put in expository writing. Without being either entirely theoretical or entirely analytical, these chapters are nonetheless primarily concerned with the nature, rather than with the exploitation, of those characteristics. The second part of the book reverses emphasis: it does not disavow the theoretical and the analytic, but it gives its main attention to the practical matters of actual composition. It does not attempt to provide a complete account of English grammar or an exhaustive rehearsal of every rhetorical figure. Rather, it tries to deal thoughtfully only with those matters of composition, whether grammatical or rhetorical, which most frequently arise in students' expository writing. Throughout it eschews the hard and fast rule, except where rules—or conventions, as they might more properly be called—are the only explainable grounds for standard practice. In place of rules, it offers such reasoning about the effects of each locution or structure as seems to the authors sound. Because the authors, like their readers, come from a place and a time, their preferences will undoubtedly be more apparent than they wish or intend. And, the subject being what it is, they will undoubtedly fail, by omission or commission, to please any reader all of the time. The second part of the book will serve its purpose well enough, however, if it proves to be an enlightening and useful guide to those who take their thinking seriously enough to desire its expression in a form capable of adequately containing and effectively transmitting it.

❁ PART 2

☀ *The Grammar and Rhetoric of the Sentence*

> *Most of the occasions of this worlds troubles are Grammaticall.*
>
> MONTAIGNE, *Trans. by John Florio*
>
> *What grammarians say should be has perhaps less influence on what shall be than even the more modest of them realize; usage evolves itself little distorted by their likes & dislikes.*
>
> FOWLER, *Modern English Usage*

IN THE PAST FIFTY YEARS more and more people (linguists, then teachers, then their pupils) have come to regard grammar as a matter of record, not of rule. They speak of it as *descriptive* rather than *prescriptive,* and they have ample historical justification for doing so. Just as Aristotle's *Poetics* is an account of the drama *as it was* in his day (with observations by the author and some expression of preference), so grammar is generally considered today to be an account of what is acceptable and accepted in the language of contemporary society. It is a fact that a good many of the "rules" generally considered sacrosanct are themselves of recent origin. So it is with the "shall-will" distinction for the future tense, the distinction between "which" (to introduce nonrestrictive clauses) and "that" (to introduce restrictive clauses), the distinction between "farther" and "further." But it must not be forgotten—and the defenders of the descriptive point of view sometimes do forget—that the question of rules is a complicated one.

There are at least four ways in which rules enter into discussions of language, and they should be kept distinct. First, people sometimes use "rule" in the sense of "regularity," the sense it has in the phrase "as a rule." Thus, one might say, "It is a rule in English that an adjective precedes the noun it modifies," which means simply: "Speakers of English regularly say 'terrible nuisance' and the like rather than 'nuisance terrible.'" There seems to be little harm in this use of "rule," though of course anyone rigorously studying language must prefer the plainly descriptive statement to the ambiguous one. The first statement is ambiguous because it might also mean something like this: "Any grammar that attempts systematically to specify the sentences of English, and distinguish them from nonsentences, will have to contain a rule saying that the adjective precedes the noun." This is the second sense of "rule": "rule in a descriptive grammar." In neither of these senses does "rule" have any prescriptive force; it simply points to ways in which people actually do talk. Rules of the third kind, by contrast, are patently prescriptive. They are in effect *legislation* by supposed authorities on the way people should talk—often in self-righteous defiance of the way the language in fact works. Such was the rule about "which" and "that" noted above, a rule which taxes the ingenuity of even such an authority as Fowler, author of *Modern English Usage*. Rules like that sometimes take hold, and become part of the language, but more often they do not, as Fowler himself remarked in the passage which introduces this chapter. (Both of the preceding two sentences violate the rule, but we venture a guess that most readers did not even notice the violations, much less sense them as ungrammatical.) Rules of this third kind are what make the linguist's gorge rise, and indeed the writer, like the grammarian, may safely ignore them except when they offer useful advice about *clear* writing and do not pretend to establish standards of *grammatical* writing. Nor, in general, will the writer need to learn rules of the first two kinds, for he already knows a great deal about how his native language actually works in daily conversation.

But there is a fourth kind of rule, one which does merit the writer's attention. Such rules begin as descriptive, but what they describe is the careful speech and writing of educated people, not the casual speech of the whole language community. And since a writer, when he takes up his pen in earnest, usually wishes to emulate fluent and respected writers, he must take such rules as having a certain prescriptive authority. In a formal essay he will write "it does not," in a less formal one "it doesn't"; but except in humor or mimicry he should never write "it don't," since to do so will mark him for his reader as one who does not know the rules of Standard Formal English. The blunder is not a moral one, not a logical one, nor even a sin against the English language. It is more like a social lapse: "it don't" is simply the wrong thing for the occasion, though it would do well enough in other circumstances. In a sense, every child, when he learns to read and write, begins learning a partially new dialect, and upon his eventual mastery of this formal dialect depends his admission into the fellowship of educated men.

Rules of the fourth kind, then, distinguish formal writing and speech from casual talk, and the writer must be acquainted with them if he is to perform adequately. For the most part he will have little difficulty with them; no reader of this book is likely to treat "he don't" as Formal English. Yet there is a large area of indeterminacy, for of course even Standard Formal English is not nearly so homogeneous as the label makes it sound.

Moreover, even the relatively firm rules of formal usage have a way of changing. James Boswell sometimes wrote (to himself) in his journals at the end of an exciting day, "You was the great man today." The use of "was" with the second person was common in the eighteenth century and served to separate the singular from the plural "you." Less than two hundred years later, however, a biographer of Walt Whitman reproached the poet with "a rather meager education" for writing, in a letter to his mother, "I wish you was here." What happened in those two centuries was that the intervention of grammarians fastened "was" to the first and third persons only. Very possibly another two centuries will make even "it don't" respectable. Some of the currently popular (but not standard) forms will take longer to come into formal usage or may never get there at all. The prejudice against "ain't" and against such double negatives as "can't hardly" is so great that there is little likelihood of their early absorption. The point to be made is that forms of language alter. Changes usually come first in speech; they make their way into personal letters and diaries, then into creative expression (the dialogue of realistic drama and fiction, for example), and later into more somber studies and documents. The proliferation of ephemeral printed material in newspapers and popular periodicals hastens change; so also do the unceasing flood of words from radio and television and the constant mixing of cultures that results from easy, fast transportation. Formal education retards the process, yet even in a country like ours, which boasts of universal education, change goes on. There are new words constantly pushing into general use, old forms disappearing (and, curiously enough, reappearing), a vast unchartable mutation delightful to lexicographers and infinitely upsetting to the native learner, the foreign visitor, and the lover of things as they are.

Where, then, is the student to turn for guidance when in doubt? The answer is not an easy one. On the other hand, it is not nearly so complex as the last two paragraphs may lead him to fear. In the first place, he can always play safe, that is, observe the "rules" in any good handbook. His language may seem stiff at times, but it will always be acceptable and even respected. The one danger in this strict adherence to the guide books of language is the development of a kind of linguistic snobbery, a "purism" that too often leads the adherer to make essentially moral judgments on his fellows based solely on the degree of their respect for what are, after all, matters not necessarily of character or of conscience. If the student chooses this "safe" way, the history of language obligates him not to be unduly proud of his choice: he has picked the conservative gray flannel, knowing that it will serve him for most occasions, in preference to a garment somewhat less adaptable but more self-expressive.

If he adopts a purely descriptive standard, if he determines that any form now in use is good enough by virtue of its existence, he will find his sensitivity to nuance dulled and his capacity to communicate markedly diminished. By this extremism, he impairs the power language has to sharpen his own intellectual processes and he impairs the power it has to provide communication with the thoughts and actions of others. If he is intellectually curious and naturally inventive and adventurous, he may, however, wish to free himself somewhat from the kind of minimum standard that a handbook provides. In that case, his course will be risky though exhilarating. Much of the richness of language lies beyond the rules, and it is there that this combination of historical knowledge and intelligent respect for current standards occurs. But the student who chooses this way must know more, not less, than the handbooks tell. Fortunately, the student ambitious enough to want such an acquaintance with language has today many good sources at hand. The *Oxford English Dictionary* traces changes in form and meaning, providing dates and examples in profusion. H. L. Mencken's *The American Language* is packed with information about the development of English in this country. Its style is at times witty, at times indignant and scornful, but its learning is generally sound, and its scope broad. Margaret Nicholson's *A Dictionary of American English Usage,* though sometimes finical, Eric Partridge's *Usage and Abusage,* and Bergen and Cornelia Evans's *A Dictionary of Contemporary American Usage* are volumes that every student should have on his desk alongside his dictionary. With these reliable resources at hand, almost any student with enough diligence to turn pages and enough interest to watch for the questionable spots in his own writing can venture with confidence into what someone on the staff of the *New Yorker* has called "the brier patch of English usage."

Since the sentence is the basic unit of discourse, examination of specific matters of grammar and of rhetoric can begin with it. The basic type of English sentence is most simply analyzed:

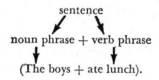

(The boys + ate lunch).

In our example the noun phrase is further analyzable:

noun phrase

article + noun

(the + boys).

and the verb is expanded thus:

(ate + lunch)

Of course either noun phrase or verb phrase may be expanded in other ways, which indicate other common subtypes of the basic sentence. Taking the verb phrase, for example:

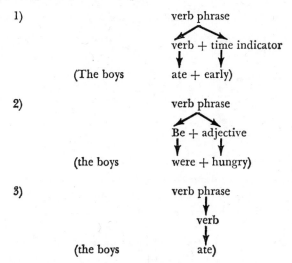

1)   verb phrase

                                    verb + time indicator

          (The boys   ate + early)

2)   verb phrase

                                    Be + adjective

          (the boys   were + hungry)

3)   verb phrase

                                    verb

          (the boys   ate)

And there are a number of other types.

From simple sentence forms such as these through several grammatical processes (the most important of which are called *transformations*) all English sentences derive. Some transformations rearrange the elements of simple sentence forms to produce sentences of other types. The passive transformation, for instance, if applied to "The boys ate lunch," would produce "Lunch was eaten by the boys." Two different question transformations would generate "What did the boys eat?" and "Did the boys eat lunch?" More interesting still are the transformations that combine simple sentence forms into more complex, for such operations generate most of the expressive richness of English. Consider the two sentences "The boys ate lunch" and "The boys were hungry." Depending on which transformations are applied, the product might be any one of the following:

The boys were hungry, and they ate lunch.
When the boys were hungry they ate lunch.
Being hungry, the boys ate lunch.
The hungry boys ate lunch.
Lunch was eaten by the hungry boys.
The boys who were hungry ate lunch.
The boys who ate lunch were hungry.
The boys ate lunch because they were hungry.
The boys eating lunch were hungry.
Hungry, the boys ate lunch.

And so on.

Here, in the presence of such grammatical alternatives, lie the writer's opportunity and his dilemma. With so many available ways of saying even a simple thing, he can hardly complain that the language constricts him. Rather, he may fear that it will overwhelm him with possibilities. Clearly the alternatives, though they all share a common core of meaning, differ both in precise significance and in rhetorical force. What will the writer gain or lose by choosing one form over another? The problem becomes even more graphic when we move from the rather trivial sentences above to a more puzzling set of alternatives:

1) The richest man is the one who has the cheapest pleasures.
2) He who has the cheapest pleasures is the richest.
3) That man is richest whose pleasures are the cheapest.

The three sentences have a common vocabulary and say the same thing; yet there are distinguishable differences among them. The first uses the syntax of contemporary prose, adjectives preceding the nouns they modify, the relative clause ("who has . . .") following directly its referent ("one"). The second substitutes a pronoun for the noun "man" and attaches the relative clause to it in a fashion which sounds slightly stiff and over-formal to the modern ear. The third (a statement by Thoreau in his *Journal,* March 11, 1856) places the relative clause apart from its referent. Apparently Thoreau's intention is to take advantage of the heightened contrast that comes from balancing "richest" against "cheapest" in identical positions in their respective clauses, and to use the emphatic position at the end of the sentence for the word which is the key to this unconventional assertion. His sentence is meant to ring in our ears, to take on some of the power of the proverb, and it succeeds in doing just that.

So simple a matter as the arrangement of clauses or the substitution of a noun for a pronoun is, then, a proper consideration for the careful writer. He will learn to appreciate the precise effect of various word patterns only as he extends his reading and as he practices achieving specific effects in what he writes. Such a prognosis may not seem particularly helpful to the present reader, however, if his concern in the matter is already acute. For that reason, some positive suggestions are clearly in order.

1) KINDS OF SENTENCES

The diagrams above may be summarized by this definition: "A sentence in English is a combination of a noun or noun phrase with a verb or verb phrase, or combinations of multiples of each." That definition is, you will notice, based on form and element content, not on meaning. To define sentence as "an utterance that expresses a complete thought" is to define by meaning; it is also to get us into a thicket where we shall need more than a machete to get out. "Not a jot" and "Never, never, never, never, never" both "express a complete thought," and satisfy our sense of completeness. "Until I come" expresses a complete thought (if any thought can be called "complete") and even has the characteristics of form and element content listed in the first definition; yet it does not satisfy our sense of completeness. On the other hand, the first definition alone may be satisfied and still produce nonsense: "A corns but these beetle pacify awkward grace."

To reach a definition that is useful, we had better ask what use such a definition is called on to serve. In books of this kind, at least, and for those who are expected to read them, definitions serve teachers as a short-hand way of directing students to information sufficient to correct errors in the student's paper or faults in his style. For such a purpose, the definition by meaning more often than not begs the question: a student who has put a capital at the beginning of and period at the end of a clump of words probably senses completeness in that clump or he wouldn't have marked them off as he did. A definition like the second one will not be very helpful to him. A definition like the first, however, is clear-cut enough to provide specific instruction. It will not be foolproof ("Until I come"), but it can be made to work in conjunction with other instructions so that it becomes nearly foolproof. If we set up a series of definitions at once, we can use them in combinations for the full discussion that follows. (The basic elements—word, noun, verb, adjective, and so on, we shall not define at all. For one reason, a solid definition would take much space; for another, anyone who needs a simple working definition of those words is either unready for this book or has reached a stage of sophistication that makes it superfluous to him.)

Some definitions:

PHRASE: a group of words not a sentence but forming part of a clause and separable from other parts by reason of mutual dependency; classifiable by elements, or by function, or by both.

> The man with the blue guitar stood in the street singing a plaintive ballad, twanging away fit to raise the dead, and rattling the gourds suspended from his belt.

by function

> The man with the blue guitar (noun phrase)
> stood in the street (verb phrase)
> with the blue guitar (adjective phrase)
> in the street (adverb phrase)
> the blue guitar (noun phrase)
> fit to raise the dead (adverb phrase)

by elements

> with the blue guitar (prepositional phrase)
> singing a plaintive ballad (participial phrase)
> to raise the dead (infinitive phrase)
> suspended from his belt (participial phrase)

by both

> in the street (prepositional phrase used as adverb)
> with the blue guitar (prepositional phrase used as adjective)
> twanging away . . . (participal phrase used as adverb)
> suspended from his belt (participial phrase used as adjective)

CLAUSE: a group of words forming part or all of a sentence, containing in either case the elements of a sentence; classifiable by kind and by function.

> When he had sung the ballad through, he opened his gnarled hand like a cup and passers-by dropped coins into it.

by kind

> he opened his gnarled hand like a cup (independent clauses, also called
> passers-by dropped coins into it   "main clauses")

> When he had sung the ballad through (dependent clause also called
>   "subordinate clause")

by function

> When he had sung the ballad through (subordinate clause used as adverb)

Drop "when" from the subordinate clause, and "and" from the second main clause. The three clauses are now roughly the same. The dependency or independency of a clause is sometimes indicated and determined by the conjunction attached to it, if any.

> no introductory conjunction *and*   (independent clause)
> these   introductory   conjunctions:
>
> and, but, or, nor, yet, only, for, so,
> either . . . or, neither . . . nor
>
> these (and like) introductory con-   (dependent clause)
> junctions:
>
> if, when, after, until, because,
> since, although, provided that

Some subordinate clauses are linked to main clauses by pronouns rather than by conjunctions:

> The village has three churches *that can be seen from a distance.*

> Three churches, *of which the villagers are proud,* can be seen from a distance.

These are relative clauses, clauses with the function of adjectives. They cannot stand alone, either as they are or with the pronouns deleted. To get at the independent clauses from which they are derived, one must substitute for the pronoun the noun or noun phrase to which it refers and make appropriate adjustments in order:

> *Three churches* can be seen from a distance.
> The villagers are proud of *three churches*.

Another important group of subordinate clauses functions as noun:

> *That the party ended in chaos* surprised no one.
> I said *what you say*.

Notice that in such sentences the main clause is not independent, as it stands ("surprised no one"; "I said"). A noun, noun phrase, or pronoun has been omitted where the subordinate clause now stands:

> [The fact] surprised no one.
>
> I said [it].

Now, for the sake of making use of the terminology familiar to most teachers and students, sentences may be classified as simple, complex, compound, and compound-complex. A simple sentence contains one independent clause. A complex sentence contains one independent clause and one or more dependent clauses. A compound sentence contains two or more independent clauses and no dependent clause. A compound-complex sentence contains two or more independent clauses and one or more dependent clauses.

The nomenclature is for reference only. The relevant question, as always, is "What difference does it make?" Or, to put the question so that it will provoke a more useful answer, "Why does the language have these combinations?" Obviously, it has them because they serve different purposes or produce different effects. Discussion of those purposes and effects can best proceed by study of characteristics beyond the purely formal ones.

A *simple sentence* may be short (Jim swims.) or long:

> Born to wealth and station, nurtured in a culture as refined and articulate as any known to man, blessed at the outset with intelligence, good health, a large store of energy and uncommon good looks, he illustrated with every passing year of his life the genuine advantages of the man with a good start in life.*

---

* This sentence is simple according to traditional grammar, but not simple in the sense explicated on pages 172–173. The phrase "nurtured in a culture as refined and articulate as any known to man," for instance, is derived through several transformations from the simple sentences

> [They] nurtured [him] in a culture   Man knows [other cultures]
> [The culture was] refined   [Other cultures are refined]
> [The culture was] articulate   [Other cultures are articulate]

Thus there can be a good deal of grammatical complexity in sentences that contain only one clause.

It may be "periodic," like the one above, or loose—like this one:

> He illustrated, in every passing year, the genuine advantages of the man with a good start in life by reflecting constantly his distinguished and wealthy parentage, the refined and articulate culture of his home, the initial gifts of intelligence, good health, a large store of energy, and uncommon good looks.

Or it may be a mixture of periodic and loose or an adaptation of either. (For fuller discussion, refer to pages 183–185.)

Since one of the noticeable characteristics of good modern prose is a tendency to use the loose rather than the periodic sentence and to limit sharply the complications even of the loose sentence, you will seldom find (and should seldom compose) a sentence as strung out as the one just cited. It can easily be made into two sentences, and probably should be:

> He illustrated the genuine advantages of the man with a good start in life. Year after year his actions constantly reflected. . . .

A particular reason for keeping the simple sentence short is that its main assertion is likely to be overwhelmed if the sentence is allowed to accumulate a large number of phrases. The advantage of the periodic over the loose pattern, for the simple sentence, is that it provides a convenient way of giving that main assertion the prominence it needs, by retaining it to the end, where it has the last word, so to speak.

Brevity is not by itself an adequate canon, however. It is tedious to require a reader to assimilate a sentence like this one:

> The originator of the plan under discussion believes in the idea of keeping within bound, or at least of maintaining reserve about, the plans of others with ideas similar to his but without capacity for realizing them in the hope of preventing their making some public announcement before an announcement, accompanied by evidence of readiness and competence in execution, from his own lips.

But it is no kinder to require him to jerk through a choppy paragraph such as this:

> The originator of the plan under discussion has an idea. That idea is to keep other people's plans in bound. Or it is to maintain reserve about such plans, at least. The idea is not concerned with all other plans, however. It is concerned only with other plans by people who have ideas like those of the originator of this plan. They have similar ideas. They do not have capacity for realizing them. The originator hopes to prevent such others from announcing their plans publicly. Or, at least, he hopes to announce his first. His announcement will be accompanied by evidence of readiness and competence in execution.

What lies between these extremes? There is no sacrosanct formula, but reason will tell a writer who listens to it that a sentence that is simple in the traditional grammatical sense can seldom afford to be encumbered with more than three or four phrases beyond the noun and verb phrases that make its core.

The virtues of the simple sentence are many. It is easily made emphatic; it can isolate action and actor with dramatic vividness; it encourages succinctness. For the arguer, it is an inestimably valuable means of distinguishing assertions so that each can be separately examined. For the explainer, it is a major instrument of simple partition. For the reviser, of his own work or of the work of others, it is sometimes the only satisfactory means of untying a knot or exposing an ambiguity or contradiction. It will not eradicate stupidity or cure sentimentality, but it can powerfully aid the writer to clarify his own speculation and cure his own slovenliness.

A *compound sentence* contains two or more connected independent clauses. It is not the same, note, as the simple sentence containing a compound subject or compound predicate:

1) "Charisma" is a technical word. (Simple sentence)

2) "Charisma" and "entropy" are technical words, the first in sociology, the second in the physical sciences. (Simple sentence with compound subject and a compound modifier)

3) "Entropy" had one meaning in the nineteenth century but has a contrary meaning today. (Simple sentence with compound predicate)

4) "Charisma" is a technical word in sociology, and "entropy" is a technical word in the physical sciences. (Compound sentence)

Examples two and four above are alike in meaning, though they differ in form. The relevant question is this: why does the language supply more than one form for the same content? The question is the same as that implicit in our earlier discussion of "transformations" on the basic sentence pattern. Why so many? In the variety illustrated in that earlier discussion, some answers readily suggest themselves: questions and commands, for example, serve quite recognizably distinct purposes. But here, in examples two and four, no such distinct purposes are served. But note: the simple sentence, by putting "charisma" and "entropy" together on one side of an equation, suggests that definition is intended; and by putting the additional information in an attached phrase it makes that information only supplemental. The compound sentence, by separating the words and giving each a complete clausal structure, not only emphasizes the distinction between them but uses the information we call "additional" in the simple sentence to make that distinction.

The ideas of separation and relationship are fundamental to the compound sentence, though not limited to it. Technically speaking, this is a compound sentence:

A ruble is worth less than a dollar, but Phoenix has increased its population in the past decade.

Separateness has been achieved, but relationship has not. The connector is there ("but"); what is lacking is any discernible reason for its having been that connector rather than another ("and" or "so," for instance). Two observations emerge from this example. (1) The independent clauses of a compound sentence should bear some meaningful relationship to each other. (2) That relationship is indicated by a connecting word or phrase, placed before one of the clauses.

The effect of the compound sentence is to give each independent clause equal weight and at the same time to indicate a relationship between them other than that of simple equality. It would be convenient if the kind of relationship could be pinned down for absolute classification. Unfortunately, it cannot. In general, it is true that the relationships indicated in a compound sentence are those of (a) supplementation, (b) alternation, (c) subtraction or contrast, (d) consequence, and (e) sequence.

a) They sing and they dance.   (supplementation)
   (and)

b) They sing or they dance.   (alternation)
   (or, either . . . or)

c) They sing but they do not dance.   (contrast)
   (but, yet, although, whereas)

d) He started singing, so they began to dance.   (consequence)
   (so, and, therefore)

e) He started singing, and the others joined in.   (sequence)
   (and)

The impossibility of restricting these relationships perfectly is apparent from sentences like these:

The roof blew off, and the car was flipped into a ditch.

The roof blew off, and the rains poured in.

Clearly, the relationship in the first sentence is supplementary (x plus y) and that in the second, sequential (y after x) and consequential (y as the result of x). Both sentences are compound sentences, and both are provided for by the description above. But now compare the second sentence with this one:

Because the roof blew off, the rains poured in.

It is hard indeed to see any difference in meaning between the two, yet a good ear will detect the shift in emphasis. The latter sentence is complex; the former, compound. The former indicates consequence; the latter indicates cause. In indicating consequence, the compound sentence preserves equal stress on both actions described. In indicating cause, the complex sentence provides a different kind of stress for each of the clauses (you can hear the difference readily enough if you read the sentence aloud).

The *complex sentence* emphasizes relationship of clauses at the expense of equal emphasis. Its function is to subordinate. It may be short or long, periodic or loose; but it always lays stress on the type of linkage between its clauses. In a compound sentence, the conjunction is helpful but can often be dispensed with altogether:

> They danced and they sang and they shouted. They danced, they sang, they shouted.

> The wind blew, so he shut the door. The wind blew; he shut the door.

In a complex sentence, the conjunction, if any, is ordinarily more decisive:

>   he read the book   he planned to get married
> After he read the book, he planned to get married.
> Because he read the book, he planned to get married.
> Although he read the book, he planned to get married.

Because they do emphasize the relationship of dependency, complex sentences have an obvious value in discourse where dependency is important. In narrative prose, for example, the complex sentence is used freely. It is also used for descriptions of process, in which chronology and consequence are both fully implicated.

> As he turned the stair, he saw the figure disappear through a window at the end of the corridor.   (narrative)

> Before the wheel is attached, a wire should be run through the pin-hole to make sure that it is free of grease and dirt.   (process)

It is common in comparison and contrast, and in argument:

> While Prince Hal cavorted in London, Hotspur broke heads and lances in the North.

> Since the government of a monarchy depends on the character of its ruler, many thought Hal unfit to succeed his father.

The complex sentence is valuable in indicating the relative importance of two (or more) assertions:

> Keats, whose poetic output was not large, has long outlived the prolific Southey.

And wherever it is used, it tends to tighten and consolidate.

The *compound-complex sentence* has, perhaps, no especial rhetorical virtues save those of the patterns that compose it. Its grammatical complication does not necessarily imply complicated meaning or complicated effect:

> When he sings, she dances and the monkey rattles his cup.

It provides the coordination of equivalent elements and the subordination of others to them. The situation that requires such coordination and subordination for its description is well served by this kind of sentence, though the alternative open to the compound sentence is open to it, as well:

> She dances when he sings. The monkey rattles his cup.

What, now is to be done about such word groupings as these?

> Not a jot.

> For the king, more revenue.

Both are sometimes classed as *sentence fragments,* but they differ enough from sentence fragments that need censure to warrant some distinction from them. The first of the examples above clearly derives from some preceding sentence for which it is a response or supplementation, like this:

> Did you enjoy it? Not a jot.

Though the second group of words does not contain the elements listed above as characteristic of a sentence, it assumes those elements: "[I enjoyed it] not a jot." Because it assumes them, it adopts the demeanor of a sentence (capital letter at the beginning and a period or other terminal mark of punctuation at the end). The second example adopts the same demeanor, and therefore lays claim to status as a sentence, for a reason essentially the same, though somewhat more limited in range. Assume these preceding sentences:

> The consequences of this edict were at once apparent to the wily ex-chancellor. It promoted the security of the court and clipped the wings of dissident barons. For the Church, it meant new taxes. For the king, more revenue.

The term to describe such sentences as these is *elliptic.* Their structures are strong, not weak, for the reason that they increase coherence rather than diminish it. The same cannot be said of some word groupings:

> The prime minister waited until the last minute to announce his decision. A mild statement in form. It was, however, violent in effect. The parliament heard it without murmur at first, then broke into loud clamor. After thinking over what they had heard. The king. . . .

The test for validity of a sentence fragment is this. It is elliptic and correct if its form is clearly indicated by the nature of the preceding sentence, usually by parallelism in form, or by the fact that it has the force of emphatic and decisive repetition or rejoinder. It is disruptive and incorrect if it isolates phrases or dependent clauses from sentences to which their presence is necessary. The passage above would be correct as:

> The prime minister waited until the last minute to announce his decision. His statement was mild in form but violent in its effect. The parliament heard it at first without murmur; then, after thinking over what they had heard, they broke into loud clamor. The king. . . .

There are other ways to classify sentences than by their complication of elements. One way is by the intention of the sentence maker, which is, of course, an intention with relation to some listener or reader. A *declarative sentence* states existence, condition, or relationship. Its normal word order in English is: noun (noun phrase), verb (verb phrase), noun (noun phrase). (Men like croquet.) An *interrogative sentence* questions. Its normal word order in English is either: verb auxiliary, noun, verb, noun (Do men like croquet?), pronoun, verb, noun (Who likes croquet?), or pronoun, auxiliary, noun, verb (What do men like?). An *imperative sentence* commands. Its normal word order in English is: verb, noun. (Take it.) *Exclamatory* sentences express strong feeling in a variety of word orders. (Good! What a disaster!, and so on.) All of these definitions are tautological, and the description that follows each is, again, insufficient by itself. Taken together, definition and description will serve. But they will serve only if allowance is made for the fact that they are not exclusive. The *sign* of an interrogative sentence may turn any of the others into a question: Men like croquet? (Elliptic for: Do men like croquet? or Are you reasonable in suggesting that men like croquet?) Take it? (Elliptic for: Do you want me to take it? or Should I take it?) What a disaster? (Elliptic for: "Did you say 'what a disaster'?") And there are many ways of giving imperative force to a sentence: Take it. Do take it. Take. You take it. You are to take it. You will take it. You must take it. Let's take it. Let them take it. Like the interrogative sign, the exclamatory sign may convert one kind of sentence into another: Men like croquet! (The very idea seems preposterous.) Do take it! (I implore you, I beseech you.)

Despite the power of the mark of punctuation, it is not enough to say that the kind of sentence is determined by it. The sentence "Has he broken a bone" might be either interrogative or exclamatory, but it cannot be declarative or imperative. Word order is fundamental; punctuation is secondary.

Another way of classifying sentences is by their internal structural development. Earlier examples were given of loose and periodic sentences, but a separate discussion here is prudent.

LOOSE AND PERIODIC SENTENCES •

The terms "loose" and "periodic" as characterizers of a sentence refer to its syntax, specifically to the way in which principal and subordinate elements are arranged. In a *loose* sentence, the main clause is completed early and the qualifying elements follow.

> *The Prelude* is an autobiographical poem in which Wordsworth tried to represent the origin and growth of poetic feeling from the dim impressions of infancy through the highly formative experiences of youth into the troubled and frustrated years of young manhood.

In general, the loose sentence is relaxed and informal precisely because it makes use of the natural structure of the language, proceeding from subject (with modifiers, if any) to object (in this example, with a modifier of considerable complexity and length). The *periodic* sentence "shapes" its structure more formally, placing modifiers so that the predication of the sentence, and therefore its direction and intent, is not clear until at or near the end.

> Through the dim impressions of infancy, the highly formative experiences of youth, and the troubled and frustrated years of young manhood, Wordsworth's autobiographical poem, *The Prelude,* tries to represent the origin and growth of poetic feeling.

The purpose of the periodic sentence is twofold: a) it increases the tension of a sentence by withholding all or part of the predication, and b) it brings modifiers into prominence by gathering them within the area where the tension has been created. It is useful, then, wherever control of the reader's attention is vitally important. Because it involves some infringement on the natural course of the sentence, however, the periodic device is quickly noticed, and its prolonged use, as in Henry James's novels, marks a style as clearly idiosyncratic. Whether or not the idiosyncrasy is desirable depends largely on whether or not the kinds of interruptions introduced are suitable to the matter and purpose of the piece. A sentence as hesitant and tortured as this one is certainly ill-suited to strong assertion:

> He knew with the suddenness of insight to which he had grown accustomed in his new mental state that these, the infertile flowers of a life too long spent in what had been, from whatever point of view one chose to examine it, a manner excessively solitary, were not now, and never had been, the sort of tributes to lay at the feet, if so pagan and oriental a tradition of worship were not presumptuous and uncharacteristic for him to consider, of his beloved, and too long neglected, friend.

Nor are the balanced periods of this sentence suitable for quiet and tentative statement of opinion:

> This man, long the consort of criminals and enemy of the law-abiding, a petty tyrant of back alleys made powerful by the corruption of those in high places and relentless by his insatiable greed and vanity, has again demonstrated his cunning as well as the indifference of those charged with the public welfare by seizing in our time of greatest need the very resources on which we most depended for our sustenance.

The point of these examples is that the periodic sentence is a flexible instrument, adaptable to thunderous indictment as well as to introspection. But whatever its content and whatever its tone, it draws attention to the informative detail incidental to the principal assertion. The loose sentence is like a kite, its tail of dependencies fluttering at the end; the periodic sentence is like a ceremony in which the rolling out of the red carpet prepares for the entrance of the chief dignitary.

BALANCED PHRASING •

By the time students reach college, some have developed an ear sensitive to the poise and cadence of language, perhaps the result of direct instruction, but more likely the fruit of wide and attentive reading. Those who already have it are possessed of a principal means to rhetorical power. Those who do not can develop a rudimentary command of it by considering the various effects which the shifting of verbal structures can produce.

Since the dominant pattern of English is a simple one (subject-verb-object), it is not strange that *inversion* commands immediate attention. Its usual effect is to emphasize or dramatize the word which is moved out of its ordinary place, as in these examples:

> Had Napoleon acted, Moscow might not have been burned.
> (*Instead of* If Napoleon had acted. . . .)
>
> Reluctantly he faced the angry mob. (*Instead of* He faced the angry mob reluctantly, *or* He reluctantly faced the angry mob.)

In the first sentence, the writer throws weight on what is actually a dependent clause by inverting the subject and a part of the predicate verb; in the second, he does the same for the adverb by moving it forward. Both of these illustrations show a kind of redressing of balance, a corrective to the normal syntax which provides inadequate emphasis for the word or clause of primary importance in this context.

A less spectacular kind of balance is created by repetition of pattern, by what is known as *parallel structure*. In simplest form, this is no more than maintaining one part of speech in a series, a device that produces some of the most memorable phrases in our language:

> Life, liberty, and the pursuit of happiness.
>
> Read, mark, and consider.
>
> The world, the flesh, and the devil.

The single rule governing such structures is that each part must provide an identical grammatical pattern, even though elements in it, as in this oft-quoted excerpt from Bacon's essay, "Of Studies," may be omitted:

> Reading maketh a full man; conference, a ready man; writing, an exact man.

Actually it is possible to vary one part of each phrase slightly without damage to the parallelism if the varying is of a kind not to distract:

> Histories make men wise; poets, witty; the mathematics, subtile; natural philosophy, deep; moral, grave; logic and rhetoric, able to contend.

In this illustration, "histories," "poets," and "the mathematics" are not identical, in that the first represents the product of study, the second the producer, and the third the study itself. We can understand, perhaps, why Bacon deviated from the strict pattern (which he observes with fidelity elsewhere in the essay) if we try to rephrase the sentence more rigidly:

> History makes men wise; poetry, witty; the mathematics, subtile.

In our reconstruction "history" is ambiguous since, particularly before the pattern is established, it may be taken to mean "the study of history" or "the events of the past"; and "poetry, witty" offends the ear.

There is something valuable to be learned from this example. Parallelism is wonderfully effective, but it must not be used insensitively. Overused (as it is, indeed, in Bacon's essay), it becomes monotonous. Used without attention to other considerations, it may damage the sentence it balances by offending on some other score. When parallelism governs sentences, they are likely to be sharply rhetorical. The speeches of Brutus and Antony at Caesar's burial, speeches which many schoolboys know by heart, are examples of the power that word arrangement has to move the listener. When parallelism works with other structures, it is, though less rhetorical, no less effective. In this sentence, for example, the parallelism of the phrases following the colon brings them together into a unit which, in turn, strikes a just balance with the phrase preceding the colon:

> Rousseau's *Confessions* is a chronicle of self-pity: for the dereliction of parents, the infidelity of friends, the hostility of the world.

2) THE RHETORIC OF CLAUSES

Earlier some features of *meaning* which are functions of various clause structures were considered. The discussion that follows will note more carefully the *rhetorical* effects of such structures, and of their placement in the sentence.

INDEPENDENT CLAUSES •

One of the readily discernible characteristics of good modern writing is a tendency to shorten the sentence, sometimes to a single independent clause, a tendency carried to an extreme in the "tough" novel of our day. Whatever the complex historical and psychological causes of this shortening of the sentence may be, it is possible to credit it with the virtue of directness and, often, of succinctness.

Compare

> Jake strode into the room. The door banged behind him, hard. He stopped short in the middle of the room. "Hullo," he said. "What's that?"

with

> Jake strode into the room, banging the door hard behind him, and stopped short in the middle of the room. "Hullo," he said, "What's that?"

or

> After Jake strode into the room, banging the door behind him, he stopped short in the middle of the room and said, "Hullo! What's that?"

There is a vigor, a suggestion of abrupt action, in the first passage that is only partially conveyed by the others where the participial phrase ("banging . . ."), by subordinating one action, has the effect of reducing the separateness and therefore the abruptness of the actions.

Constant use of the short independent clause as a complete sentence has the fault, however, of its virtue. Because each clause produces a solid thump, the ear soon loses the power to distinguish between thumps. The result is a sense of sameness and of disjunction between successive sentences. Nonetheless, this simple kind of structure is a valuable one. The writer who habitually gets wound up in sentences of tortuous complexity will find temporary use of it an effective curative.

DEPENDENT CLAUSES •

The grammatical character of the dependent clause is familiar to many for whom its rhetorical functions are quite mythical. Yet the uses of dependent clauses are so many and so important to the effect of a sentence that indifference to them is fatal to effective expression. One of those functions is the indication of logical relationship. The sentences that follow need to have relationships more clearly defined:

> The Bodleian manuscript is obviously a copy of the original. It has several interpolations. The interpolations may be the work of a Benedictine monk.

Converting the second and third sentences into a dependent clause draws the information together and places emphasis on the predication of the first sentence:

> The Bodleian manuscript, which has several interpolations possibly the work of a Benedictine monk, is obviously a copy of the original.

An alternative arrangement draws the information together and places emphasis on "interpolation"·

> The Bodleian manuscript, obviously a copy of the original, has several interpolations possibly the work of a Benedictine monk.

A second rhetorical function of the dependent clause is to induce anticipation. Each of these clauses

> When Louis refused a third time to hear its emissaries

> If you add copper sulfate instead of sodium

arouses the reader's desire to know the consequence of the action described. Conversely, the feeling of the vitality of action often declines when the dependent clause follows:

> The council decided to turn directly to the people when Louis refused a third time to hear its emissaries.

> The solution may explode if you add copper sulfate instead of sodium.

The nature of the consequence will to some degree determine the placement of the dependent clause. If the conclusion of the second sentence, for instance, were "may turn green," it would be rhetorically preferable to begin with the independent clause. Since "may explode" is an adequate satisfaction of the tension created by an opening dependent clause, however, that sentence is better written thus:

> If you add copper sulfate instead of sodium, the solution may explode.

The same is true of the first example, which is better written:

> When Louis refused a third time to hear its emissaries, the council decided to turn directly to the people.

Besides providing unity and a sense of anticipation, the dependent clause may help in the *control of emphasis*. Curiously enough, it may function either to increase or to decrease the weight placed on a term. In the sentence

> Inexperienced workers naturally make more mistakes

the term "inexperienced" may be given more prominence by conversion:

> Workers who are inexperienced make more mistakes.

But a desirable de-emphasis results from creating a dependent clause in this instance:

> The sighting of the new star was made possible only by the development of a more powerful telescope, and the star was later named Pluto.

> The sighting of the new star, which was later named Pluto, was made possible only by the development of a more powerful telescope.

In the examples given here, the dependent clause achieves emphasis by expansion of an adjective into a dependent clause and de-emphasis by the reduction of an independent clause to dependency. The obvious inference from the examples is not sound for all possible situations, of course, but it is good enough as a rough generalization to warrant notice.

One caution concludes this brief discussion of dependent clauses: a writer must know the precise effect of the subordinating conjunctions with which such clauses begin. (A list of the common ones appears later, in the discussion of transitions.) Very frequently, the unintended implication that sends the reader in the wrong direction comes from nothing more than the faulty use of a subordinating conjunction, as in the passage below:

> The usual European explanation for American shyness is that Americans almost by definition have no interest in any sort of intellectual endeavor. Kluckhohn offers a more subtle interpretation *although* it is a valid one.

Clauses may also be distinguished by the function they serve in a sentence. They may in fact serve any of the functions performed by nouns, adjectives, and adverbs.

> He spent what he had and went home.   ("what he had," noun clause, object)
>
> *Compare:* He spent his money and went home.
>
> What he earns goes into the bank.   ("what he earns," noun clause, subject)
>
> *Compare:* His earnings go into the bank.
>
> The man who saves most earns most.   ("who saves most," adjective clause)
>
> *Compare:* The most saving man earns most.
>
> When he earns, he saves.   ("when he earns," adverbial clause)

The advantage of clauses used in these ways is this: clauses contain verbs and therefore generally refer to action explicitly. By introducing the idea of action into noun, adjective, and adverb, a writer is sometimes able to increase their vividness. Clauses used in place of abstract nouns are especially useful for clearing away vagueness and ambiguity, or simply for letting the fresh air of human activity blow over an arid stretch of prose:

> In the theory of action the point of reference of all terms is the action of an individual actor or of a collectivity of actors. Of course, all individual actors are, in one aspect, physiological organisms; collectivities of actors are made up of individual actors, who are similarly physiological organisms. The interest of the theory of action, however, is directed not to the physiological processes internal to the organism but rather to the organization of the actor's orientation to a situation. When a term refers

to a collectivity as the acting unit, it is understood that it does not refer to all of the actions of the individuals who are its members, but only to the actions which they perform in their capacity as members. Whether the acting unit is an individual or a collectivity, we shall speak of the actor's orientation of action when we describe the action. The concept *motivation* in a strict sense applies only to individual actors. The motivational components of the action of collectivities are organized systems of the motivation of the relevant individual actors. Action has an orientation when it is guided by the meaning which the actor attaches to it in relationship to his goals and interests.

Something certainly needs to be done to that passage not because it is meaningless but because its meaning is obscured by abstractness of language. By substituting clauses here and there for some of the abstract words, we can make the sentences more accessible. The result will not be great prose, but it will be much clearer prose.

> The point of reference for all terms in the theory of action is what people do, singly or in groups. Now it is obvious that what a man does, or what a group of men do, is in one sense a physiological matter. Theory of action is concerned, however, not with nerves and glands and bodily processes but with processes of the mind, those we call "psychological." A key word in the theory is "orientation." An oriented action is one guided by the actor's sense of the way what he does relates to his goals and interests. When any term in the theory refers to the group as an "acting unit," it does not mean to take into account all the actions of those who make up the group but only those actions they perform together. And whether we are talking about one actor or a group of actors, whenever we describe an action we shall have its orientation in mind. Now, strictly speaking, the concept of *motivation* has to do only with the actions of a single person. What we advance here is this proposition: the motivations for what many people do as a group turn out to be an organized system of the motivation each person in the group feels when he participates in the group action.

3) KINDS OF PHRASES

Phrases may be classified, as clauses have been, by form and by function. Since, however, the functions they serve are substantially the same as those served by clauses, this discussion will treat them by form and subsume function in the treatment.

PARTICIPIAL PHRASES ·

Probably more students are familiar with the classic blunder in the use of participial phrases than with the particular effects achievable by correct use of them. To move from the familiar to the unfamiliar, then, is to begin with that cardinal error, the *dangling participle*. Considering

the prominence it has in most handbooks of grammar, it is remarkable
how persistently it continues to disgrace the writing not only of students but of others who might reasonably be expected to avoid it. Part
of the persistence is due, no doubt, to its innocence and convenience.
Only in such "boners" as

> Wearing a red shirt, the bull attacked the unfortunate man

does it offend and amuse the general reader. And were it not for the
confusion a dangling participle often causes, it would not deserve further
attention. That it does cause confusion is evident in a sentence like this:

> Defending liberty with such vigor, my opinion is that Milton in his *Areo-
> pagitica* is the leading libertarian of his time.

Who or what is "defending"? The answer can be solved, of course, but
one writes to inform a reader, not to puzzle him. The construction of
such a sentence is, therefore, indefensible. Such confusion can usually be
avoided by keeping a simple rule in mind: the participial modifier should
come as close as possible to the word it modifies. Not:

> Having no grounds for his argument, it seems to me that Alcibiades de-
> cided to rely on rhetoric in order to defend his position.

But this:

> It seems to me that, having no grounds for his argument, Alcibiades de-
> cided to rely on rhetoric in order to defend his position.

Wherever possible it is wise to avoid separating subject and predicate
verb by the participial expression:

> Alcibiades, having no grounds for his argument, decided to rely on rhetoric
> in order to defend his position.

> CORRECTED: Having no grounds for his argument, Alcibiades decided to
> rely on rhetoric in order to defend his position.

The earlier sentence about Milton is so awkward that relief can be found
only in complete revision:

> Milton's vigorous defense of freedom in the *Areopagitica* makes him, in
> my opinion, the leading libertarian of his time.

So much for the abuse of the participle. What of its effective use? The
principal utility of the participle seems to lie in its power to create a
sense of *simultaneity*.

> Cassius spoke cautiously to Brutus, measured each word with care, and
> increased his fervor at each sign of impatience in Brutus' face.

> CORRECTED: Cassius spoke cautiously to Brutus, measuring each word with
> care and increasing his fervor at each sign of impatience in Brutus' face.

In these examples, "spoke" indicates an action which *includes* the other verbs. Turning "measured" and "increased" into participles makes the inclusion clear and gives the reader an almost graphic realization that the actions of measuring and increasing go on during the speaking and are a part of it.

Moreover, participles make it possible to establish clearly the relationship of two periods of time within a single sentence:

> Although he tried repeatedly to do so, Coleridge could never recapture the vision of "Kubla Khan" which came to him in a dream that was interrupted by the untimely intrusion of a visitor.

> CORRECTED: Although he tried repeatedly to do so, Coleridge could never recapture the vision of "Kubla Khan," the product of a dream interrupted by the untimely intrusion of a visitor.

Participles, present and past, also serve as instruments of *unification*. In the sentence about the sighting of a new star, revised several pages back, a further improvement might be made by reducing the dependent clause to a participial phrase:

> The sighting of the new star, later named Pluto, was made possible only by. . . .

Such use of the participial phrase is almost too common to warrant mention, and its abuses—largely those of misplacement—are relatively infrequent. The use of the participle in so-called "absolute" constructions, however, is less common though fully as useful as a unifying device:

> He climbed out of the ring, his ears nearly deafened by the roar of the crowd around him.

> Its oars rising and falling rhythmically, the first shell swept around the bend of the river and into the final stretch.

Here the participial constructions attach relevant information to the main clauses and thus unify the action described in them.

PREPOSITIONAL PHRASES ·

Mention has already been made of the important role which the position of words plays in conveying the meaning of a sentence. The need for a considerable fixity of position in English is obvious, for without it the relationships between the various nouns in a sentence and between the nouns and verbs would quickly become obscure. If position were all that English could rely on to establish relationship, however, it would be a very inflexible language. That it is not falls partly to the credit of the preposition. Although position is principally responsible for our understanding the relationships in a sentence like this

> He gave the girl the money,

it is through prepositions that relationships are conveyed in sentences like this

> The girl in the bank put her pen on the counter.

A simple test of the importance of prepositions is to block out all of them in a brief passage of prose and then try to understand the meaning without them:

> Genuine crises are rare. Various times, civil and religious disputes have filled the air lasting and deafening clamor, yet leading vital transformations. The political and social foundations State were never shaken or even called question. Hence they cannot be regarded genuine crises. We find examples this firstly the Wars the Roses England, which the people trooped one two factions nobility and the Court, and secondly the French Wars Religion, where actual fact the main issue lay the followers two noble houses, and the question was whether the King would maintain his position independently either, or which he would join.

While it is possible to guess at the prepositions omitted in many places, especially where idioms are involved ("called *in* question," for instance), the nature of the relationship between nouns and between nouns and verbs becomes ambiguous in many others. It is those relationships that the preposition clarifies when it is properly and accurately used.

As its name implies, the preposition is not used alone; it always has an object which is, grammatically, a noun or a pronoun or some word acting as surrogate for a noun or pronoun:

> We are going *to his house.*

> He delights *in singing.*

> He came *from New York.*

> *Where* did he come *from?*

This combination, known as the prepositional phrase, is generally used as a modifier (adjectival or adverbial) within the sentence:

> The man *on the horse* is a polo player. (adjectival)

> He strikes the ball *with a mallet.* (adverbial)

Its use as subject or object of the verb is either elliptic or awkward or both:

> *In the air* is better than *on the ground.*

> *At my house* will be satisfactory.

Considering the many functions of the prepositional phrase in its adjectival and adverbial roles, it seems wise, therefore, to separate it entirely from the subject-object functions, and formal writing generally respects that separation.

As modifiers, prepositional phrases act like one-word adjectives and adverbs. They name attributes of nouns (the girl *in blue*) when they are adjectival. When they are adverbial, they express one of the usual adverbial relationships: those of time, place, direction, derivation, condition, consequence, exclusion or inclusion, means, manner, or agency. Like one-word adverbs they usually precede the adjectives they modify and may either precede or follow the verbs they modify. The word "usually" is needed for any statement about the placement of prepositional phrases: because they are supplements to the "main line" of the sentence—subject-verb-object—they are relatively instable and quite susceptible to the demands of emphasis, rhythm, and euphony as well as to those of logical relationship.

The difference between the two following sentences is one of emphasis:

> He put down his knapsack in the middle of the room.

> In the middle of the room he put down his knapsack.

The difference between these is one of clarity:

> They poured the syrup which they had spent all afternoon boiling out of the bucket.

> They poured out of the bucket the syrup which they had spent all afternoon boiling.

And between the sentence immediately above and the one below the difference is one of rhythm and euphony:

> The syrup which they had spent all afternoon boiling they now poured out of the bucket.

Problems of placement do not yield readily to solutions by rule. A writer has to be alert to detect the possibilities of confusion from bad placement and sensitive to the sound of language to detect those placements which offend the natural rhythm of English or throw emphasis where it is not wanted. Although the same alertness and sensitivity would certainly prevent other abuses of the prepositional phrase, it is possible to make concrete suggestions for a few, not as a substitute for alertness and sensitivity, but as an aid where they may not be sufficiently acute to be a guide.

A. There are much worse sins than leaving a preposition at the end of a sentence. In speech even the most fastidious users of language are likely to do so on occasion; in formal writing, however, the preposition is usually joined firmly to its object. Some of the uses objected to by the overly cautious are not really abuses of prepositional unity at all but are simply emphatic placements of adverbs so closely attached to the verbs they modify that they constitute a part of the verb: "That is treatment he is not willing to *put up with*." It was a secretary's correction of such a locution that is said to have led Winston Churchill to write in the margin, "This is the kind of nonsense up with which I will not put."

B. Much worse than the "dangling" preposition is the overuse of compound prepositions, especially of those whose metaphorical ground has been obscured by time: *on the basis that, in terms of, in considera-tion of the fact that,* and so on. A paragraph full of such prepositional structures so far divorces the active words of the sentence that a kind of miasma begins to rise from it, covering its movement and its meaning:

> In respect to the terms of the agreement made on the basis of a con-sideration of the factors in the case, we are of the opinion that to act in the sense of the terms in this instance without more examination concern-ing the possible effects on the ground of damage to other parties in the situation would not be in the interests of anyone.

C. Any *succession* of prepositional phrases is likely to confuse a reader because it presents a string of qualifiers separated from the words they qualify. Even when the meaning is not obscured by such a succession, the elegance of the sentence may be injured. (See the discussion of Euphony on pp. 198–199.)

D. Occasionally the practice of separating a preposition from its ob-ject leads a writer to repeat it unintentionally:

> The shrubs along the road *in* which he had for the last two hours been crouching *in* were thick enough to conceal him completely.

To expose such a repetition is to condemn it.

E. The most serious misuse of prepositional phrases, and probably the most common, is that arising from indifference to meaning. "With," for instance, has become a jack-of-all-prepositional-trades; "in" and "into" are carelessly interchanged; "by" is used to mean "beside"; "off of" is substituted for "off" in defiance of logic. There is nothing harder for a foreigner to get used to than the prepositions in our language when they are correctly used; considering the cavalier treatment some of them habitually receive, it is not surprising that they are frequently confusing even to natives. Only a laborious catalogue would make it possible to establish the significance of each English preposition, and a complete catalogue, if it included all current usages, would undoubtedly show so much overlapping that most distinctions would become questionable. The best single piece of advice may be this: since prepositions are relational in their function, it is wise to think, whenever possible, about their relational intention in physical terms to prevent misuse. It ought certainly to elimi-nate such sentences as these:

With such people all you can do is hope they will change.

He sings *with* a high voice.

If you want to succeed *with* some other means, you are free to try.

He came back to the house *with* his hat lost.

He earns his living *with* the sweat of his brow.

INFINITIVE AND GERUND PHRASES •

The infinitive phrase is a convenient but not very flexible structure. Its most natural use is as object of a verb or as appositive:

He wants *to spend his vacation in Bermuda.*

His plan *to do so* was foiled by an accident.

As subject of the verb, the infinitive phrase is rather formal and not common to speech, in which it is likely to be replaced by a gerund.

To see is to believe. *(Seeing* is believing.)

The gerund, or verbal noun, is used as nouns are most commonly used—as subject or object of a verb, as object of a preposition:

Climbing the mountain is more fun than *descending* it.

He thinks his success comes from *waiting.*

They tried *running* in pairs but soon gave up *trying.*

Both the infinitive phrase and the gerund phrase provide ways of maintaining the vitality and movement implicit in a verb. At the same time, they make the action figure as the thing talked about in the sentence. Their grammatical peculiarities cause little difficulty except in connection with the agent of the action they imply. Despite the fact that they function as nouns, they retain some of their verbal character, grammatically speaking. Thus, although they may themselves be subjects or objects of a verb, they also have subjects and objects; and the form of their subjects is often mishandled. The logic of the distinctions may be omitted here, but the distinctions themselves need brief mention:

A. The subject of an infinitive is in the objective case:

She wants *him* to go alone.

B. The subject of the action implied in a gerund is in the possessive:

She approves *his* trying to go alone.

They like Mary's singing.

The so-called dangling or detached infinitive—

To treat first matters first, the ship is too slow for our needs

—is frowned upon by some, but its only disadvantage seems to lie in the possibility of confusion. In the example given above, no one is likely to think that the infinitive phrase modifies "ship"; in the one that follows the construction is less defensible because it does create some ambiguity:

> This is a means, to do him justice, by which some good may be accomplished.

This section began with simplification. The English sentence, it stated, is basically a simple structure. It then discussed and demonstrated some of the structural variety and the complexities possible within it. Both may be summed up in another simplistic formula that may prove useful:

> who (what)? + does (is)? what   [+ to whom (what)?]

Here, the emphasis is not on form but on the meaning of the sentence. The usefulness of such a formula will become apparent in the next chapter, where paragraph and whole essay are considered. At this point, it is mentioned only because it is one of those handy devices for testing prose already written and now ready for revision. If any of the three questions (the third is not always relevant, of course, as in "The sun shines") cannot readily and clearly be answered in the words of the sentence under examination, something is wrong. If the answer those words give, taken by itself, sounds indefinite or confused, clarification is in order. The metaphor of action which the formula uses makes a reviser sensitive to unnecessary abstractness and abstruseness. If he has it in mind, he will not in conscience be able to retain a sentence like this one:

> The motivational components of the action of collectivities are organized systems of the motivation of the relevant individual actors.

The help such a simple formula can give is considerable, but it is not enough to make good prose, even if "good prose" is a term limited to style. Part of what a sentence accomplishes, it accomplishes by other means than soundness of statement, correctness and appropriateness of structure, aptness of vocabulary. Because language, as written and as spoken, involves the continuum of time, one of its characteristics is movement, pace, *rhythm*. Because the written word is associated with the spoken word, another of its characteristics is *sound*. Neither is easy to discuss, but neither can be ignored in a serious treatment of the writer's problems and opportunities.

4) RHYTHM

The effects which the structural devices discussed above have on a reader are partly the result of the meaning conveyed within each and partly the result of the rhythm, or cadence, of the structure itself. Although it is not possible, short of writing a treatise on the subject, to present an adequate account of prose rhythms in English, it is worth while to note that there are such rhythms and that they do affect the total meaning of a prose passage. The words generally used to describe various rhythms are largely metaphorical—such words as "leisurely," "crabbed," "sonorous," and "labo ed"—and hard to define in specific terms. The fact that English is an *accented* language, however, and that words commonly have only one major accent suggests that these adjectives must refer, in some measure, to the succession of accented and unaccented syllables.

In poetry we are accustomed to "scanning" lines according to accentual patterns, and there is no reason that one cannot scan prose in the same fashion. Many scholars and critics have indeed done just that, but their findings do not as yet provide enough evidence to make it possible for a writer to rely on the effect he may produce from a particular succession of accents—not that a writer is likely to go about the business by counting on his fingers anyway. The inadequacy of the analyses made so far is attributable to many causes. As noted above, rhythm accounts for only a part of the total meaning of a sentence, and it is hard to separate that part from the rest; even could it be separated, so little has been known until recently about the role of pitch in conveying meaning that a further separation between the effects of rhythm and of pitch must still be made. And, finally, modern prosodists are convinced that beneath the accents indigenous to each word there are other kinds of accents which arise from the association of words into meaningful utterances, subaccents which may be quite as important to the rhythm of poetry and prose as those which would be indicated by a traditional scanning. The most that can be said in such brief space may take the form of two general observations: (1) a long succession of monosyllabic words creates some sense of the unrelatedness of parts, perhaps because so large a number of the subordinating conjunctions and prepositions in English are dis- or trisyllabic; (2) attempts to imitate the regularity of poetic meters are nearly always detrimental to prose.

5) EUPHONY

Like rhythm, euphony is a characteristic of prose to which no good writer is indifferent but one about which very little advice can be given. The exploitation of sound is particularly noticeable in poetry, of course, where it often serves for emphasis and for confirming the relationship of words in the poem as well as for more special effects. In prose, the attempt to make "linkèd harmonies" is seldom worth the effort it requires. At the same time, there are conjunctions of sound which a fastidious writer of prose will avoid: a series of words ending in -ion ("The notion that there could be provision of equal portions of the spoils for every nation is so serious an evasion of intelligent speculation that . . ."); a succeeding pair ending in -ing ("He stayed through the meeting seeming not to care what . . ."); a succession of polysyllables of any termination ("The prodigious celerity and ingenuity characteristic of reactions stimulated by . . ."); accidental alliteration ("They knocked not noticeably louder than anyone else, but . . ."), especially of sibilants ("Since separating silver from baser metals is scarcely as easy a process as . . ."); successive prepositional phrases beginning with the same preposition ("At the middle of the bottom of the lower half of the sheet of graph paper he put . . ."). The generalization deducible from such specific cases is that repetition of sound is often dangerous in prose. Again, the generalization is subject to many exceptions and has no value except as a general caution. Of so-called harsh or uneuphonious sounds, nothing need be said save that they have their uses and are perhaps less likely to be abused, in the long run, than those which are thought to be "sweet."

The final matter in this chapter on the grammar and rhetoric of the sentence is a compound of both. It deals with the grammatical elements known as *person, number, tense, mood,* and *voice;* but it deals with them primarily as factors in a rhetorical situation. The situation may be roughly described in this way. No matter what its length, a sentence undertakes to coordinate words so that the objects and actions to which they refer fall together meaningfully in the reader's mind. The coordination is always difficult and customarily tenuous. It takes only a slight jar—the result, perhaps, of inattention—to disturb that coordination and to throw the reader into momentary, or permanent, confusion. The coordination must therefore display consistency throughout, and the consistency it displays is, inevitably, that which the writer's mind imposes through language. Hence, the grouping of these grammatical elements under the heading that follows.

6) CONSISTENCY IN VIEWPOINT

The devices so far discussed generally do their work of providing balance in a sentence by calculated management and are therefore more the mark of the studied than of the natural style. Even in the free flow of language, however, balance is desirable and necessary. There, it comes primarily from consistency in viewpoint, a matter which may be examined under five separate headings.

Person. There are, grammatically speaking, three persons in English: the first person (speaker), the second person (person spoken to), and the third person (person spoken about). Consistency demands that there be no unmeaningful shifts in person, and that sentences be so constructed as to eliminate ambiguity of person. To write

> Everyone likes pleasure, but you shouldn't be its slave

is to move, for no adequate reason, from the third person ("Everyone") to the second ("you"). A proper choice of pronoun for the second clause not only corrects the grammatical error but improves the rhetorical quality of the sentence:

> Everyone likes pleasure, but no one should be its slave.

The phrase above, "for no adequate reason," is meant to catch the eye. As a matter of fact, there is *a* reason for the shift in the illustrative sentence, even though it is not an "adequate" reason. Modern English actually uses *two* persons for the indefinite pronoun rather than the traditional *one*. In colloquial speech we commonly use "you" to indicate the indefinite, saying, "When you try to figure out a problem like this, you invariably discover the depth of your ignorance." The "you" of this sentence is not the person-spoken-to but the person-spoken-about. Actually, the person-spoken-about in this situation seems to make a more intimate inclusion of the speaker himself and of the person-spoken-to than does the indefinite "one." In more formal discourse, we adopt a generic noun ("a man," "a person") or an indefinite pronoun ("anyone," "someone"); more and more rarely, in American English, does the once-traditional form "one" appear. No matter which form is used, however, the rule of consistency stands; it is bad to shift persons unmeaningfully.

Number. Like shifts in person, shifts in number generally stem either from carelessness or from the confusion that still marks the activity of the indefinite pronouns in English. That a student, after years of the study of English, should write

> The practice of simony, like that of granting indulgences, were common in the medieval church

is inexcusable; that one should get tripped up in a sentence like

> Everyone has their own way of doing things

is, considering the double suggestion in "everyone," not entirely surprising. A careful grammarian would point out that "one" is singular and is so considered by the writer since he employs a singular form of the verb; pragmatists point out that "every-" obviously implies more than one and has good cause to assert its plurality in the adjective "their" even if it does not do so in the verb. The debate about these pronouns rages wherever English is taught, and differences in use occur wherever it is spoken. But the practice of treating what the textbooks consider to be singular pronouns as though they are plural if the sense of plurality can be inferred appears to be increasing and now occurs even in the speech of educated people. It is not, however, commonly encountered in the serious writing of those people, and it is on such ground that a stand affirming the rightness of the singular concept of the indefinite pronouns *everyone, anyone, no one* must rest:

> Everyone has his own way of doing things.

Maintaining consistency in number is necessary not only within the sentence but also in the sequence of sentences. If not absolutely wrong, it is at least confusing to write:

> *Soldiers* highly trained in the convention of traditional warfare *are* often terrified by the irregular. *This soldier* cannot accommodate *himself* to the tactic which *he has* never encountered. So it was with the Roman *troops* when *they* faced the unorthodox attacks of the barbarians from the North.

Tense. Consistency in the use of tenses does not limit the writer to the use of a single tense within a sentence or passage, but it does limit him to a sequence. The most common errors in tense found on students' papers come from failure to understand the relationships indicated in this grouping.

I		II	
present tense		past tense	
perfect tense		past perfect tense	
future tense		conditional tense	
auxiliaries:	may	auxiliaries:	might
	can		could
	shall, will		should, would
	has, have		had

Crossing the tenses of one group with the other may disturb the time balance in a sentence:

> If Arnold *had not used* the phrase "sweetness and light" so frequently, the importance he *attaches* to it *would be* less apparent than he *wanted* it to be.

> CORRECTED: If Arnold *had not used* the phrase "sweetness and light" so frequently, the importance he *attached* to it *would have been* less apparent than he *wanted* it to be.

The ramifications of tense order are many but the little chart above is a simple and handy guide for the most common perplexities of this sort.

One further note about tense is relevant here. The present tense is a particularly lively one in English. It not only indicates current action:

> *I see* your books are new

and habitual action:

> I *hear* the opera every Christmas

and future action:

> He *goes* to Paris next spring

but is also useful in animating the past, particularly in narrative passages:

> Lincoln *strides* into the committee room, his face rigid with anger

and in presenting textual analysis:

> In this episode, Homer *introduces* the goddess who is to watch over the fortunes of Telemachus and Odysseus throughout their adventures.

The use of the present tense in textual analysis is so important to the writer of critical essays that it deserves emphasis. If he is referring to a source and his interest is in the content of the source, not the historical situation in which it appeared, he should use the present tense:

> Professor Wilson *suggests* that "solid" is actually a misreading for *"sordid"* in Hamlet's famous lament, "O that this too too solid flesh would melt!"

This use of the present tense is proper whether or not the author is still alive:

> Goethe's interest in Faust-the-man *is* greatest of all in the last act of Part II where care overwhelms the proud humanitarian Faust has become.

Both of these illustrations use the present tense because emphasis is on the text and the text is, in some sense, always alive.

Where emphasis is on the author and the historical situation in which statements are made, the situation changes:

> A few months ago, Professor Wilson *suggested,* in an article in *PMLA,* that. . . .

> As he grew older Goethe's interest in Faust-the-man *deepened.*

The historical situation and the textual analysis may, and frequently will, occur together:

> Crèvecœur *was* the first to attempt a definition of the independent spirit of the colonists. His popular book *depicts* the emergence of . . . .

Mood.   Traditional textbooks list three moods for English: the indicative, the subjunctive, the imperative. These they distinguish as referring to definite action (indicative), probable or desired or predicted action, or action contrary to fact (subjunctive), and command (imperative). The indicative and imperative moods are firmly fixed in the language:

According to report, Carlyle *rewrote* his history of the French revolution from memory after the manuscript was accidentally destroyed. (indicative)

Bertrand Russell's advice is this: in matters of thought *distrust* all authority. (imperative)

Of the subjunctive, however, there seem to be only vestigial remains. The contrary-to-fact condition still exerts influence on the verb *to be,* as in

If Ptolemy *were* right, there would be no way to account for the behavior of heavenly bodies in galaxies distinct from our own

but, even there, ordinarily only in the past tense. The action denoting probability or wish or prediction may be subjunctive, but there is today very little use of the "subjunctive" form of the verb, save as that term is applied to the use of certain auxiliaries (as in *"may be* subjunctive" in this sentence).

The demise of the subjunctive need not concern us here. The one point to be made is that undiscriminating shift of mood within a sentence is a troubling matter to the reader because it requires him to follow a shift in attitude-toward-action for which he is not prepared. Such shifts are particularly annoying when they are from the imperative to either of the other moods. This sentence is bad for that reason:

It *may be* that Toynbee *is* right about repetition in history, but *take* the similar idea of Spengler and you *will see* how different the conclusions from such an idea *can be.*

CORRECTED: It *may be* that Toynbee *is* right about repetition in history, but Spengler *had* a similar idea and *reached* a very different conclusion.

Voice. Some modern grammarians are as dubious about there being two "voices" in English as about there being a "subjunctive," and they prefer to talk of a "passive construction" rather than a "passive voice," since the verbs used for such a construction do not alter their form. Whichever term one chooses, it is clear that there are two patterns in our language which differ in the relationship of their grammatical subject to the predicate verb.

In the active voice, the grammatical subject performs the action:

James I created a new dynasty in England.

In the passive voice, the grammatical subject receives the action:

Charles I was beheaded in 1649.

Both voices have their usefulness, naturally, or they would not exist. Here, for example is an order produced by the Office of Price Stabilization for display in restaurants and stores during World War II:

Quality and Quantity Are Required To Be Maintained.

The reason for the passive construction in that order is obvious enough. *Who* requires? No one is named, but the downrightness of "Required" indicates that it is Someone or, more likely, SOMEONE. Such impersonality has its uses, but it can readily become a device for making matters seem more important or imperative than they really are.

The problems of *person* and *voice* often combine to annoy the writer of expository prose. If he is describing or explaining an activity or condition in which human participation is implicit, he has these choices: (1) to create a semifictitious personage to whom he can refer ("the writer" is the one often used in this book); (2) to reify abstractions, making them the subjects of active verbs ("Such an analysis requires careful examination . . ."); (3) to use the "editorial *we*" ("If we examine this analysis carefully, we see that . . ."); (4) to avoid "we" by using "one ("If one examines this analysis carefully, one sees that . . ."); (5) to employ direct address ("You must examine such an analysis . . ."); (6) to resort to impersonal constructions ("From an examination of such an analysis it becomes apparent that . . ."; or (7) to use the passive voice ("If such an analysis is carefully examined . . ."). There is no rule of thumb for deciding among them, and within a long piece of prose a writer will ordinarily use several. Such differences as are discernible alter from context to context, and generalizations about them are likely therefore to be somewhat misleading. Nonetheless, a few recommendations are warrantable to accompany the choices just listed.

1) A semifictitious *persona* often becomes a trap for the writer simply because he has no real existence as a flesh-and-blood being, even in the writer's imagination. Gradually he is transformed from a generalized being into a prototype to which all vices or virtues can with impunity be attributed. The reader, meeting this bloodless character on page after page, develops an independence from him rather than the identification with him which was the author's aim in introducing him in the first place.

2) Making abstractions act as vital agents in a sentence is, on the whole, a good practice, principally because it is forceful and economical. The active verbs brighten and give movement to matter which might otherwise be heavy and static. The danger in this procedure is that the abstractions will become so independent that they obscure their derivation from separate events, that is, from the "facts" which are their ground and reason for being.

3, 4) The "editorial *we*" and the formal "one" are both such obvious conveniences that they have little vital juice in them. "We," particularly, is a convention which has lost much of its original weight. The true "editorial *we*," like the "royal *we*," is meant to convey the power of concerted action. The critical essay which uses "we" to mean "the author" is probably making the best of a bad situation: the writer wants to avoid the intrusion of himself-as-a-person which takes place if he uses the pronoun "I," and he wants also to avoid the awkwardness and heaviness of passive and impersonal constructions. There is one "we" which seems to have a better argument for existence, that which a writer uses when he *joins* the reader in speculation. If misused, however, it is likely to sound patronizing ("We don't want to make that sort of error, do we?"), but judiciously and honestly used it helps to strengthen the communication between writer and reader.

5) Direct address is proper for commands but likely to be annoyingly avuncular or magisterial when it is used to point out the application of statement to the reader's own life. When "you" is a substitute for the third-person indefinite pronoun, it does not carry those overtones, but it is still rather colloquial for formal expository prose.

6, 7) Impersonal constructions and the passive voice depend on the static verbs of equivalence (copulative verbs) and therefore have a certain rigidity about them. Moreover, as noted above, they tend to obscure the *real* agent of whatever relationships are predicated. Certainly they are not always to be avoided; neither are they to be preferred if alternatives readily present themselves.

The grammar and rhetoric of the sentence are, of course, to some extent also the grammar and rhetoric of the paragraph and of the essay or book. Increased dimension raises additional problems for the writer, however, and at the same time offers him scope for more complex effects. Those problems and effects are the subject of the following chapter.

❂ *Idea and Order in the*
Paragraph and Essay

There is no good way of writing well and also of writing easily.

ANTHONY TROLLOPE, *Barchester Towers*

THE PARAGRAPH may best be described as Dr. Johnson described a woman preacher: the triumph of art over nature. There are no paragraphs in nature. They are the product of art, though—as Polixenes remarks in *The Winter's Tale* about cultivated flowers—it is "an art that nature makes."

The best way to consider the paragraph is to think of it as the result of deliberate arrangement, a calculated disposition of parts. Paragraphs are not often written that way; but that is the way they have to be re-written, and the sooner a writer learns to bring some of the discipline of revision to the original process of writing, the better off he will be. A risk is involved, of course, and sometimes the risk is greater than the possible gain. In the full flood of inspiration or of overpowering conviction, restraint may be unwise or even futile. The result is likely to be greater need for revision later, but that may not matter. When, however, the mind is not so much fired to the job of writing as set to it—a condition more ordinary, by far—skill at order is not only a saver of time and energy but an important provoker of thought.

Typographically, a paragraph is simply several lines of type, the first of which usually begins some distance to the right of the margin. Logically, it is a coordination of related assertions. Rhetorically, it is a series of sentences so ordered as to achieve a single major effect. The range is from fact to hope, of course, but it is with the ideal that we must grapple to make any progress at all. We shall not worry about typography, but as elsewhere logic and rhetoric claim our attention. If a paragraph is a progression of sentences, how can the separate claims of logic and of rhetoric most efficiently be realized?

What is needed here is some governing metaphor, and the one we propose is theatrical. The paragraph is a scene from a play. As a separate scene, it has characters and action; as one of many scenes in the play, it has some meaning and function beyond itself. The writer is playwright. His concern is to make the scene-paragraph represent something that is happening. That means distinguishing actor from action from acted-upon. It means supplying sufficient matter to give the action appropriate size; it means providing motivation and sequence and result. It means forecasting and concluding and connecting. And, perhaps most of all, it means keeping the actor in focus throughout—a matter that will be discussed quite specifically later, under the heading of "Coherence."

The metaphor may seem fanciful, but it is far from that. These are the central matters of structure and development (the thesis statement or topic sentence, devices of expansion, systems of arrangement, opening and closing and connecting strategies, coherence). And the writer with a sound sense of craft is constantly aware as he writes not only of what he is saying but of what he is doing. He deploys sentences, which is precisely what the playwright does with characters.

1) *THE TOPIC SENTENCE*

The topic sentence (or thesis statement, as it is sometimes called) is a more or less fictitious entity. It does sometimes make an appearance in so many words, of course, but fully as often it is not something written but what is meant by what has been written. That is, the topic sentence is something a reader extracts from a paragraph and something a writer has in mind as the unity he wants to achieve. The schoolboy notion of a topic sentence as the big firecracker from which a string of little firecrackers is suspended, each due to go off with a tiny "pop" when the big one is ignited, has little relationship to the truth. An accomplished writer of prose is much too well aware of the weaving required for a good representation of his thought to lay it out, thread by thread, with no regard for the original design. But accomplished writers no longer need to read analyses of this kind, so it is wise to consider, even in half-fictional terms, the problems of those who do.

Paragraphs can be written, of course, in firecracker order. For some purposes, that may be their best order. An explanation of process, for example, is most efficient if the steps of the process are chronologically catalogued:

> An omelet requires strictly fresh ingredients and a skilled hand. The yolks and whites of the eggs are separated first and the yolks beaten slightly with a fork until they are well blended. To the blended yolks is then added. . . .

Even in this simple process, a strategy is apparent, and a part of that strategy is the opening sentence which serves as a kind of warning and summary-in-advance.

A more helpful view of the topic sentence comes from thinking of it, not necessarily as some single grammatically complete utterance in a paragraph, but as a central proposition which it is the business of the paragraph to develop. It is, in this view, a succinct summary of the paragraph; or, to return to the metaphor introduced above, it is the meaning of the scene.

Consider, for example, the uncomplicated sentence that follows as the "core" or "topic" to be developed:

> The battlement speech in *Macbeth* expresses perfectly the despair that follows discovery in a tragedy.

As discussion will show, there is plenty of matter in this sentence for more than a paragraph, but at this point we can examine its possibilities for expansion without concern for the eventual product. Simple grammatical analysis will give us a start.

SUBJECT	The battlement speech in *Macbeth*
VERB	expresses perfectly
OBJECT	the despair that follows discovery in a tragedy.

Now the subject of a sentence is always the "given" of the proposition. It is the thing of which something is to be predicated and is therefore above suspicion, so to speak, for the moment. Its being above suspicion does not mean, however, that it is necessarily self-explanatory, and a certain amount of information may be needed in this example to identify the speech, as a preliminary to satisfaction of other obligations implicit in the sentence. The verb makes the first step beyond what is to be taken for granted in the proposition, and in this instance that step is a big one. The meaning of "expresses" as it is used here must be explained and, one would expect, illustrated as well; but it cannot be adequately elaborated apart from its object, which requires some attention to the generalization that despair follows discovery in a tragedy as well as elucidation of the terms "despair," "tragedy," and particularly "discovery." Since verb and object are both, as parts of a proposition, that which is "to be proved," they can be linked in the single term "predicate" and the sentence redivided in this fashion:

SUBJECT	The battlement speech in *Macbeth*
PREDICATE	expresses perfectly the despair that follows discovery in a tragedy.

Now what is gained by this division? Simply a separation of two distinct obligations which the writer takes upon himself when he writes the sentence: 1) to explain the subject, and 2) to explain and defend ("prove" in the sense used earlier in this book) the predication. If the core sentence is to be expanded only into a paragraph, the writer will limit explanation and defense accordingly. If it is to be expanded into an essay, he will plan to take one paragraph or several for each of his obligations. If it is into several paragraphs that the expansion is to fall, each of those paragraphs, too, will have its core sentence, and each core sentence will likewise be divisible into subject and predicate, laying upon the writer obligations like those already illustrated.

As long as he fulfills his obligations, the writer is free to devise whatever strategy he thinks most likely to suit his matter, his purpose, and his reader. For that reason, what is conventionally called the "topic sentence" may be broken into parts or, if kept intact, may be placed at one of several places in the paragraph, or be so transformed by rhetoric that its presence comes more through the "sense" of the paragraph than through any explicit statement. A paragraph picked almost at random from the writing of an English essayist and novelist will illustrate the point:

> No, I distrust Great Men. They produce a desert of uniformity around them and often a pool of blood too, and I always feel a little man's pleasure when they come a cropper. Every now and then one reads in the newspapers some such statement as: "The *coup d'état* appears to have failed, and Admiral Toma's whereabouts is at present unknown." Admiral Toma had probably every qualification for being a Great Man—an iron will, personal magnetism, dash, flair, sexlessness—but fate was against him, so he retires to unknown whereabouts instead of parading history with his peers. He fails with a completeness which no artist and no lover can experience, because with them the process of creation is itself an achievement, whereas with him the only possible achievement is success.
>
> E. M. FORSTER, *Two Cheers for Democracy*

The paragraph is not so much an expansion of any stated proposition as the progress through several propositions which, taken together, culminate in a core of meaning, a something which we might say the paragraph is "about":

> Those men who are conventionally called "great," unlike those who act out of love or out of the desire to create, leave nothing behind them if they fail.

The author's assertion of distrust, his many ironic turns of phrase, his fiictitious Admiral Toma are all stratagems, and it is to them that the richness of the paragraph is almost entirely indebted.

The sentence which comes closest to being a "topic sentence" in the paragraph just quoted is the last one. In another paragraph, it might be the second or a middle sentence. The location of the topic sentence, then, if indeed it is ever stated in so many words, will vary. The paragraph may move from or toward it, or it may rise to it and fall away from it like a wave sweeping the shore.

2) DEVICES OF EXPANSION

Whatever the location of the core sentence, its work is carried on by the other sentences of the paragraph. The division of that work—explanation of subject, explanation and defense of predication—has already been presented. Now it is important to examine the means by which writers do the explaining and the defending. The warning that appears again and again in this book deserves repetition at this point: to describe the devices of expansion is not to suggest that writers think of them as devices or that they consciously "fill out" each statement as though they were stuffing a pillowcase with feathers. To repeat, the expansion is (a) a necessary explanation of the core substance and (b) a part of the strategy by which the author contrives to render his full meaning. It is not separate from the core of the paragraph but is actually the medium through which the core of meaning is transmitted. Treating each device in isolation falsifies the actual situation somewhat, but it is the most convenient and useful procedure and is therefore the one chosen.

The explanations that follow are intended to fill out and sharpen a section of the chapter on persuasion. There, these "devices" are presented as persuasive forms that subject matter takes. In this chapter the focus has shifted to what the writer himself can do to make his paragraphs develop their core richly and decisively.

The writer's most common device for development is *restatement*. Despite the dangers of repetition, the simple fact is that a certain amount of repetition is necessary in the use of language, not only for emphasis, but quite as much for full expression of whatever is to be said. Restatement is not a completely literal repetition, of course, and that is why it succeeds. It is a second or a third attempt to weave a design from the strands of thought; if the first does not succeed, one of the later ones may, or all of them together will give a fuller reproduction than any one. Note how restatement works in this paragraph:

> Each generation takes a special pleasure in removing the household gods of its parents from their pedestals and consigning them to the cupboard. The prophet or pioneer, after being at first declared to be unintelligible or absurd, has a brief spell of popularity, after which he is said to be conventional, and then antiquated. We may find more than one reason for this. A movement has more to fear from its disciples than from its critics. The great man is linked to his age by his weakest side; and his epigoni, who are not great men, caricature his message and make it ridiculous. Besides, every movement is a reaction, and generates counter-reactions. The pendulum swings backwards and forwards. Every institution not

only carries within it the seeds of its own dissolution, but prepares the way for its most hated rival.

W. R. INGE, *Outspoken Essays*

No one would characterize this paragraph as repetitive; yet it is full of restatement. The second sentence is the first sentence looked at in different perspective; the "pendulum" sentence uses a metaphor to restate the one that precedes it; and the final sentence, which is as close to being the topic sentence of the paragraph as any, is an accumulation and repetition of parts of the first, the fourth, and the fifth sentences. Good restatement enriches and colors explanation and is therefore invaluable as a means of conveying the complexity of thought.

Example provides the most obvious means of expansion, and just because it is obvious it is uniquely suited to the job of clarifying the obscure and of making the general specific and the abstract concrete. Although they do not constitute formal proof—one swallow does not make a summer, as the saying goes—examples are really attempts at proof because they display the phenomenal evidence which is the ground for general statements. For that reason, they must be treated with respect; a faulty example is bad not simply because it is in itself inappropriate but because its failure detracts from the authority of the generalization it is supposed to support.

Whether or not an example needs to have attention called to its character as example depends on its context and its length. An example which is only a phrase or single sentence will generally not need any indicator of its presence:

> The most enlightened members of the state—*the scribes, the councilors, and the wise men of the inner temple*—have for a long time predicted this event.

> Men of lofty vision and deep conviction are often regarded with suspicion by their fellow men. *Socrates was condemned to die for corrupting the youth of Athens; Jesus was crucified for blasphemy.* Yet vision and conviction, being themselves incorruptible, have their way in the world.

Examples of greater length are sometimes treated more formally. Either they are set off from the main body of the text, as the examples above are set off, or they are preceded by a signal of some sort:

> The life of a President is so exacting that it must be relieved by regular periods of physical exertion. Every President within recent memory has found need for the stimulation of muscle tone and the relaxation of nervous tension which come from a vigorous hour or so of brisk activity. Mr. Eisenhower, *for example,* played golf several days a week; Mr. Truman used to take a fast morning walk; Roosevelt swam daily in the White House pool, and his predecessor, Hoover, was an ardent fisherman.

> The fable has a double tradition in Western literature. From Æsop it inherits a certain moral solemnity; from La Fontaine, the habit of

ironical reflection on the disparity between appearance and reality and between precept and practice in human affairs. Although the fable is no longer so popular as it once was, its modern practitioners have found it a useful instrument for satire of man and morality alike. *The two modern fabulists who come most quickly to mind*—Edward Lear and James Thurber—are both swift to detect the ludicrous in action and precept, but neither is so blunt as La Fontaine in exposing it.

The use of *supporting data* for statements, like that of examples, is a convenient and obvious means of clarifying and documenting whatever is predicated. The kind of data will be determined, of course, by the nature of the statement, and no illustrations are necessary here: statistics, tables, graphs, enumerations, diagrams, and citations of text, for instance, are all relevant. The means of handling such material within an essay are as varied as the nature of the material, and generalization about procedures is therefore difficult. The practice of relegating extensive documentation to footnotes or appendixes is, in the main, a wise one, particularly if the exposition in the text itself does not depend on such documentation for its clarity. Where clarity is at stake, the supporting data should remain in the text and there be exposed as economically and attached as organically as possible.

Both example and supporting data are largely substantive, though they have strategic value, too. Some other devices of expansion have less to do with support, or proof, of assertions than with their illumination. Among them, *anecdote* is one of the most valuable. Now it is clear that an anecdote is, in one sense, also an attempt to insist on the soundness of a statement by showing its representation in experience. But the sense of the particular and informal which is part of an anecdote detracts from its value as documentation at the same time as it adds to its value as illustration. Whether the anecdote is historical or contemporary, about the actions of someone well known or about the writer's personal experience, it adds the power that storytelling has for all readers. Abstractions, after all, are the dried leaves of event; to use anecdote as an expansion of a general statement is therefore to do no more than bring it back to life.

Like anecdote, *quotation* and *allusion* are more dramatic than substantive in character. They are different from anecdote, however, in being oblique aids to clarity and completeness. They suggest the rightness or the meaningfulness of preceding statements by proposing corollaries in the experience of writer and reader, corollaries which are called to mind by a familiar phrase or by mention of some figure or event which has taken on a particular character in the public consciousness. To describe Woodrow Wilson as "America's Robespierre" is to clarify and, at the same time, to add information so extensive that it would take pages of exposition to equal it. The problem which rises from the use of allusion is readily apparent from the example: if the allusion is within the reader's range of experience, it may be wonderfully effective; if it is outside that range, it may be annoying and will certainly do little to clarify. To some extent, the same thing may be said of the use of quotations, especially when they are presented elliptically:

> The medieval warning, *De gustibus* . . . , is more pertinent to fashions in clothing than to styles in art.

Many quotations, however, are so much a part of the public treasury that a writer may be almost sure of his reader's familiarity with them. The problem with them is that their very familiarity may annoy. A writer must simply steer his way carefully between obscurity and triteness if he chooses to amplify meaning by the use of allusion and quotation. Moreover, if he is wise, he will be sparing of both, for a text which relies on these two devices very heavily is likely to look like a connoisseur's display of dainties rather than a firm and rich elucidation of thought.

3) ORDER

The classical structure of the oration was for a long time the model for ordering expository prose. Its three main divisions provide a scheme which is at once handsome and comprehensive: introduction (*exordio*), body (*præcognitio, partitio, explicatio, amplificatio, applicatio*), and conclusion (*peroratio*). There is a brief rhetorical opening; then a careful statement and dissection of the thesis, followed by an analysis of each part, an elaboration and a direct application to the life of the listener; finally, a summation designed to bring the weight of the thesis to bear on the listeners' feeling and on their desire for action. Implicit in the scheme is a recognition that reason is paramount but that it must be linked with feeling before it will produce action. And implicit also is the condition of argument—an assertion whose truth it is the purpose of the exposition to prove beyond question. Everything is taken care of in the most orderly fashion: terms are defined, possible ambiguities eliminated, implications and assumptions explained, proofs adduced, and examples provided. Beneath the formal structure an almost infinite variety is possible in the organization or order of matters in each part. One section may proceed by classification, another by contrasts, a third by chronology, and so on. Yet, whatever the internal variety, the enclosing structure remains firm and almost relentless.

The formal pattern of the classical oration is no longer in fashion, not even in sermons, which for a long time continued to exploit it after it had largely disappeared from general use. In its place—partly, no doubt, from analogy with discoveries in the natural sciences—there has grown a tendency to make even expository writing "express" in its form the nature of its substance. It is not easy to say how form and substance can be made one, and it may be an exaggeration to speak of equivalence where only appropriateness is possible. Yet, whatever the formula, it is certainly true that some material, used for a particular purpose, is better dealt with in one form than in another. A particular argument, for instance, may achieve its greatest clarity and power in the form of a dialogue; one sort of proof may be most appropriately presented by the orderly tracing of cause and effect, another by the uninterrupted accumulation of supporting data; classification may best suit analysis; or chronology, narration. No general rule is possible, of course, for writers' intentions vary so widely that only ingenious combinations of form are sufficient to satisfy them. It is possible, however, to describe several kinds of organization and to point out uses and abuses of each.

Order by *classification* is the most obvious means of organization for expository prose, and it comes closest to the oratorical pattern mentioned above. The proposition which is the core of the essay (e.g., "Washington's policy of avoiding 'foreign entanglements' is no longer possible for any civilized country") is first divided, as suggested above, into "subject" and "predicate." The subject ("Washington's policy of avoiding 'foreign entanglements' ") is explained by reference to his Farewell Address and, in order that the policy may be accurately represented, by some account of the events during his tenure of office. Then the predicate ("is no longer possible for any civilized country") is developed—in this case, "proved"—by a presentation of arguments classified, let us say, as "economic," "political," and "moral." The classification itself arises from an initial listing of arguments and from the observation of similarities among those arguments. A decision about which of the three classes to present first depends in part on the strength of the evidence for each and in part on the particular emphasis a writer wishes to provide. A contributor to the *Christian Century,* for instance, might discuss all three classes but elaborate only "moral" intensively, placing it third in the series so that it might come as a climax to the whole line of argument. A political analyst in *The New York Times* might subordinate "moral" and "economic"; an editorialist for *New Masses* would undoubtedly make "economic" the climactic classification. Classification always depends in part on the observer's way of looking at a matter, so it is not surprising at all that various writers will classify and develop the same matter differently. Nor is it undesirable that they do so. The important thing is that the classifications, whatever they are, be borne out by the material and that they be sufficient to encompass it.

It is clear that order by classification requires that the subject matter

be such as to lend itself to categories, to more or less watertight compart-
ments. Classification is the handmaiden of analysis when analysis is concerned with what is static. To use it as the order for explaining a process
is therefore inadvisable, for it reduces emphasis on action, which is the
heart of process.

A second, and also common, order is that of *cause and effect*. Where
classification throws emphasis on substance, cause and effect throws it on
the active relationship between substances, on the alteration which results
from their coming into contact with each other. Obviously, then, it is
particularly useful for the explanation of process. At its simplest, this
kind of order may seem to present no problems: cause precedes effect in
fact and should therefore precede it in report on fact. Yet even to explain
the chain of events which turns water into ice requires attention to more
than one cause—to pressure as well as to temperature. Perhaps it is the
term itself that misleads one into thinking of cause and effect as simple;
"causes and effects" would be far more accurate, for few things happen
in this world as the result of a single cause and few causes have only a
single effect. This multiplicity and variety require that the writer select
among causes and effects those relevant to his purposes (all are relevant
to the action itself), and it is in the act of selection that trouble is likely
to occur.

The writer who uses cause and effect as a principle of order must be
alert to causes and effects which do not at once meet the eye. He must be
ready to explore for more of both and should perhaps begin from the
assumption that apparent causes and effects may or may not be the most
important or even the real ones. Once he has made his selection, he can
proceed from one to the other in either direction, making the choice of
direction depend on whether he wants emphasis to fall on causes or effects.
If he finds, and decides to deal with, a plurality of causes and effects, he
will also find the order of cause and effect insufficient and will almost
certainly have to call on another principle of order to act in subordinate
capacity. Think, for example, of the problem of explaining the causes
of so simple an event as a summer shower. Do we begin with today's wind
and heat or with the warm front which began to develop last week in
Texas and the breakup of an ice pack in Greenland? For practical purposes the writer must restrict the causes and effects he considers according
to their proximity to the event and according to their necessity; those
that are distant and, though relevant, either not absolutely necessary to
the effect or not of major importance, he must perforce ignore or skim
over lightly. Those that are immediate and essential he retains or brings
to the fore, marshaling them in such fashion as to make their relationships apparent. The dominant connection which he must exploit in this
procedure is a hybrid, a cross between "therefore" and "thereafter" which
unites time and cause. Where relationships are purely associative, of

course, that order is manifestly improper; but even where they are derivative, it may be misleading. Unless the lines of causation and response can be clearly sorted and exposed, it may be better to limit oneself to simple succession, carefully avoiding any indication of another relationship. The cumulative effect will be much the same, and the particular links of the chain will not then be subject to criticism.

In human experience, events seem to be inevitably related in time, whatever their other relationships may be. It is natural, therefore, that *chronology* should be an important principle of organization, even in nonnarrative prose. Its importance is enhanced, however, by the fact that all writing and speaking are also involved in duration so that even in pure description of a static object chronology is implicated: "What shall I describe *first?*" the novice asks. There would seem, then, to be two kinds of chronological order: that which records the actual progression of events (real chronology), and that which represents the experience of the observer (subjective chronology).

Real chronology may be manipulated for effect, the writer beginning, as Horace advised poets to do, in the middle of things, or at the beginning, or at the end. Subjective, or psychological, chronology is already a manipulation of the fact, generally a manipulation for the sake of emphasis: the writer begins by describing the nose because it is the nose to which he wishes to give prominence, or he holds back from describing the nose until the end of his account for the very same reason. Most expository prose stays within the sphere of real chronology, but the informal essay and, in recent years, even the speculative essay have shown a disposition to take liberties with it, to fuse the time of conscious, rational experience with the time of memory and feeling in which conventional order is inverted, distorted, or reduced to simultaneity. The effects achieved by such freedom are its best defense; like syncopation in music, they are achievable only when a strong sense of real chronology lies behind them. The amateur writer does well, then, to make sure that he can manipulate the patterns of ordinary chronology before he attempts to represent the extraordinary chronologies of subjective experience.

Aristotle noted that the ability to detect likenesses is one of the sure signs of intelligence, and it is on this ability (which, of course, implies the ability to detect differences) that he based his system of classification and his theory of definition. The habit of creating order by *comparison* and by *contrast* seems, as a matter of fact, to be almost as natural to man as thought itself. Metaphor lies at the root of language and is fundamentally comparative in nature, exposing a linkage which is not patent but which is nonetheless real. To some degree all comparisons are useful in the same way—they call attention to characteristics which might otherwise escape the eye. An exposition of the concept of piety in The Book of Job may be greatly enriched by a comparative exposition of the same concept in Aeschylus' *Prometheus Bound,* the details of one revealing the absence or transformation of those details in the other. A discussion of a republican government's right of eminent domain profits from comparison of that right with a king's prerogative of entry and use for defense of the realm, the extent and power of the former becoming apparent only when the much more limited royal authority is described. Besides calling attention to detail, comparisons are particularly useful when the purpose of an exposition is to aggrandize or to demean; setting two objects or events against each other makes one into a touchstone or foil, a standard by which the other can be measured.

Managing a comparison is not easy, whether its purpose is simply to describe likenesses and differences or to solicit approval of one matter at the expense of another. If the explanation of each is developed separately, the force of comparison is diminished; if the objects or events are developed concurrently, each characteristic being balanced immediately against its foil or counterpart, the comparison becomes an annoying seesaw. Somehow the sense of integrity and the force of relationship must both be retained, a feat best accomplished by a judicious use of both procedures, coupled with another ordering device, perhaps that of classification. To return to the "piety" example mentioned above: the comparison might begin with a brief account of the cultural context of each of the works, using their approximate dates of composition as the initial links between them, then touching on the differences in the cultural context, and finally drawing the two together again on the subject matter of the essay—the embodiment in each of a concept of piety. At this point there comes an opportunity for further unifying by definition and by classification: determining the meaning of "piety" for this essay and stating the considerations relevant to exploration of the concept in these two works. The "body" of the essay may well continue the alternation between union and division: for each of the considerations to be developed, a sentence or more to point out the relevance of that consideration to both the Greek and the Hebrew work, then a point-by-point comparison of passages which illustrate the similarity or difference. And so on until the entire ground is covered.

Most comparisons, of course, are a compound of likenesses and differences, and the order of presentation is affected by the general rule of emphasis: the subordinate precedes the principal. This is true of a whole essay as well as paragraphs or sections within it. By the same token, the place for concession or qualification is early rather than late. In the example given, if the differences between the two concepts of piety outweigh the likenesses, it is with the likenesses that the essay should begin. The essay thus falls "naturally" into two major divisions. Within each, subdivisions will more or less imitate the arrangement of the larger unit to which they belong.

Because comparison implies a balancing, this kind of order provides opportunities for rhetorical parallels of all kinds, an opportunity not really satisfied by bare connectives like "on the other hand" and "in contrast."

> The uppermost idea with Hellenism is to see things as they really are; the uppermost idea with Hebraism is conduct and obedience. Nothing can do away with this ineffaceable difference. The Greek quarrel with the body and its desires is that they hinder right thinking; the Hebrew quarrel with them is that they hinder right acting. "He that keepeth the law, happy is he"; "Blessed is the man that feareth the Eternal, that delighteth greatly in His commandments";—that is the Hebrew notion of felicity; and, pursued with passion and tenacity, this notion would not let the Hebrew rest till, as is well known, he had at last got out of the law a network of prescriptions to enwrap his whole life, to govern every moment of it, every impulse, every action. The Greek notion of felicity, on the other hand, is perfectly conveyed in these words of a great French moralist: *"C'est le bonheur des hommes"*—when? when they abhor that which is evil? no;— when they exercise themselves in the law of the Lord day and night? no; —when they die daily? no;—when they walk about the New Jerusalem with palms in their hands? no;—but when they think aright, when their thought hits: *"quand ils pensent juste."*. . . The governing idea of Hellenism is *spontaneity of consciousness;* that of Hebraism, *strictness of conscience.*
>
> MATTHEW ARNOLD, *Hebraism and Hellenism*

Because comparison emphasizes extremes of likeness and of difference, its strategies are useless when emphasis on *degree* is what the writer wants to achieve. Pairing the abstract and concrete, for example, calls for the procedures of comparison. Pairing the general and particular calls for something quite different. Abstractness is a matter not of degree but of kind: a word is either abstract or concrete. But a word may be more or less general, more or less particular. For this condition of more-or-less, a rhetoric of gradualism is necessary. The scale from particular to general may begin or stop wherever the writer finds his purpose best served. A girl in Thornton Wilder's *Our Town* awes her friends by displaying a letter addressed to: "Jane Crofut; The Crofut Farm; Grover's Corners; Sutton County; New Hampshire; United States of America; Continent of North America; Western Hemisphere; the Earth; the Solar System; the Universe; the Mind of God." The rhetoric in this instance is that of completeness. Whether complete or partial, the only cautions necessary are against confusing the distance between leaps and against leaping in both directions at once or successively in opposite directions.

The five principles of organization discussed so far rely more or less heavily on a sixth, that of *climax,* or order of importance. It is no secret that emphasis, in a sentence as in a paragraph or an essay, is stronger at the beginning and at or near the end than in the middle. The order of the English sentence is partly responsible for that fact, no doubt, but more responsible is the human habit of expectation. Impressive climaxes and satisfying resolutions depend on the preparation that precedes them, and for that reason the usual order of matter is from the less to the more important. Now, as in chronological order, a writer may achieve special effect by doing the unexpected, by using an anticlimactic order. In general, however, that practice is useful only for surprise or for brief and violent emphasis, and it imposes upon its user the problem of retaining the reader's attention and of developing a stable perspective on the subject matter once the opening cannon has been fired.

Few essays of any length depend on a single organizing strategy for the good reason that readers expect a measure of variety in prose just as they expect a measure of uniformity in verse. Moreover, a single principle of order is seldom sufficient to provide for the complexity of the matter it is intended to control. A flexible strategy, on the other hand, makes it possible for a writer to exploit the full resources of whatever material he has at hand. The professional writer is able to shift from one kind of order to another without taking thought. The tyro may have to lay out his strategy well in advance and follow its successive maneuvers scrupulously to avoid a rout. For him an *outline* is important and often essential.

4) THE OUTLINE

As the underlying metaphor implies, an outline describes the circumference of an essay and of each of its various parts. If, then, the earlier contention about topic sentences is sound, an outline is the orderly presentation of main assertions, those which are to be expanded by various devices. To make it any less than that is to respect form and to ignore substance. An outline for the projected essay on piety, for example, is little short of useless in this state:

    I. Introduction
    II. Body
        A. Similarities
            1. Idea of God
            2. Idea of man
            3. Idea of punishment
        B. Differences
            1. Idea of God
            2. Idea of man
            3. Idea of relationship
            4. Idea of afterlife
                .   .   .
                .   .   .
    III. Conclusion

Yet that is what "outline" means to many who have been taught to look upon it as a kind of ritual preliminary to writing. A good outline is not a ritual; it springs from thought and should capitalize on its origin. In its early state it may be no more than a series of assertions, set down (elliptically, perhaps) just as they occur to the writer:

1) Job and Prometheus know their inferiority in power
2) Job habitually dutiful, Pr. habitually resentful
3) Greeks thought of afterlife as a dark continuation of existence, not punishment or reward
4) Job patient under affliction, rationalizing at first
5) Both fall from high to low estate: Pr. for deliberate acts of rebellion, Job not
6) Hebrew idea of Sheol (afterlife) as a comfortable extension of life after death
7) Both pieces probably written in 5th century B.C.
8) Hebrew and Gr. culture separate but both East Asian
9) Hebrew culture more isolated than Greek
10) *PB* a religious drama; Job half drama, half poem?
11) *PB* not a speculation but a demonstration of agreed-upon concepts

One assertion suggests another and the accumulation soon suggests the possible combinations and the appropriate means of organization. From the list an outline grows which not only guides the writing of the essay but stimulates it and provides a clearly focused test for its achievement. An outline developed from such a series of assertions is immediately useful to the writer. With the outline before him, he can work swiftly and efficiently, explaining and expanding each assertion, "filling in" the outline with the corroborative and illustrative data he has accumulated by research and reflection.

THESIS: The treatments of piety and impiety in *Job* and *Prometheus Bound* reflect the most important differences between traditional Hebraic and early Greek religious belief.

1) Although Hebraic culture is more isolated than Greek, both are East Asian.
2) Fatalism, strong sense of human inferiority, common to both; so also a vigorous tradition of the hero and saviour of a group or people.
3) Hebraic view of afterlife (Sheol), like Greek Hades, reflects uncertainty about judgment hereafter for acts committed here. Importance of justice vs. rule of inscrutable God.
4) Main difference between concept of single God and of a pantheon; distance between Job and God greater than that between Prometheus and Zeus.
5) Difference reflected in the two works.
   a. Job habitually dutiful; Prometheus independent.
   b. Job patient under affliction; Pr. resentful.
   c. Job finally distrustful of reasoning; Pr. full of reasoning on his own account.

6) Idea of a "testing" of Job consistent with relationship (See 4); Prometheus' ordeal not a test but a punishment.
7) Forms of the two works also reflect difference.
   a. *Job* part drama, part poem of speculation; its drama full of suspense (wagers, tests, peril, victory, reward).
   b. *PB* a religious drama designed to illustrate orthodox concepts; drama ritualized, outcome foreknown.
8) Form and content together develop attitude toward piety in each work.
   a. *Job*—piety is waiting patiently to understand will of God.
   b. *PB*—(by negative illustration) piety is obedience.

There is another use of the outline which must not be overlooked. Besides serving as a guide to composition, it may be a tool for reorganizing what has already been composed. Some writers like to release the pressure of thought within them by writing it out without preliminary concern for neat and efficient order. When they have temporarily exhausted their resources, they turn a critical eye on what they have produced, summarizing it in outline form just as it occurs and then rearranging sections for clearer directions and sounder emphasis. The procedure is attractive insofar as it allows a writer to rely on the rush of thought as long as it lasts; it is perhaps less attractive in the later stage, when by rewriting and reorganizing he must make up for the inadequacies of what he has produced. An early outline will reduce the amount of reconstruction necessary when the first draft is completed, though it may not eliminate all reconstruction and certainly will not eliminate some amount of rewriting. Most people who have something to write use outlines both at the head and the tail of their work, even when they do not write them down. The form in which they cast the outline, if they do write it down, is of relatively small importance as long as the principal assertions are precisely stated and then arranged so that their relationships are made clear and so that the whole plan displays a steady forward movement.

5) COHERENCE

The three traditional goddesses of rhetoric—unity, coherence, and emphasis—are, suitably, the deities which all of the matters discussed in this section are supposed to serve. Of the three, *coherence* calls for special attention. Although sheer bulk may impose emphasis and a rough unity on the matter of an exposition, it is no aid—and is often a detriment— to coherence. Now coherence can be best defined by reference to its etymology; literally, it means a "sticking together," and in rhetoric it is the term used to designate the connectedness between parts large and small. Although it is clear that coherence will be affected by the degree to which the materials of an essay are congruous (a discussion of three battles of the Civil War would achieve some coherence simply as a by-product of the unity of its subject matter), congruity is not alone sufficient.

The basic means of achieving coherence is by rational *arrangement* of material, a matter already adequately discussed. A second means is by the judicious use of *connectors,* a matter treated at the end of this chapter under the heading "transitions." Both means are largely structural, that is, concerned with the manipulation of blocks of expository matter. Within the blocks, of whatever size, and controlling their internal chemistry, several other means of achieving coherence may come into action. *Repetition,* for instance, whether of a key word or of the pattern of phrases, clauses, and sentences (parallel structure), calls attention to the relationship between parts and thus increases coherence. The use of a *key metaphor,* whose terms are introduced obliquely and unostentatiously over a long passage of prose, may draw the whole passage together most subtly. More effective and less "literary" than either repetition or the use of a key metaphor, however, is the development of coherence by control of *actor and action.*

A subject—personal or impersonal—performs an action which begins, proceeds to climax, and ends. The essay remains coherent as long as the actor and the action make their presence constantly felt; it becomes disconnected and diffuse when their presence is obscured. This theatrical metaphor shows its relevance most clearly, of course, when the subject is personal:

> With regard to this system, Ammianus has but two general comments to offer, and, of these, the first concerns the Roman aristocracy. In a number of striking passages, which have been used by Gibbon as the basis for a brilliant portrayal of contemporary imperial society, Ammianus lets himself go in a scathing indictment of this class. With Juvenalian scorn he stigmatizes the aimless frivolity of lives made possible only through swollen incomes derived from the exploitation of the provincials and consecrated to no purpose worthier than the ostentatious display of wealth and pride. He describes the incessant round of amusements, bathing, driving, hunting, yachting, and the exchange of hospitality, whereby the worthless aristocrats of his day sought to conceal the futility of their existence. He points with disgust to their moral and spiritual shortcomings, their cowardice and effeminacy, their avarice and wastefulness, their quickness to borrow, their slowness to repay; above all to the childish superstition which prompts them to resort, on the slightest pretext, to diviners and soothsayers who prey upon their fears. This superstition he attributes to the lack of any serious principles of conduct, a defect for which they have themselves to blame, inasmuch as they have turned from the cultivation of the mind, rejecting the heritage of philosophy through which alone such principles may be attained, in order to immerse themselves in mere sensationalism. Accordingly, among their retainers, the crooner has replaced the philoso-

pher, the teacher of histrionics that of oratory; they seal their libraries like tombs, but construct for themselves hydraulic organs.

CHARLES NORRIS COCHRANE, *Christianity and Classical Culture*

Any subject may be treated as though it were personal and thus become the dominant presence in its development. Obviously, a lavish sequence of "he did" or "it did" sentences will be as annoying as a series of abrupt movements on stage, and it is to avoid abruptness that Cochrane varies the structure and length of sentences so carefully in the excerpt just presented. But there is no need for a slavish sequence in the first place. The actor may be given many names, by use of synonym and paraphrase; a series of actions may be so attached that only one mention of the actor is necessary for all; artful manipulation of syntax can place the actor at other than initial positions in the sentence without altering his grammatical and logical authority. All that is necessary is that the central figure and the central action dominate.

Now there is no denying that this formula for coherence is oversimple. It is nonetheless a useful one, often useful for actual composition, nearly always useful for clearing up passages which have become muddled and directionless. Its weakness is that it operates from a fixed element, the actor, and this limits flexibility and movement. Some of that weakness is easily overcome by taking liberties with the "actor." For instance, in this opening paragraph from an essay about an English novelist, "novel" is the actor for the first two sentences and "novelist," for the ones that follow:

> The English novel has traditionally admitted of no exact definition, no generic purity. Written by all sorts and conditions of men, as was the poetic drama of the Elizabethans, it has been designed for as many kinds of readers. The responsibility of the nineteenth-century novelist was to offer his readers a "story"; apart from that, and within the bounds of Victorian taste, he might provide what *extras* he would—sociological, psychological, moral. Sweeping his puppets aside, he might preach the new ethics, expound the nature of things, prophesy the future actions of his characters or the future of human character; returning again to his puppets, he was free to pass in and out of their minds, now seeing through this pair of subsidiary eyes, now through that, now exerting the omniscience of his own sight.
>
> AUSTIN WARREN, *Rage for Order*

In the end, coherence is always a quality of thought rather than a manner of expression. The confused mind cannot produce coherent prose. On the other hand, the deliberate effort to make an obscure or muddled passage coherent by the use of rhetorical procedures often helps to reduce the mental confusion in which it originated.

6) INTRODUCTIONS

The frustrating experience of trying to find "a way to begin" is common to amateur and professional writer alike. Basically, it is usually a compound of dread and perplexity: dread of the labor involved in translating thought into language, and perplexity about which spring to touch first in order to set the machinery of composition going. Most writers resign themselves to the fact that they will begin a half-dozen times, throwing away one effort after another, until something satisfies enough so that writing can continue. Not infrequently, the sentence or paragraph which succeeded will later be abandoned entirely or completely altered, but if it has served its purpose the loss is a gain of one kind.

Because most serious writing goes through several stages, what is said about composition may apply to one stage but not to all. That is particularly true of introductions. It is more important to a writer that he get started than that his introduction be, at the outset, all that he wants it to be. Later, when he is revising, he can afford the energy to "polish up the handle on the big front door" of his essay, and these remarks are therefore directed to that final stage of his work.

The cursory glance taken in an earlier chapter at the articles in a single issue of the New York *Times Magazine* disclosed several strategies for introducing the subject and for engaging the reader's attention. The more "popular" the magazine, the greater will be the effort to relate the text to the reader's casual experience and the less will be the effort to make him rise out of his casual concerns into the particular world of the article before him. Ordinarily, the superficiality and sensationalism of an introduction will be consistent with the quality and manner of the exposition which follows it. For the writer of serious expository prose, directed in the main at those who may be assumed to have an initial readiness to be informed, it is therefore not necessary to provide further discussion of the opening maneuvers of less sober writing.

The aim of the introductory sentence or paragraph of a critical essay should be to get things moving: to indicate the topic of discussion, to give information about the limitations to be placed on that topic, and to set, or at least hint at, the tone of what is to follow. All this should be done as compactly as possible. Purely mechanical interposition of the writer is the sure mark of the amateur. This does not necessarily mean that use of the first person is bad, although it is true that "I" is a difficult pronoun to manage in many ways. Consider this example:

> I firmly believe that the honor system should be substituted for the present proctored examination system. I shall attempt in the following paragraphs to convince the reader of this.

Now, the first "I" is without question justifiable because this is an expression of opinion, and the writer wants the reader to know that it is his own opinion he is expressing. He could have done so, of course, by writing, "An honor system should be substituted for the present proctored examination system," and before he is done, having hunted for phrases to keep the "I" going—"in my opinion," "it seems to me," "as I see it"— he may wish he had. But "I firmly believe" is not entirely bad and even has the advantage of directness and simplicity on its side.

The same cannot be said for the second sentence. Here the writer enters though his presence has no value. At the moment he should be getting on to defend his revolutionary proposal, he is holding up a placard which reads, "This way to the main works."

The series of introductory sentences below illustrates clearly the process of improvement in the making of introductions which a student might practice in his own writing.

1) In the following paragraphs I shall compare and contrast views on American society as they were expressed by two foreigners writing about one hundred and fifty years apart.

2) Although one hundred and fifty years separate their views on American Society, there are many similarities between the observations of Crèvecœur and Müller-Freienfels.

3) Although their observations are separated by one hundred and fifty years of extensive social change, both Crèvecœur and Müller-Freienfels see that the most distinguishing characteristic of American society is the leveling process.

CONCLUSIONS

There are two common faults in the concluding sections of students' papers. One is the reintroduction of the mechanical "I."

Thus I have shown how one can obtain a synthesis of Martius yellow in shorter time by a reduction of the number of steps in the initial process.

The other might be called the "pious hope." It usually appears in some such form as this:

If more men today would capture the great vision of St. Augustine's *City of God,* there would perhaps be no need for a United Nations.

The faults point to their own correction. A conclusion should be no more general than the essay it concludes; its job is to restate, as adroitly as possible, the principal matter and the tone of the preceding text. Rewritten, the examples given above might read:

This eliminates a third step in the initial process for synthesizing Martius yellow and reduces the time for the whole operation to two hours and thirty-five minutes.

The *City of God* is all of these things—history and theology, philosophical speculation and textual criticism—but above all it is a vision of the world redeemed by a "new Adam," Jesus Christ.

7) TRANSITIONAL WORDS AND PHRASES

If there is one difficulty that harasses students more than any other, it is the linking together of sentences and paragraphs. In large part, good transitional structures are a corollary of good organization; the author who is completely in command of his work, who knows just where he is going as he writes, will have no trouble with transitions. But even for the professional writer, the occasions are few in which he knows exactly where his writing will lead him. For him, transitional words and phrases are a means of tacking down the gains he has made, the ground he has covered. For his reader, they become signals of considerable importance.

Literally, "transition" means "a crossing." In the practice of exposition, the transition acts as a bridge between sentences, between groups of sentences, between paragraphs and sections. Moreover, it is a bridge with a direction sign: it not only takes the reader across but it tells him where he is going and where he has been. Explicitly, *a transition reveals relationship*. The possible relationships are many: cause to effect, general to particular or particular to general, supplementation, restriction, concession, and so on. The writer can readily decide which relationship exists between units by asking such questions as these:

> What do I want to accomplish in the sentence I am about to write? Am I simply adding information to that already given? Am I presenting conflicting matter? Do I wish to make a concession? prove a point? present a reason for something's being so? show the next step in a process? Is this sentence to be illustrative only or will it further the discussion? Does it define? assert? support?

Once the relationship is known, a proper connective can be selected. To make that selection, one must know the precise effect of conjunctions and other transitional words and phrases. Even the most common ones regularly suffer misinterpretation and should, for that reason, be listed here.

and moreover furthermore	These expressions indicate that what follows is supplementary to what precedes. They should, therefore, link matters of like kind and grammatical form.

but however yet	These mark a change in direction or the introduction of material which conflicts with what has gone before. Since opposition is intended, they, too, should link matters of like kind and grammatical form.
still nevertheless notwithstanding	The sense of an opposing current is conveyed by these words, also, but they generally come after some sort of concession has been made.
although though while	These words are concessive. They always require a balancing principal statement.
for because	Both introduce the *reason for* another statement or condition.
then since as	As conjunctions, these three words may be used to show cause or they may simply indicate a relationship in time.
in order that so that	These show purpose.
provided that in case that	These restrict.

Complete command of these connectives is a requisite of good writing, but they will not alone give all that is needed for free and forward movement of discourse. In fact, overuse of them can easily become an impediment to the easy flow of good prose. A page spattered with *however*'s and *for*'s and *then*'s is as unsightly as a garment held together with safety pins. The kind of transition that does best service is the unobtrusive one, the one that comes from making the language of the text provide its own connections, the transition known—for want of a less pretentious word—as the "organic transition." It is not nearly so mystical as it sounds, and a little practice will give any student confidence in its use.

To create an organic transition, a writer may think of it as looking in two directions at once: back to what has been said and forward to what is to be said. The trick—and it is a kind of trick—of delivering that sense of double awareness lies simply in picking up a word or a phrase or the main idea of the preceding passage and touching it lightly, with or without some change, in the connecting term. Examples will make that procedure clearer than will further explanation.

The student who wrote the following paragraph has used both formal and organic transitions within the paragraph.

> For several reasons the convention is sometimes considered better than the primary system. *In the first place,* it is obvious, from the small number of voters in primary elections, that the public generally cares little about them. *Moreover,* the convention system allows selection of candidates so

that the ticket is balanced to give all groups representation. *This kind of selection* has the *additional* advantage of providing a guarantee against the nomination of "crackpot" candidates and of sharply curtailing campaign expenditures, itself an important matter if one realizes that, in politics, support is always accompanied by the expectation of favors and patronage. *All these* are valuable considerations. *Yet,* in the face of the one great objection to conventions—machine domination—they lose their importance.

This kind of selection uses a key word in the preceding sentence and leaves to *additional* the work of showing that this statement is supplementary to its predecessor. *All these* gathers the four arguments advanced in favor of party conventions, and the sentence it introduces reinforces the tone of approval.

The following selection is another example of a tightly knit paragraph:

> . . . and throughout the first chapter of *Walden* there is a note of impatience, sometimes an almost feverish desire to get the world to shake itself clear of clutter and complication, to give up the velvet cushion for a pumpkin, to stop the trains from running, the newspapers from pouring out their daily rush of words, the housewives from adding to the useless piles of stuff in the attic, and their farmer husbands from adding shed to outhouse and barn to shed and mortgage to all. The *impatience and the fever* well up in a great cry, "Simplify! Simplify! Simplify!"
>
> But simplification was the one thing the world had no intention even to consider. The steam engine had come, and soon there would be. . . .

In the foregoing passage, a good part of the unity of the paragraph is achieved by the series of parallel phrases. The repetition of "impatience" and "fever" adds to the unity by drawing the examples together in the generalization originally proposed; and the turning of "Simplify" into a noun gives the paragraph that follows an emphatic but unmechanical link with the paragraph just concluded.

The more skilled the writer, the more subtle and varied will be the devices he employs for binding sentences and paragraphs together. The relationships conveyed by those devices will nonetheless be the same as those mentioned earlier, and a student can for that reason properly begin with them and with the rudimentary transitions as a means of coming to realize which connections between statements are common. Once he has those connections firmly in mind, he can learn to handle the many devices for making a paragraph or an essay appear as inevitable in its progress as a river.

❋ *Words and Style*

*No more would I tell a green writer all his faults, lest I
should make him grieve and faint, and at last despair.*
BEN JONSON, *"Praecipiendi Modi," Timber*

"STYLE IS INGRATIATION." That is, style is the means of giving pleasure, most obviously of giving pleasure to the reader. Were there no pleasure in writing for the writer, however, little would get written. Yet the writer's pleasure is not simply a satisfaction in the product or even in the fact that what he has written gives delight to someone else.

In one part of the chapter on persuading, style is described as a two-layered matter, one layer reflecting the writer's conscious deployment of language, the other reflecting a habit of mind and of utterance so deeply ingrained that he is seldom more than half aware of it himself. Pleasure is important in both senses of the word "style." Because style expresses that under layer, it pleases a writer much as any release of energy pleases the man in whom it is released. Style is, in this sense, an extension of self. On the upper layer, that of deployment, style provides pleasure because it is an exercise of skill, a demonstration of self-control and of control over matter.

If style gives pleasure, developing a style ought to give pleasure, too, and it does—as much as developing skill at tennis or acting or piano playing. It is pleasurable activity, but it is also difficult, time consuming, painstaking. Writing is not a "natural" act. "I spoke in numbers, for the numbers came," Pope said of his youthful gift for versifying. Perhaps so—for Pope. For most of us, the "natural" flow of language is patterned only enough to meet the minimal demand of communication. Everything beyond that—and it is the "beyond" that is at issue here—requires knowledge, skill, and imagination.

Still, the writer has only words and words-in-order to work with. (Add punctuation and paragraph indentation, if you will, though the addition has less to do with style than with convention.) With order, large and small, the preceding two chapters have dealt at some length: one with the order, and relevant rhetorical concerns, of the sentence; the other with the order of paragraph and whole essay and with the relevant rhetorical concerns of that order. This chapter deals with words, and with words as a vital element in style rather than as instruments of reference.

1) DICTION

Otto Jespersen, a great grammarian of the English language, is said to have remarked that the direction of change in a language is from ditch to castle. Since he made that remark (if he did) there have been many efforts by serious students of language to make sociological classifications of one kind or another. Thus, within the great classes of origin (Indo-European, and so on) and within the national and regional classes (French, Germanic, Arabic), additional classes have been sorted on the basis of characteristic vocabulary, syntax, and conformity to traditional or "approved" usages. Obviously these classes are of very different kind from the ones grounded on the historical development of linguistic forms, and they lack the neatness and reliability of those earlier classifications. Yet they have a particular interest for the writer because they attempt to distinguish, among the various patterns of speech in a given language, those patterns which are distinctive indicators of the economic status, the cultural experience, and the social position of the speaker. An analogy to this kind of classification can be found in the highbrow-middlebrow-lowbrow metaphor used a few years ago to describe social habits and tastes in clothing, cigarettes, movies, magazines, and alcohol.

People have undoubtedly made social distinctions about the forms of language since culture began. Attempts to teach young people to speak and write "correctly" imply established forms and corruptions of them, and the forms considered "established" are necessarily those which the teachers themselves are accustomed to using. If this were the complete story, however, there would be little difficulty in determining correct language: the language which the tradition bearers (teachers, priests, hereditary chieftains) learned from the tradition bearers who preceded them would continue to be the correct language. In isolated and strictly hierarchical societies, if there are any left, that may still be the case. But most societies have experienced frequent disruption of hierarchies and almost none are really isolated today. Certainly, as far as Western culture is concerned, it is not possible to consider any society of the past three thousand years as either rigidly hierarchical or culturally isolated. Wherever a society is at all mobile and flexible, its language will undergo change; and wherever language undergoes change, some of the changes that occur will develop in small groups and come to be identified with them. Quite naturally, those who receive formal education in their youth will be exposed to the traditions of language-as-it-has-been-used, and those who do not will derive their norms of language from the speech they hear about them.

Now, although it is true that formal education often tends to perpetuate forms and distinctions that have lost currency even among educated people, it is also true that it preserves forms and distinctions which have developed in the language as aids to clarity, precision, and beauty. Given the fact that no absolute authority exists for distinguishing good from bad diction, right from wrong usage, our best recourse is to the spoken and written language of educated people. The obvious question, then, is this one: do educated people agree in matters of diction and usage? And the obvious answer is: Not always. Here it is important to note that the obvious answer is not a flat negative. A rough guess would be that ninety-nine out of a hundred expressions in any piece of writing by an educated person will go unchallenged by an educated reader. But the hundredth may be disputed vigorously.

A short time ago, the advertising writers for a cigarette manufacturer produced copy in which "like" figures as a conjunction. Indignant letters immediately began to pile up on editors' desks everywhere, protesting against debasement of the language, corruption of the young, countermand to the labors of schoolteachers, and so on. Sober consideration of what is at stake in a dispute of this kind will bring us close to the root of this whole business.

There can be no denying that "like" has often been used in the past by great writers exactly as it is being used in the advertisement. (There are examples in any historical dictionary.) This does not by itself mean that the usage is acceptable now, of course. Nor can there be any doubt that respectable writers so use it today, as the same dictionary will show. It does not seem possible, then, to discriminate on simple grounds of use. The next possibility is to quantify: do more use "like" as a conjunction than use "as"? There may be no way of getting a satisfactory answer to that question, but if there is, something further must be considered: is it better to do what most do or what few do? Another possibility is to qualify: do people I admire and wish to imitate use "like" as a conjunction? If that seems absurdly petty, the final possibility is to take the precise line: how does "like" compare to "as" in terms of precision, clarity, even euphony? But this produces a blank.

If all this speculation produces no certainty, why the fuss? As was noted in the second chapter, assertions of preference often arouse more fervor than those about which some common validation is possible. The same is true about a matter of this kind. It cannot be said that "as" is more precise than "like"; it is, in fact, likely to be less so simply because "as" has a temporal and causal sense as well as a comparative one. It cannot be very convincingly shown that more educated people use one form than the other, and even if it could, something more is needed to make mere majority become the ground for action. There is really no alternative to this conclusion: that, in matters of disputed usage, it is a waste of time to argue about rightness and wrongness because it is a matter in which preference is the ground of arbitration, not fact.

This is not at all the same as saying that the choice between "like" and "as"—or any similar choice—does not matter. It matters a good deal, but it matters as a feature of style, of the conscious choices made by a writer, of his self-expressiveness, not as virtue or duty or moral goodness. When Fowler (*Modern English Usage*) describes some uses of the conjunctive "like" as evidence of a "slovenly parsimony of words," and divides the world into those who have an "instinctive objection" to the form and those who do not, he has in mind the style of a select group of writers whom he admires. Without arguing any superiority for "as," he prefers it to "like"—partly, no doubt, because he likes nice discriminations. Such a taste is not to be despised. Neither is it to be taken as adjunct to moral law.

Taste, then, is implicated in style, but taste is notoriously private even when, as in the matter just discussed, it has the weight of pedagogical consensus with it. No one can legislate taste; people cannot even talk helpfully about it without setting themselves up as arbiters of many specific literary forms for which there is neither clear historical sanction nor distinct rhetorical or semantic advantage. "Like" is used and has long been used as a conjunction by good writers; it is fully as serviceable as the alternate word "as": these two facts argue for it. Against it is another fact: that most writers who pride themselves on propriety of expression do not use it. Given this knowledge, a writer chooses, and in choosing reveals something about himself. His choice affects his style, and his style suggests the grounds of choice.

There is, of course, no responsible choosing unless there is also knowledge. A writer steadily accumulates distinctions among words and phrases, and the distinctions most valuable to him are often those about which no dispute is useful. For his purposes, he prefers "in back of" to "behind" and uses "rest" and "remainder" interchangeably. Below the level of these distinctions, however, most writers recognize and respect a conventional body of usage. When they deviate from it, they deviate quite consciously in order to gain some rhetorical advantage. To knowledge of the convention and knowledge of variants, they bring specific intention and conscious judgment. They may choose unwisely, of course—in which case the meaning and effect of their work will not be what they intended —but at least they choose.

"STANDARD ENGLISH" •

For better or for worse, "Standard English" is defined here as the English most educated users of the language commonly employ. There is some difference between standard *spoken* and standard *written* English. There is some difference between what is standard in Texas and what is standard in Vermont, and even more between what is standard in Chicago and what is standard in Leeds, England. But in the main the differences are not great, rarely cause confusion, and rather please than dismay. This book is written in Standard English, though some of its locutions are undoubtedly quite different from, even if not incongruous with, those of a history textbook. Its differences are differences of choice, therefore of style; the book has only one of the many possible styles in Standard English.

DIALECT •

Dialect is language peculiar to a locality. It ranges from expressions used by all persons of the locality (like "I was graduated high school") to those used primarily in speech alone and retained for the most part by speakers of limited formal education ("a fur piece," meaning "a long distance" in rural localities all over the United States). It may be the special language of a cult, even a signal of recognition among members (as in the Beat "Like man I got this misery feeling from too much tea"). Dialect has considerable charm for the ear of the person to whom it is not native, and for that reason a writer may find it useful at times. He will not, however, expect to conduct much serious exposition in it. The *Iliad,* for example, would not be very well served by summary of this kind:

> Helen was still right pretty, but Menelaus was too tuckered out from fighting to pay her any mind.

For purposes of humor, irony, surprise, emphasis, a writer may find dialect valuable as a supplement to standard diction. He will not find it useful as an alternative to standard diction.

VERNACULAR •

The basic meaning of "vernacular" is "native"; the vernacular tongue is to be distinguished from a foreign tongue which, for one reason or another, may be the official or prestigious language of one's country. In Dante's time, Latin was the proper language for the writing of learned and literary men; Dante's defense of Italian for such writing was a defense of the vernacular. When Chaucer wrote *The Canterbury Tales,* the language of the church was Latin, that of the court was French; Chaucer chose the vernacular, a hybrid of Romance and Saxon origins. Until the first World War, most Chinese writing was in Mandarin, though many vernacular dialects flourished for the ordinary purposes of life. During the War a vigorous program was initiated to displace Mandarin with a vernacular, both for purposes of communication and of education, and it is now fully established.

Because a conflict between the official tongue and that spoken and written by most of the populace is less and less common, the word "vernacular" has gradually taken on a slightly less specific meaning, though one that goes back to its Latin origin (*vernaculus,* born in one's house). When scholars speak of a poet of the vernacular today, for example, they have in mind someone who uses the language of the "common man," the man-at-home. Again, the use that is made of the vernacular, as defined in this sense, is a conscious choice of the folksy over the formal; it is justified if it serves a purpose.

COLLOQUIALISM •

The practical difference between colloquialism and the vernacular is likely not to be very great. "Colloquial" means "used in speech." It implies "used only in speech, not in writing." But, of course, speech is not thought of as colloquial; the term refers to written use of the vocabulary or syntax common to speech but not to writing. In modern prose, the distinctions are much less severe than they were a few decades ago. There has, indeed, been a conscious colloquializing of written prose in American English for over a hundred years. Still, the colloquial is uncommon enough to academic exposition, at least, so that its use there, like the use of dialect (though not so strongly), provokes attention and is therefore suitable mainly for emphasis and the like.

An early part of the book discussed the gradual assimilation of the pronoun "you" to the third-person-singular, even in formal written prose. That assimilation is undoubtedly one effect of the colloquializing of our written language. Another, more striking, is the notable reduction of connectives. Because speech can easily be fortified by gesture and intonation, it is possible to indicate many relationships with a few connectives (and, but, so, when, if). For a variety of reasons, some modern writers have tried to strip their prose to these few colloquial connectives, largely in order to de-emphasize the presence of the writer's analytical and synthesizing mind.

> Josephine was very sorry. It was not her fault. She was eating and a dog slipped and a man was hurt. This has happened in Spain. Joseph is so sorry. They told him they applauded him. He is not nervous. He is easily hopeful. There was no use. The accident was hurtful. I remember Paul told me that it had happened and he remembered. Poor Joseph he will be alright again but it is unfortunate.
>
> GERTRUDE STEIN, *Painted Lace and Other Pieces*

The effect is a special one, certainly, and not one of great value to most exposition, though something can be said for the objectivity gained by such exaggeration of a colloquial practice.

Slang has its natural habitat in colloquial language, but it is not identical with it. Slang is the codification of exuberance. Like ginger ale, exuberance begins to lose its fizz as soon as it is poured out, and slang is for that reason short-lived. It either disappears completely (Would anyone describe a dance as "mellow" today, and what would he mean if he did?) or becomes idiomatic and is assimilated into the main current of the language, colloquial, written, or both. "Beat" is a dialect word that has become general slang. It may itself derive from another slang usage, the past participial form "beat" meaning "exhausted." Right now, as an adjective, the term is precise and respectable—"the beat generation." Whether that usage will be recognizable a generation from now, it is hard to say. It may become as archaic as "flapper," or it may assume some midstation between colloquial and standard, as "deadbeat" has done, or solidify its credentials with Standard English, like the verb ("He beats every opponent he plays").

While it lasts, slang often has extraordinary power to make us see matters in a new light. It exposes hidden properties, challenges fixed assumptions, and revitalizes words. But like this spring's hat, it looks dowdy by summer and old-fashioned by fall. For that reason a writer uses it sparingly and only when he believes the gain from freshness is greater than the loss by tarnish.

Idiom is different from slang, though slang may become idiom. The soundest definition is in this case the simplest. An idiomatic expression is a construction of two or more words in which the sense of the whole construction is not predictable from the meaning of its parts. People say that they "catch cold" from sitting in a draft although the sense of "catching" is not in their minds as it might well be in the expression "catch your cold." Others talk of "getting by without effort," of "getting on in business," of "getting at the job immediately," of "getting ourselves up for a party," of "getting out of town" and "of getting tired," in each instance indicating a shift of meaning for "get" by the preposition used with it. In a cow "eats up" the grass, a girl "washes up" the dishes, and a driver "slows up" at an intersection, a different meaning is given to "up" in each phrase.

Not all idioms involve prepositions, of course. In the sentence "We used to use the words we were used to," the first and third uses of the verb "to use" are idiomatic, the second is not. In such a phrase as "going the whole way," the idiom reflects a submerged metaphor both in verbal and in noun; in "bearing up," a metaphor that is still potent works in both verbal and preposition. The use of idiom, more than any other matter of diction, requires sensitivity and memory: the former to detect nuance and the latter to record what even the best dictionaries cannot always capture. Good writing is always idiomatic writing, for idiom is the living tissue of a language.

2) *CHARACTERISTICS OF STYLE*

The brief accounts of kinds of diction given above are accompanied by a minimum of prescription. The main requirement is to be alert to the variety, to be interested in the possibilities it offers for expression, and to understand the grounds for choice when choice must be made. Even if a set of commandments could be drawn up on irreproachable premises, it would not serve half so well as the kind of self-education implicitly recommended above. In this matter of diction, there is simply no satisfactory shortcut for alertness and a lively interest in words.

About the general characteristics of style it may nonetheless be possible to make some helpful comment, even though that comment may entail a good deal of emphasis on what is commonly done wrong rather than on what is commonly done right. Some faults are so characteristic of amateur writing that the best way to deal with them is to face them openly, and that is what we do below.

REDUNDANCY •

The English language inherited both from Romance and Anglo-Saxon sources the characteristic of repetition as a means of emphasis—repetition sometimes of a single word or phrase, sometimes of a meaning in different words. Thus, the conventional expression "wear and tear" indicates nothing more than "wear" but achieves a kind of reinforcement from the addition of "tear." Consciously used, repetition has great power, but there are kinds of repetition that come from no conscious use by the writer. They result rather from his ignorance of the full force of a word he uses or from inattention to what he is doing. Such ignorance or inattention produces what is called "redundancy" or "pleonasm.."

> A hero is usually distinguished in bravery, fortitude, and courage.

The three nouns are not quite identical ("bravery" is derived from a word meaning "fierceness"; "fortitude," from a word meaning "strength"; "courage," from a word meaning "heart"). But the characteristic they refer to here is probably a single one. Unless the writer has a reputation for nuance, his reader will undoubtedly take this for mere wordiness.

> The deliberate, planned lie is generally less successful than the spontaneous one.

How are "deliberate" and "planned" other than synonymous here? It is conceivable that, in speech, a certain emphasis might be achieved by this repetition. If the same force is desired in writing, however, some change must be made. Such a simple change as this might do the trick: "The deliberate, the planned lie . . ."; or better: "The deliberate lie—planned with care and executed with calculation—is. . . ."

> He is an author contemporary with the modern time.

The verb is in the present tense, so there is no need that "contemporary" be reinforced by "with the modern time." "Contemporary" can, of course, be used with times other than modern: as in "St. Francis, the founder of medieval mystical piety, was a contemporary of St. Dominic, the founder of the Inquisition."

> Neither the big magnates of the corporations nor the specialized experts nor the trained technicians realize what is at stake.

By derivation, magnates are big; by necessity, experts are specialized; and by definition, technicians are trained. In this example, the writer doesn't seem to care that his reputation with his reader is also "at stake."

ELEGANT VARIATION • Fear of repetition occasionally leads students to avoid it at too great cost. They escape the frying pan of monotony only to fall into the fire of overingeniousness and affection. A right balance between repetition and variation is not a matter for prescription, but examples may help to suggest the nature of the disease and the character of a cure.

> *Prohibition* seems to be a stimulant to most people. Even if they have no inclination toward doing what is *forbidden,* they feel an urge to resist *proscription* for the sake of resistance; or they assume that what is *interdicted* must be worth investigating or it would not have been *disallowed* in the first place. And the more strict the *ban,* the more subtle will be their efforts to outwit it.

In this illustration, the effort to avoid repeating derivatives of "prohibit" is so noticeable that a reader is more likely to concentrate on the writer's ingenuity (or his capacity for using a book of synonyms) than on what he is saying. Such a laborious procedure is bad not only because it distracts the reader and lends an air of pomposity to the passage but because it fails to make effective use of the key word. The passage is better on all three counts if the writer shows moderation in the use of synonyms.

> *Prohibition* seems to be a stimulant to most people. Even if they have no inclination toward doing what is *forbidden,* they feel an urge to resist *prohibition* for the sake of resistance; or they assume that what is *prohibited* must be worth investigating or it would not have been *forbidden* in the first place. And the more strict the *prohibition,* the more subtle will be their efforts to outwit it.

Elegant variation may actually cause misunderstanding as well as distraction and annoyance, as in this example:

> *Power* is the basis of political action. Whether *control* is exerted by elected or self-appointed or hereditary officials, *authority* conditions and manipulates action at will.

Are we to understand the italicized words as synonyms, or is some distinction suggested? If the former, then surely the passage will be more effective if written thus:

> *Power* is the basis of political action. Whether *it* is exerted by elected or self-appointed or hereditary officials, *power* conditions and manipulates action at will.

It is not fair, however, to condemn a practice because of its abuse. Repetition is too valuable an aid in good expression to discard because the incompetent use it without discrimination. A better procedure is to look to the ideas; if *they* are not idly repeated, one need have little worry about the repetition of words. To show how effective sheer repetition may be, this discussion closes with a passage well known in English literature. It is the work of an author whose deliberate use of repetition consorted magnificently with his deliberate limitation of emphasis to a few great ideas and made his voice a dominant one in the culture of half a century.

> The pursuit of perfection, then, is the pursuit of sweetness and light. He who works for sweetness and light, works to make reason and the will of God prevail. He who works for machinery, he who works for hatred, works only for confusion. Culture looks beyond machinery, culture hates hatred; culture has one great passion, the passion for sweetness and light. It has one even yet greater!—the passion for making them *prevail*. It is not satisfied till we *all* come to a perfect man; it knows that the sweetness and light of the few must be imperfect until the raw and unkindled masses of humanity are touched with sweetness and light. If I have not shrunk from saying that we must work for sweetness and light, so neither have I shrunk from saying that we must have a broad basis, must have sweetness and light for as many as possible. Again and again I have insisted how those are the happy moments of humanity, how those are the marking epochs of a people's life, how those are the flowering times for literature and art and all the creative power of genius, when there is a *national* glow of life and thought, when the whole of society is in the fullest measure permeated by thought, sensible to beauty, intelligent and alive. Only it must be *real* thought and *real* beauty; *real* sweetness and *real* light. Plenty of people will try to give the masses, as they call them, an intellectual food prepared and adapted in the way they think proper for the actual condition of the masses. The ordinary popular literature is an example of this way of working on the masses. Plenty of people will try to indoctrinate the masses with the set of ideas and judgments constituting the creed of their own profession or party. Our religious and political organizations give an example of this way of working on the masses. I condemn neither way; but culture works differently. It does not try to teach down to the level of the

inferior classes; it does not try to win them for this or that sect of its own, with ready-made judgments and watchwords. It seeks to do away with classes; to make the best that has been thought and known in the world current everywhere; to make all men live in an atmosphere of sweetness and light, where they may use ideas, as it uses them itself, freely— nourished, and not bound by them.

MATTHEW ARNOLD, *Culture and Anarchy*

Both redundancy and elegant variation are failures in economy. The writer is guilty of wastage in both. When his language is redundant, it vitiates attention: why should a reader pay close attention if he can count on being told and retold? And it annoys the reader who has the habit of being attentive. When the writer resorts to elegant variation, he vitiates attention in another way, by sending the reader off on tangents rather than leading him to the point. The economy of a piece of writing need not be austere, as spare and dry as sea biscuit. It may, in fact, be luxuriant. But it is important that it be an economy—that is, a conscious management—not a thoughtless rattling on or a hyperfastidious avoid-ance of the obvious and useful.

VAGUENESS AND AMBIGUITY · Most of the much-lampooned repeti-tiveness of legal language is the result of trying to make watertight state-ments. The danger of vagueness and ambiguity in legal documents is too obvious to need illustration. Perhaps it is only this life-and-liberty-saving importance that can make a writer hunt for ways of making perfectly clear whatever he has to say—unless pride in his craft is enough to impel him to do so. The authors of these sentences are certainly slipshod in their work:

1) This seems to be just inconsistency in American philosophy. (Is "just" adjectival or adverbial? It makes a great deal of difference.)
2) This word designates any person who acts in a civil.way. ("In a civil, that is, courteous, manner" or "in his capacity as a citizen or employee of the government"?)
3) The ordinary man must act as a check on any usurpation of the expert's powers. ("Usurpation of power by the expert" or "usurpation by someone else of power rightly the expert's"?)
4) He says that since all Americans have equal rights, no one goes out of his way to get out of that class, and that the people who were out slowly descended back due to their own lack of ambition. (This one needs a complete rewriting: "He says that, since all social classes in America have equal rights, almost no one goes out of his way to get out of the class into which he was born, and that those few who, for one reason or another, do move out return gradually because the advantages prove not to be worth the effort.")
5) Humor is a very effective means for communicating discontent when used satirically, but when humorous analogies are applied to serious subjects, the humor becomes devoid of its purpose and indeed detracts

from it. (Any reader patient enough to work over this sentence will finally discover that clearing up "its purpose" will do more than anything else to clear up the confusion in the sentence. "Its purpose" must be understood, apparently, to exclude satire. That makes the statement completely illogical, but at least it is no longer ambiguous.)

The corrective to vagueness and ambiguity is, in part, a taste for precision. This taste is not a natural one, and its acquisition is not easy. Nor is it invariably attractive. There are writers, and would-be writers, for whom precision is so important that they may engage in an infinite deal of haggling over a matter of little import. Henry James managed to make an art out of such haggling, though not an art unreservedly admired for that characteristic, as numerous parodies of it demonstrate. Precision seems to be compulsive for some people, and compulsiveness is always unattractive to the beholder. Yet there is too much virtue in exactness to allow abuse of it to demean its role in a writer's attitude. A writer cannot afford to ignore *le mot juste,* or a word as *juste* as he can manage without taking such pains that the effort rather than the meaning attracts attention.

A second corrective to vagueness and ambiguity is knowledge of the choices available, for they are not exclusively choices between the "right" and the "wrong" word. They may be choices between the concrete and the abstract, or choices along the spectrum from general to particular and along that from sensory to nonsensory.

  a. *Concrete and Abstract.* A concrete entity is one that has mass; an abstract entity one that does not. There is no shade of either, though some nouns may be used for both: "humanity," for example. "Appetite," "rigor," and "beauty" are abstract nouns; "chair" and "lead" are concrete. Despite the arguments advanced in many quarters, it is clear that abstract words are valuable and cannot readily be replaced by concrete ones. To begin with, abstract words are a convenient shorthand ("rigor" as a word summing up an attitude perhaps compounded of precision, punctuality, neatness, self-discipline, and sternness of demeanor —a great deal to make a word mean, as Humpty Dumpty remarked, but that's the way with abstractions) . They also identify common properties (as "beauty" does whether the word is used of a horse, a rose, or a woman). It is true, however, that abstract words may increase vagueness unless they are coupled with concrete words as supplements:

His life is rigor itself—up at five, at work within the half-hour, unremitted laboring until mid-afternoon, then off for a brisk walk and a quick swim before sitting down to a spare meal punctually at four.

Or they may be coupled with verbs that contain a strong sense of action:

Not "the composition in this painting is a reflection of . . ." but "the composition in this painting reflects. . . ."

b. *General and Particular.* There is a spectrum from general to particular, not a simple line of division between them. The most general word is the one that is most inclusive in its reference; the least general, or most particular, word is the one that refers to a single entity. The spectrum is valid not only for nouns but for verbs, adjectives, and adverbs as well. It is safe to say that writers run greater danger of vagueness and ambiguity at the general, rather than the particular, end of the scale, though there is, to be sure, the possibility of so much particularity that no general statement emerges at all where one is intended. An adjectival scale, from particular to general, might run: perfect, unexcelled, superb, excellent, good. Discrimination among such words stimulates a reader's confidence that the writer is taking care.

c. *Sensory and nonsensory.* Although the proportion of sensory to nonsensory language is necessarily a matter of taste, it is a simple fact of experience that appeal to sense increases the vividness of imagery and therefore the evocativeness of a word or phrase. "A rosy future" holds more promise than one that is only "promising."

INFLATION • The undisputed master of the inflated style is Dickens' Mr. Micawber.

> The blossom is blighted, the leaf is withered, the God of day goes down upon the dreary scene, and—and in short you are ever floored. As I am!

It is funny in print; in life, it is often offensive and sometimes pathetic. There is a marked tendency among good prose writers today to write with as much simplicity as they can manage. (Churchill is a notable exception.) But not all things can be said simply. And, more to the point, not all people want to say things simply. It is no heinous offense to write "Anyone who has a fair position in industry . . ." instead of "Anyone who has a decent job in industry . . ." but the inflation, the slight pomposity, is there all the same. This is more noticeably stiff: "Higher education of excellent quality can be had at very lenient terms at state universities." Coupling a passive verb with "at very lenient terms" marks this ineradicably for what it is—an attempt to make something simple sound imposing. Like "Those who uphold the negative side of this question," it represents a kind of shrinking away from rude contact with things-as-they-are.

It is a somewhat different psychological attitude that leads a writer to load his text with phrases which send up their echo from a previous century. He seems to know the rudeness of things-as-they-are but to have turned to a golden past for words with which to enhance their dignity. He never "uses" but "avails himself of"; for him, people are "wont" to do things. A third kind of inflation is that which seems to have no cause other than the love of abstractions for their own sake. Although it may be indicative of a potentiality in the writer, it is certainly as annoying to the reader as any device one can name. One example should be enough:

> The Editor claims that the two advantages of the proposal have since been rendered improbable, and, hence, the presence of the House Deans is *conducive to a feeling of surveillance.*

EUPHEMISM • Euphemism is the use of a mild or vague or roundabout expression as a substitute for blunt precision or disagreeable truth. Some euphemisms are simply matters of propriety. (See H. L. Mencken's amusing remarks on "mortician" and on the invention of "ecdysiast" to meet the professional demands of a certain Miss Sothern, *The American Language, Supplement One,* pp. 569 ff. and 584 ff.) Probably most of the euphemisms that appear in students' papers, however, rise from hypersensitivity, a vain fastidiousness almost as repulsive as its counterpart, vulgarity. Hypersensitivity and vulgarity are both bad in writing because they keep the writer from making honest contact with his material, that is, they make him *insensitive* to its real character. The student who wrote "position" instead of "job" (see above, Inflation) has imputed to "job" certain unpleasant suggestions of meniality; he hopes to dignify by a name, feeling that there is a kind of magic power in words which can alter the objects to which they are attached. The hope is illusory, and the act pretentious. A salary is not made bigger or better by being called an emolument, nor is a luncheon made more delicious by being called a collation.

Another kind of euphemism, a vicious kind, is that which attempts to put a fair face on foul matter. "Liquidation of undesirable elements" is murder, plain and simple. A "deliberate defection from known truth" is a lie, nothing more or less. Such terms, unless used mockingly, are attempts to hide the facts, not reveal them, to complicate rather than simplify communication.

Both euphemism and inflation point to their own correction. Language that is direct and at the same time restrained bespeaks composure and control, not simply of language, but of attitude and character. Drawing back from unadorned and accurate expressions suggests a basic uneasiness in the writer's relationship with the world and with his reader. Inflation may stem from like uneasiness, but it adds a certain callousness and false energy to language that repels as much as euphemisms do.

JARGON • Of all the faults of style dealt with here, use of jargon is the most common one in the writing of college students. It is not hard to see why. For one thing, they inhabit a society in which imitation is not only hard to avoid but often rewarded. They sense that one way to sound well informed or learned is to use the language they take to be that of well-informed and learned people. They rarely take all of it and often seize only what is new to them; therefore, their shortcomings are not due to their environment alone. Every writer, young or old, experienced or not, is responsible for his choices, and choosing jargon is no exception.

The term itself has three meanings: (1) any outlandish and unintelligible speech (from its root, Fr. *jargon, gargon,* a chattering, warbling— *Webster's Collegiate*); (2) the specialized language of a trade or profession, of a special skill or science; (3) any hybrid language. What all three definitions have in common is unintelligibility from the point of view of the outsider. Jargon is, then, a word of reproach leveled against those in the know by those who are not. As such, it would need no discussion here. Those in the know have a right to special language, among themselves at least, and jargon in the second sense (above) is obviously useful. The vocabulary peculiar to printers, to doctors, to miners, whatever its origin, is a shorthand for them. "Galley" is one thing to a printer and another to a sailor, and each usage is a form of jargon. Moreover, jargon is a means, within a specialty, for controlling reference and avoiding ambiguity. "Party of the first part" is not simply legal unction.

It is when such specialized vocabulary is used by those outside the specialty or when it is abused, for purposes of show, by those inside it that jargon becomes offensive. Then it not only keeps the outsider out, it gives him a strong suspicion that he is being patronized or bamboozled. This example, from a book on business management, was picked out for spoofing in the *New Yorker* of July 21, 1962:

> The Golden Rule is another codification of considerations which should govern our choice of actions lest we end by suboptimizing in terms of our interpersonal objectives.

The *New Yorker* queries: "What would you say if we told you that we already *had?*" The jargon here is from the social sciences, and the question a reader raises about it is whether or not the distinctive vocabulary is necessary to what is being said. Does it sharpen definition? What is lost if the sentence is simplified?

> If we don't obey the Golden Rule, we may not get along with people as well as we'd like to.

The aura of science is lost, but what kind of science is it that depends for its communication on aura? Jargon of this type is something very close to the occult language of astrologers, medical quacks, and circus spielers, surely.

A conscientious writer can test his own sentences for jargon in several ways. If a considerable number of abstract words accumulate in any passage he writes, especially words ending in *-ion, -ogy, -ical,* he is probably flirting with jargon. If he *feels* superior about using this or that word, if the word charms him by its suggestion of specialized knowledge, he is carrying on a full-fledged courtship. And if he has reached the stage of writing what he himself cannot paraphrase succinctly, he is already victim of the sirens and will need some rhetorical Odysseus to reclaim him.

What can he do? The simplest corrective is to ask himself several questions about each word or phrase: "Is this necessary?" Then: "Can it be said more simply without losing accuracy and completeness?" Finally: "Is the complexity or lack of complexity in the matter referred to represented by the language used about it?"

Here is another example of jargon:

> To form a rule or formula so as to evaluate the causation of this bane of humanity, wars, one would have to evolve a psychometer, so to speak, with which the occurrences of certain attitudes and involved coordinating factors could be gauged, compared, and in the ultimate contrast made self-evident in a social-science general rule.

That sentence is from a student's paper. It shows how imitative use of jargon (evaluate the causation, evolve, occurrences of attitudes, coordinating factors) not only muddles a statement but deprives it of clear rhetorical effect. A reader cannot tell whether this sentence is meant to be ironic (the invention of a psychometer suggests that it may be) or solemn (as the final clause seems to indicate). Nor can a reader be entirely clear about what is being proposed. A sentence like this one would be no clearer to the full-fledged social scientist than to the outsider; it is probably not more than half-clear to the man who wrote it.

Jargon is more than an irritant to the reader. It is an insidious friend to the writer, for it gives him a sense of power and facility that he has not earned by thought. He can compose in jargon without reflection and with almost no reference to reality. In doing so, he produces prose that has everything but sense, as the final example will show.

> The involute texture, the superb annealing tensions and interlocking ambiguities of this poem make a cloistral threnody in which overtone and undertone transfuse and permeate the whole. Symbolically, the paradoxical voice shields the meaning, sheds the half-light of ironic reflection—or deflection, to be more exact—over the argument, binding the velleities of rhetoric ineluctably with the sinuous evaluative renderings of thought. This is suspension of disbelief superbly collated with recollection in tranquillity, a shaping spirit of the secondary imagination.

In such a swell of language, writer and reader alike go under.

TRITENESS · An accomplice to jargon is triteness, the use of expressions so worn out that they produce no reaction in the average reader and only weariness in the person who is widely read. Moreover, like jargon, they close the eyes and numb the minds of those who use them. A person who writes as the author of the following passage did not only *sees* nothing and *thinks* nothing but *tells* nothing to his reader:

> It was with a *feeling of awe* that I first entered Harvard Yard. A *mist came before my eyes* and I spoke *in hushed tones* to the man who had brought me with him, the *mentor* of my school football team. Before me the brick and stone buildings *reared their heads* proudly into *the wide blue yonder.*
>
> Across the *velvet sward* moved *bright youth and gray-headed age.* From beyond the walls came the *busy hum* of traffic and of the *daily round of life* on the Square. Here all was *as silent as the dead.* My *heart caught in my throat* and I said *in muted tones,* "So this is Harvard Yard!"

Happily, so disastrously bad a piece is rare. Yet, the trite term—or cliché, as it is often called—is always a temptation to the writer because it relieves him of the responsibility to probe his consciousness for a more precise expression of his thought. The temptation is increased for the student by the fact that the cliché may be new to him and therefore, from his point of view, not really trite at all, an unfortunate situation admirably described by Fowler in these words:

> The hackneyed phrases are counted by the hundred, & those registered below are a mere selection. Each of them comes to each of us at some moment in life with, for him, the freshness of novelty upon it; on that occasion it is a delight, & the wish to pass on that delight is amiable; but we forget that of an hundred persons for whom we attempt this good office, though there may be one to whom our phrase is new & bright, it is a stale offence to the ninety & nine.
>
> *Modern English Usage*

If, as Fowler says, the trite phrase does not always sound trite to the man who uses it, how is a writer to know what to do? The plain fact is that no one escapes triteness entirely; we all live, in part, by clichés, moving from one set to another more sophisticated set (which generally means another set used by fewer people). Yet a conscientious writer does have some check on himself. For one thing, he can watch for frequent recurrence of phrases in his own work and check them for aptness and accuracy of reference. He can force himself to paraphrase. He can keep an eye out for overuse of such "blanket words" as *field, aspect, area, level, element, factor.* He can cock an ear at conversation around him, for in it he is almost certain to hear stock phrases tumbling out to suit the stock responses most people have to whatever situations they meet. And he can watch particularly for the metaphorical expression that has gained currency by its liveliness and is already well on the way toward the dustbin of cant (like "keep an eye out" and "cock an ear," above).

❄ *Glossary of Usage*

IT IS NOT at all easy to make definitive statements about this or that matter of usage, for three reasons: (1) "proper" usage varies from place to place and group to group; (2) it changes from century to century, even from generation to generation; (3) it develops variations and changes, especially in these days of wide and rapid communication, quite unsystematically. Yet it is also true that the basic sentence patterns and basic grammatical structures, those that govern nine-tenths or more of our speech and writing, are fairly stable from one part of the country to another, from social group to social group, and even from century to century. It is also true that writing is more stable, more "standard," than speech.

The distinctions and judgments recorded below deal only with matters of usage, verbal and grammatical, that are sufficiently argued about to make their separate listing worth while. Now the fact that they *are* argued about means that people do not agree about them—or, at least, do not make the same choices when they speak and write them. Therefore, there would seem to be two obligations paramount for a book of this kind. First, it should specify what its authors observe to be the usage of writers who, in other ways, display respect for language as a vehicle of accurate expression. Secondly, it should give some indication of allowable differences, defining "allowable" as "sanctioned by the fact that even among writers of excellent reputation usage varies." The analogous obligations for the student are these: to respect the language of those who use English most carefully; and to distinguish between allowable differences, as defined above, and those that have no sanction but general currency. In short, the purpose of this short check list is not to teach you to write like everyone else, but to keep you from doing so.

References in these listings to Fowler and others may lead you to acquire one of several useful handbooks of usage. Some good ones are: Fowler, *Modern English Usage;* Nicholson, *American-English Usage;*

246

Partridge, *Usage and Abusage;* Hook, *Guide to Good Writing;* Bryant, *Current American Usage.* Wherever in our discussion, the epithets *over-used, pretentious, hackneyed* and the like appear, we rely on such hand-books as well as on our own experience for the advice implied.

ability, capability, capacity. *Ability* means *power to perform; capability* adds a sense of endowment: *capacity* means *power to receive* or *hold.* Idiomatic: ability to swim (*not* ability of swimming); capabil-ity for unremitting effort; capacity to absorb, or capacity for absorb-ing (*not* capacity of absorbing) ; able to, capable of.

age, aged (as adjective). In modifying expressions: seven men, *aged* forty or over. . . . The jargon of advertisement (from classified advertise-ments to information-wanted posters in the post office) has led some to substitute *age* for *aged* in such expressions.

aggravate, irritate. *Aggravate* means *increase; irritate* means *excite anger in, cause soreness:* He *irritates* me and then *aggravates* my anger by pretending not to notice that I am *irritated.* Obviously, a useful distinction but one often ignored in speech, where *aggravate* is a common synonym for *irritate.*

all ready, already. *Already* is an adverb; *all ready,* a pronoun modified by an adjective: They are *all ready* to go; they are *already* there.

all right, alright. Conservative editorial practice rejects the second form, which seems to have developed by analogy with *all ready, already,* though the ground for such analogy is not a semantic one.

all the time. When the time is clearly defined by context (She sat there *all the time* he worked), the expression is unquestionably acceptable. When there is no such clear definition and the phrase means some-thing like "constantly" (Actors act while they are on the stage, but he acts *all the time*), Fowler classifies it as slang. The distinction is so nice that few observe it, though placement of the undefined phrase does, in some instances, give it an unidiomatic ring (*All the time* he takes money from the till; he *all the time* looks at her). Place the phrase at the end of either sentence, and the expression becomes idiomatic, though still informal.

almost, most. *Almost* means *nearly; most* means *preponderant part* or *to a high degree.* He was *most* eager to criticize what *almost* every-one else approved. *Most* of his remarks showed little more than irritation.

and/or. This shorthand expression, once the subject of legislation in Georgia (where *andor* was temporarily given legitimacy), has crept into general use probably from law and business. Its purpose is to indicate a double set of alternatives. "Eat this food with butter or with mustard or with butter and mustard" becomes "Eat this food with butter *and/or* mustard." We have seen very few instances of its use by literary men, but the expression occurs with increasing frequency in political and sociological writing, even in conservatively edited journals. It is called "unlovely," "un-English," and "ugly" by various arbiters, and that should be warning enough about the displeasure it provokes in many readers. "Eat this food with butter or mustard, or with both" solves the problem—but does not satisfy the argument, of course.

and etc. Redundant, since *etc.* is the abbreviation for *et cetera,* meaning "and others."

and which. As a coordinating conjunction, *and* requires an element of the same kind on each side of it. The common error involving *and which* goes like this: They read all six of the books *and which* I didn't really expect them to do. Two corrections are possible: omission of "which" and "do"; omission of "and." This sentence, of course, is correct. The six books which he read, *and which* I expected him to read, cover the field satisfactorily.

anxious, eager. As for *aggravate, irritate* the distinction between these words, though little observed, is worth preserving since it gives a meaningful discrimination between states of mind. *Anxious* means *worried; eager* means *keenly desirous.* I am *anxious* about his health and *eager* to see him recover.

any (place, thing, one, body, where). *Any* combines with these words— though not regularly with *-place*—when there is no special stress (*Anything* you can do, I can do better). When emphasis is desired, the words separate (*Any one* of us would have done as well). Fastidious writers used to avoid *anybody,* preferring *anyone,* but few are so fastidious now. One use, with *more,* is colloquial but is occasionally found in respectable writing: He doesn't do it *any more.* What is true of *any* in such constructions is true of *some.*

apt, likely, liable. The distinctions here are less tenuous than that between *anyone* and *anybody* but not so clear-cut as that between *anxious* and *eager.* The expression *likely to* is reserved by many writers for matters of more or less agreeable or neutral outcome. He is *likely* to show up before noon. *Liable* to, by contrast, introduces unpleasant consequences. He is *liable* to be left behind. In careful usage, *apt* is an adjective meaning *quick to learn* (an apt pupil) or *appropriate* (an apt solution). Its use as a synonym for *liable* is colloquial (He is apt to come late).

area. The metaphorical use of *area,* like that of *field* or *region,* is convenient but jargonic and sometimes pretentious. "In the *area* of concern for social welfare," will reduce to "Concern for social welfare" without loss.

as, like. Conjunctive use: *as* is so ubiquitous in its temporal sense that its conjunctive use in a causal sense often makes rereading a line necessary and should therefore be avoided (Compare: "The duchess swept into the room *as* he was leaving" with "The duchess swept into the room, *as* she intended to make a good impression at once). In the comparative sense, it has long shared honors with "like," though writers who are punctilious about diction scorn "like" in any conjunctive situation (Compare: "They came home *as* they said they would" with the rejected "They came home *like* they said they would"). Anyone who cares can keep that distinction in mind. The difficulty comes when following pronouns are involved. "They know me *as* well *as* she" means something different from "They know me *as* well *as* her." In the following pair of sentences, however, meaning is the same: He is twice *as* heavy *as* I; He is twice *as* heavy *as* me. In "He is twice *as* heavy *as* me" the conjunctive rule (see *and which*, above) is ignored; the sentence is ungrammatical though well on its way to becoming idiomatic in speech. To avoid such an error, Nicholson faces the most strained construction without a tremor: You dressed up *as* she. Any American writer of English would try to avoid that strangeness. You dressed up to look *like* her.

being that, being as. In constructions like "*Being that* he has no more money," the phrase is apparently a vestige of some formal locution possibly derived from schoolboy translations of the Latin absolute construction. Use *because* in its place.

between, among. The simple distinction that requires *between* for two instances and *among* for more than two is not enough. *Among* emphasizes participation in a group: He is one *among* many. *Between* emphasizes particularization, distinction, difference, even opposition of members of a group: There is no way of discriminating fairly *between* the seven owners. It is true, however, that *among* is never used when fewer than three are in the group referred to.

beside, besides. *Beside* is a preposition meaning *near by* and, therefore, from force of fact, *compared with:* sitting *beside* me; looks cheap *beside* this one. *Besides* is a preposition or adverb meaning *in addition to* or *other than: Besides* running the store, he acts as postmaster (prepositional); *Besides,* he is a boxer (adverbial).

bi-, semi-. Though dictionaries disagree, soundest practice appears to sanction *bi-* as two and *semi-* as half. *Biennial* means *every two years; semiannual* means *every half-year.* However, *Webster's Collegiate* lists *biannual* as meaning the same as *semiannual.* Informed use equates *biweekly* with *fortnightly;* popular use is ambivalent. One way out is to avoid the Latin prefixes altogether: twice a week, every two weeks, yearly, every other year. If used, the prefixes are hyphenated only before proper names (semi-Socialist) and before the letter *i* (semi-incapacitated).

burst, bust. *Bust* is a corrupt form for the past tense both of *burst* and of *break* (for which *busted* is an additional corrupt form). It has made its way into a good many rather slangy expressions and is unchallengeable within them: fit to *bust*. By some sort of alchemy, the corruption has also become a noun (The whole effort is a *bust*), but the use is slangy.

but that, but what. The first is preferable to the second on sheer grammatical grounds, but both are widely used in good writing: I don't know *but that* you are right.

can, may. The traditional distinction remains a useful one, though frequently ignored. *Can* deals with ability, power (*Can* he move his injured arm at all?); *may* deals with permission (*May* he attend, too?). In either of these examples, a substitution may be made, and that is exactly the point of the distinction: a substitution can be meaningful if the distinction is preserved.

can but, cannot but, can't help but. The first two locutions sound very formal to the American ear: He *can but* consent (can only consent); He *cannot but* consent (cannot do anything other than consent). The third is a loose construction substituted for a tighter one: He *cannot help* (can't help) but think; He *can't help* thinking.

case. The word has uses but it is much overused and often conceals vagueness. Fowler and Quiller-Couch object to *in any case,* but on no very satisfactory grounds; it is clearly an idiom. *In the case of* is usually superfluous altogether (In the *case* of the third member of the group, we think . . . ; We think the third member of the group . . .). As a substitute for *often* or *usually,* such a phrase as *in many cases* is wordy; as a substitute for nouns of specific reference, *case* is lazy ("in such *cases*" for "in such situations, operations, places, examples etc.").

certain. Loosely and inelegantly used simply for emphasis: I have a *certain* distaste. Curiously enough, in this use, *certain* seems to indicate a considerable degree of uncertainty, indefinability. This use, like that of *definite* to mean *strong* (He has a *definite* tendency . . .) is rather faddish.

common, mutual. *Common* means *shared* (our *common* heritage); *mutual* means *reciprocal* (their *mutual* hatred, i.e., of each other). But *mutual* may also be used as a synonym for *common* (our *mutual* preference for quiet).

[comparatives]. Two faults are common: doubling of the comparative form (These are far *more richer* forms than those); omission of a needed element in the comparison (Capitalism is *more* successful in developing means of production). For the second example, the comparison may develop either the subject (. . . more successful *than* communism) or the predicate (. . . means of production *than*

in controlling means of distribution"). It should not fail to do one
or the other.

compose, comprise. *Compose* means *make up; comprise* means *include.*
Five members *compose* a basketball team; Great Britian *comprises*
England, Wales and Scotland. The passive form of *comprise* (*is
comprised*) usurps the meaning of *compose.*

contact. The most careful writer undoubtedly limits *contact* to use as a
noun. Therefore: "He made a contact with the enemy agent," and
not "He contacted the enemy agent." But like *blame* and a hundred
other nouns-made-from-verbs, this one is accepted in even the best
company today.

consensus. The meaning of the word makes a following *of opinion* unnecessary.

continual, continuous. Another useful distinction, though much ignored.
Continual means *occurring in steady but not unbroken succession;
continuous* means *without interruption:* a day of *continual* interruption, an hour of *continuous* quiet.

contrary. In an introductory or connective phrase, the idiomatic expression is *on the contrary.* In an adjectival phrase, the idiomatic expression is *to the contrary: On the contrary,* the simple truth is
that . . . ; Whatever he says *to the contrary,* the simple truth is
that. . . .

contrast, compare. *Contrast* emphasizes difference; *compare* emphasizes
likeness. Idiomatic: *contrast with; compare to* or *compare with,*
tenuously distinguished according to the breadth of the comparison
(Shall I *compare* thee *to* a summer's day? If we try to *compare*
practices of the reigning monarch *with* those of his predecessor. . . .).

couple together. Like *combine together* or *attach together,* redundant.
When redundancy produces emphasis, it is excusable, though
emphasis achieved by such means raises some question about the
general economy of the prose in which it occurs.

criteria. Plural only. The singular is *criterion.*

data. Used for both singular and plural. This liberty with a grammatical
form is the result of ignorant borrowing. *Datum* is singular in
Latin; *data* is plural. Therefore, by derivation: this *datum* is, these
data are. However, the distinction between these words is not strictly
observed even in edited written prose.

decimate. Strictly, *reduce by one-tenth.* Loosely used to mean *destroy the
greater part of.*

deprecate, depreciate. *Deprecate* means *disapprove; depreciate* means
make less, reduce in quantity, quality or stature: His father *depre-
cated* his decision to study law. He *depreciates* every noble motive
to the principle of self-interest.

desirous of. High-flown for want: He is *desirous of* obtaining some assistance; He *wants* some assistance.

discussant. A relatively new word, apparently built on analogy with *inform, informant* or *participate, participant*. Its sudden fashionableness has given offense, but the word is here to stay.

disinterested, uninterested. The distinction, abused by many, is a useful one. *Disinterested* means *impartial; uninterested* means *lacking interest:* The best judge is a *disinterested* one. The worst audience is an *uninterested* one.

dive, dived, dove. In the United States, at least, this weak verb is becoming a strong one, hence *dove* is an acceptable though not required past-tense form. The past participle remains *dived:* He *dove* (*dived*) into the pool. He has *dived* ten times already.

different from, different than, different to. The cultivated idiom in American English is *different from:* His theory is *different from* any other I have heard. *Different than* frequently introduces a clause, as an alternative to *different from what:* College life is *different than* (from what) I thought it would be. His way is *different from* mine. He does it *differently than* I do. Colloquially, *than* frequently replaces *from:* His theory is *different than mine. Different to* is strictly British idiom.

due to. *Due* is an adjective. It therefore needs, and originally had, a noun which it modified: His illness is *due to* exposure. The idiomatic use of *due to* as alternative to *because of* (*Due to* unforeseen circumstances. . . .) is, however, so widespread that grammatical origin has been all but overwhelmed.

each, every. Two errors are common: use of a plural verb with these singular pronouns (*Each* of them *have studied*), and use of a related plural pronoun or a pronoun of the second, rather than the third, person (*Each* of them will take *their* lessons alone. When *each* of you stood up, *you* volunteered). Despite slack colloquial usage, edited written prose holds firm for these correct forms: *Each* of them *has studied.* Each of them will take *his* lessons alone. When *each* of you stood up, *he* volunteered. Formal use requires a matching possessive adjective when *each* follows the verb (They have rendered *each his own* talent), but a more natural phrasing would be: *Each* has rendered *his own* talent.

end up. In this expression *up* is an intensifier and otherwise meaningless. It is common in modern speech, frequent in written prose, but rare in the prose of literary writers.

enormity, enormousness. Dictionaries allow the words as synonyms, but commonly *enormity* means *great badness* (the *enormity* of his crime) and *enormousness* means only *greatness in size* (the *enormousness* of the universe).

enthuse. A verb developed from the noun and adjective but abhorrent to many. Still, it is common in speech, even in the speech of cultivated people, and it occasionally appears in prose of indisputable propriety.

equally as. The words overlap completely (He is *equally as* tall as I am). Corrected: He is *as* tall as I am. His height is *equal* to mine.

evaluate. A perfectly good word, meaning *judge* or *measure,* which has been so much abused, especially in the derived form *evaluation,* that sensitive writers often avoid it.

except. As a conjunction, the word is now unacceptable (He would go *except* she doesn't want him to) though it was once not only acceptable but elegant (*Except* ye become as little children, ye shall not enter . . .).

extra. This is a short form for *extraordinary,* therefore *something in addition to or beyond the normal.* It has long been used in combination with some adjectives (*extracurricular, extramural*) and has in recent years extended itself to other adjectives with somewhat altered meaning (*extra-special* means very special, *extra-heavy* means very heavy). In this adulterated sense, the word is gaining currency but is still rare in conservative prose.

fact. From *factus,* past participle of *facio,* I make; *something made.* Facts are. Therefore, the expression *true fact* is a tautology. A factual statement (that is, one that purports to contain a fact or facts) may be true or false, but a fact simply is a fact.

farther, further. The traditional limitation of *farther* to physical distance lingers, but general practice in the best modern prose seems to make choice more by personal preference of the sound of one over the other than by any semantic distinction. The words have a different origin and once had distinguishably different meanings, but context appears to serve well enough to identify the specific meaning so that the two have blurred.

feature. As a verb in the passive (This is *featured* by), this word has come into colloquial currency through its jargonic employment in advertising. It doesn't mean anything very precisely, is already hackneyed, and therefore offends a discriminating reader on two scores. As a noun meaning *aspect* or *lineament,* it is, of course, standard: His *features* are sharp, almost ferret-like. As an adjective or noun-surrogate (the *feature* story, the page-ten *feature*), it is the jargon of journalism for *main* or *principal* or *special.*

firstly. Though *secondly, thirdly,* etc., have survived, *firstly* became obsolete in respectable prose decades ago. It is common now for the other ordinal forms to receive similar reduction; therefore: *First,* it should be noted that . . . ; *second,* it must be admitted. . . .

flammable, inflammable, nonflammable. The first two words are synonyms; the third is antonym to the other two.

forward, forwards, toward, towards. Reputable practice is to use the form without -*s* for all purposes.

future prediction. A tautology, easily corrected by omitting *future*. There is a sense, it is true, in which this phrase is acceptable, meaning *a prediction yet to be made*.

graduate. For good usage as a verb meaning *leave after completing a course of study,* it requires the preposition *from:* He will *graduate from* high school, *not* He will graduate high school. Stricter use in such an expression requires the passive: He will *be graduated* from high school.

guess. Used to mean *estimate,* or *calculate,* the word is entirely acceptable in all contexts; used to mean *suppose* (I *guess* so), it is colloquial at present, but may not remain so (If he is, as I *guess,* a sympathizer, I want nothing more to do with him).

had better, had rather, had ought. *Had better* is used for command and warning. (He *had better* get ready); *had rather,* and its alternative form, *would rather,* for wish or preference (He *had rather* stay than go). *Had ought* is a solecism (He *had ought* to go), corrected by dropping either of the words, depending on the intent. He *had* to go. He *ought* to go.

hang, hanged, hung. The verb *to hang,* meaning *to suspend by the neck until dead,* is a weak verb. Therefore: they *hang* him, they *hanged* him, they have *hanged* him. The verb used with reference to inanimate objects is a strong one. Therefore: They *hang* it up, they *hung* it up, they have *hung* it up.

hardly, scarcely. Negative in force as adverbs, these words are therefore complete without *not, none, etc.* They have *hardly* begun. She had *scarcely* any money left when she came.

healthy, healthful. A distinction, seldom closely observed even by good writers, uses *healthy* to mean *having good health* and *healthful* to mean *health-giving*. A *healthy* mushroom might be anything but *healthful*.

human, humane. The tendency to use *human* as a noun (These *humans* are . . .) as well as an adjective (These *human* beings are . . .) is increasing and will undoubtedly prevail. As adjective, *human* means *characteristic of man, humane* means *kindly, decent* (the *humane* thing to do).

hurt. Only colloquially used as a noun, and then either entirely uncultivated or unbearably arch: Does it have a *hurt* in its paw?

identical same. Tautological, colloquial, uncultivated.

imply, infer. Implying is the action of the speaker or writer; inferring is the action of the listener or reader: Do you *imply* that he is a fool, or am I making a false *inference*?

individual. Colloquially used as substitute for *person* (This *individual* thinks . . .). In such use the special referential aspect of the word— to distinguish one from many (An *individual* may achieve more than a group)——is lost.

in, into. As prepositions, *in* is for position, *into* for direction of movement: He was *in* the dining-room and went directly *into* the kitchen. The use of *in* for both meanings is common in speech, rare in careful writing.

inside of. So written, and not as a single word. But *on-to* has achieved union (He steps *onto* the terrace). A related expression is *in back of,* or *back of;* it, too, remains ununited. *Inside of, onto, back of,* and *in back of* are almost universal in speech and very common in writing, but some very good writers resent the prepositional doubling and either drop one preposition altogether(*inside* the room, *to* the terrace) or use another word (*behind* the barn). Though common in speech, *in under* is not yet used by any serious writers. Obviously, no rule will hold here. The matter is one of gradual shifts and developed tastes.

irregardless, disregardless. Vulgarisms.

interpretative, interpretive. Some arbiters admit only the second form, but both are widely used without difference in meaning.

kind, sort. As nouns, singular and therefore to be used with singular adjectives and verbs: This kind is less expensive than that. *Kind of* and *sort of,* used to mean *somewhat* (He is *kind of* soft-hearted), are colloquial and uncultivated.

last, latest. A useful distinction assigns *last* to the terminal member of a group or series (the *last* game of the year) and *latest* to the most recent one (the *latest* effort to embarrass this country). *Last* is widely used, however, where the distinction would require *latest* (His *last* operation was unsuccessful, but his next . . .).

lay, laid, lie, lain. *Lay* (past form *laid*) takes an object: He *lays* the tie on the table; He *laid* it there; He *laid* his hand on the board. *Lie* (past forms *lay* and *lain*) is intransitive: He *lies* down; They *lay* without moving; We have *lain* asleep too long.

lend, loan. As verbs, interchangeable now, though once *lend* was reserved —by handbooks, at any rate—for the verb, *loan* for the noun (*Lend* me some money. Make me a *loan*). *Lend* shows no signs of becoming a noun (but see *hurt,* above).

less, fewer. Like *amount, number,* a pleasant distinction widely ignored. *Less* is used of amount (*less* money), *fewer* of number (*fewer* coins): If *fewer* members attend, we shall need *less* food.

may, might. *May* is used in the present-tense sequence, *might* in the past-tense sequence: If he *may* enter, she will want to; If he *might* enter, she would want to. *May of* and *might of* (He *may of gone*) are corruptions of *have* into *of*.

maximize. A relatively new word, developed by analogy with *minimize*. See *discussant,* above).

moral, morale. The adjective *moral* means *right and proper*. The noun (with an -e added from the French form of the adjective and the accent shifted) means *spirit.*

neither, nor; either, or. One careless construction is common: failure to observe the coordinates (He is not *either* clever *nor* honest. Corrected: He is not *either* clever *or* honest. He is *neither* clever *nor* honest). One awkwardness is almost unavoidable: selection of verb form when the nouns coordinated are of different person or number (*Neither* he *nor* I is? am? *Neither* the Senator *nor* his constituents has? have?). The best solution, not entirely arbitrary since it exploits proximity, is to match the verb form to the nearer of the two nouns or pronouns: *Neither he nor* I am. *Neither* the Senator *nor* his constituents have. If *Neither he nor I am* sounds too precious to be borne, avoid the problem: *Neither of us is.* But if the significance of *neither* amounts to anything at all, not *Neither of us are.*

nice, nice and. An exhausted adjective at best (a *nice* day) and, at worst (*nice and* helpful), merely a colloquial intensive.

none. Since the word is a shortening of *no one,* the argument for its use with a singular form of verb is logical. But *none* is so widely used in plural references and with no intention to sort the group into single units that a plural verb is common, both in speech and in cultivated writing: *None* of them are more convinced now than they were before he spoke.

no one. So written.

noted, notorious. *Notorious* has a pejorative sense (a *notorious* gambler); *noted* and *famous* are roughly synonymous (a *noted* author, a *famous* person).

nowheres, noways, anywheres, anyways. In all four words the terminal -*s* is colloquial and uncultivated.

off of, off from. See *inside of,* above.

official, officious. Both adjectives obviously derive from *office*. The distinction between them is that between what genuinely belongs to an office (an *official* communication) and what merely assumes the airs of official authority, with or without warrant but always with imperiousness (an *officious* manager). We admire, or at least put up with, what is official; we resent what is officious.

old-fashioned. So written. *Not* old-fashion.

one of. A common mistake is this one: He is *one of those men who spends* more than he makes. The position of *one* coerces the verb-form even though the subject (who) of the verb clearly refers to the plural noun *people* and requires a plural form of the verb. Equally common is an error involving person: You are the person who are responsible. Corrected: He is *one of* those men who spend more than they make. You are the person who is responsible.

oneself. Preferred to *one's self* unless an attempt is being made to create a distinction (*one's self* and one's body, *one's self* and all the other selves in the world). Note the trouble this reflexive suffix makes in English. We say *myself* (*my*, possessive) but *himself* (*him*, objective). By analogy, then, *meself* (now obsolete) and *hisself*, *theirself* (uncultivated but far from obsolete). Since the reflexive is also intensive, you may hear and read *Between him and myself*, but fastidious writers retain parallel pronouns: *Between him and me*. The plural pronoun requires plural reflexive form: *ourselves, themselves*, not *ourself, themself*.

overall. Imprecise and overused word meaning *general* (*overall* tendency) or *comprehensive* (*overall* view).

over with. See *inside of,* above.

owing to. A genteel, and grammatically questionable, substitute for *due to* (see above), apparently intended to regularize an idiom into decency. Two resolutions are possible. Instead of "Due to the heavy rain" or "Owing to the heavy rain," write "Because of the heavy rain"; or, better, make the construction unnecessary: "The heavy rain obliterated all tracks," rather than "Because of the heavy rain, all tracks were obliterated."

particular. See *certain,* above.

party. Legal jargon for *contracting person.* Colloquially, *any person* (A certain *party* is interested in knowing more about you). In this use, uncultivated.

percent, per cent., per cent. Alternates, equally acceptable. All derive from *per centum,* L., meaning *by* (or *calculated in terms of*) *the hundred.*

personal. Coupled with some nouns metaphorically used (personal equation, personal factor, personal coefficient), it is jargonic.

personal, personnel. *Personal* is an adjective (*personal* affairs). *Personnel* is a noun meaning *employees* or *staff* (military *personnel*) and, by derivation, an adjective meaning *having to do with employees or staff* (*personnel* officer). A *personal* adviser and a *personnel* adviser may have very different relations with those whom they advise.

phenomena. Colloquially used for both singular and plural, but in written edited prose plural only (These *phenomena* indicate that . . .). But for the future of this word, see *data,* above. *Phenomena* suffers from another misuse. It means *objects known through the senses* and is meant to distinguish those objects from *noumena, objects known through thought or intuition only.* To use *phenomena* as a synonym for *facts* or *events* is both inaccurate and pretentious.

plausible, feasible, conceivable. *Plausible* means *believable; feasible* means *practicable; conceivable* means *within the range of rational understanding.*

plenty. Used colloquially to mean *for the most part;* resembles *maybe* in its growing acceptance in edited written prose (There is *plenty* of competition but *maybe* not enough to suit a real scrapper).

plan on. *Plan on doing* is primarily colloquial; *plan to do* is more common in good written prose.

potful. As for all such compounds (cupful, handful), the plural adds *-s* (potfuls) unless the intent is to indicate plurality of the noun itself, in which case the compound disappears (He has his *pots full* now; *But* He has two *potfuls* of dirt).

potential. As a noun (He has a great *potential*), perhaps jargonic, certainly pretentious. Better: He is a promising athlete, student, musician, etc.

premium. By etymology, *only.* Its use to mean *of high quality* (a *premium* food, a *premium* performance) is hackneyed in advertising, reviewing, and the like.

pretty, pretty much. American idiom for *rather,* more colloquial than not.

prone, supine. *Prone* means *lying face down; supine* means *lying on one's back.* Metaphorical: *prone* means *inclined* (He is *prone* to hesitate); *supine* means *passive* or *cowardly* (He takes her remarks *supinely*).

proof, evidence. *Proof* is evidence sufficient to establish a conclusion. *Evidence* is whatever is brought forward in the attempt to establish a conclusion.

provided (-ing) that, if. Either *providing that* or *provided that* is an acceptable form, when the form is desirable at all. In the main, its formality suggests something contractual rather than something casual, for which *if* is more appropriate: If the rain falls, we shall get wet. *Provided* that you supply the funds, we agree to let you use our name as sponsors.

queer. As a verb (Their conduct *queered* the deal), both slangy and colloquial.

quote. A verb of unimpeachable reputation, but as a noun a colloquial shortening of *quotation* (This *quote* is taken from . . .). Also, a shortening for *quotation marks* (Put it in *quotes*).

raise, rise. As verbs, these words distinguish actions in the same way as *lay, lie* and *set, sit* As nouns, they are more interesting. They seem to be synonymous, but they are not in all instances interchangeable. We say *a raise in pay* but *a rise in the cost of living.*

reason is because, reason why. *The reason is because* is obviously redundant, but that does not keep it out of general colloquial use. It is seldom found in edited written prose. *Reason why,* on the other hand, though almost as obviously redundant, is common in both cultivated speech and cultivated writing. For the tender of ear, *reason is that* and *reason that* sound better.

refer back. So obviously redundant as to be admissible only for emphasis.

regarding, as regards, in regard to. Overused as synonym for *about.*

respective, respectively. Words meant to clarify relationship (Henry and John presented their gifts, a tin of ham and a pound of coffee *respectively,* and then left). The most common abuse reflects misplaced preciseness (They put their *respective* coats on the rack). Not to be confused with *respectfully.*

right off. Colloquial only, as are *right away, right now, right then. Right soon, right pretty, right new,* and the like are colloquial and regional.

round. Or *around.* Needs no preceding apostrophe since *round* is the older form.

Same. With or without a preceding *the,* this word is jargonic if it is used as a substitute for *it* (Having gathered this matter, we shall now assess *same* in the light of . . .). As elliptic for *the same thing* (The *same* may be said of . . .), it is common in good speech, perhaps a little less common in good writing, where the noun is more likely to be supplied (the *same* remark, the *same* intention).

said. Used as an adjective meaning *previously mentioned* (*said* document), the word is legal jargon. See *party,* above.

sensual, sensuous. Though efforts have been made to link *sensual* with the psychology and *sensuous* with the physiology of sense impressions, actual distinction now seems to be one of value. *Sensual* is at least mildly pejorative; *sensuous* is neutral or approbatory.

shall, will. Though a moderately useful distinction is commonly taught (*shall* for first person, *will* for second and third, except when determination or promise is involved), it is little observed and has no strong historical sanction. *Will* has largely supplanted *shall,* and the distinction between simple future and indication of promise or determination is left to context.

size, sized. As hyphenated to make an adjective, the proper form is *-sized* (pint-*sized*). See *age,* above.

slow, slowly. *Slow* is both adverb and adjective; *slowly* is an adverb. As adverbs, the two may or may not have exactly the same sense (same: drive *slow,* drive *slowly;* not the same: *slow*-moving car, *slowly* moving car).

soluble, solvable. Some writers use *solvable* only in referring to problems, *soluble* only in referring to physical elements. Negatives are *insoluble, unsolvable*. The noun *solution* serves both.

[split infinitive]. For strong emphasis, an adverb may sometimes split the *to* and verb of an infinitive (If you want *to* really *destroy* the program . . .). Generally the infinitive is best left intact (He decided *to read* through the last chapter hastily, *not* He decided *to* hastily *read* . . .). Except for eccentric stylistic effects it is almost never separated by more than a word (They hope *to,* in a manner of speaking, *"subsidize"* the enemy).

status. Has two common uses, the first one derived from the Latin original, *status quo* (His *status* at the time of the incident was entirely regular). The second use is apparently an extension of the first (They are trying to get *status* by moving to a suburb).

superior. Followed by *to,* not by *than.*

suspicion. Colloquially, both verb and noun; but in edited written prose, usually a noun only (He suspected me of perjury, *not* He *suspicioned* that I had perjured myself).

that, which. This distinction is sometimes made: *that* for restrictive clauses (The box *that* you want is there); *which* for nonrestrictive clauses (The box, *which* you need not take unless you want to, has no cover). The demonstrative adjective should not be used to modify a word also modified by a restrictive clause (The box *that* you want, *not That* box *that* you want). It is only fair to admit that these usages are not always observed even by impeccable stylists, partly because the discriminations are not essential and partly because euphony sometimes overrules.

till, until. Equally acceptable in speech or writing, but *until* is more common in writing.

too, very. *Too* is superlative; *very* is intensive. Colloquially, *too* is common as a substitute for *very,* though it obviously begs the question (He isn't feeling *too* well). When *very* is used with a passive participle, conservative usage requires an intervening *much* (very much improved), though some unsupplemented uses of *very* are now idiomatic (*very* interested, *very* tired). A rather recent substitute for both *very* and *too* is *that* (He isn't *that* serious about it), but it remains colloquial.

try and, try to. *Try to read* makes better sense for what is meant than *try and read,* but colloquially *try and* is used frequently.

type. As an adjunct word, it is jargonic (Hollywood-*type* setting, roller-*type* bed); it is hackneyed as a noun meaning no more than *kind* (that *type* of person).

unpractical. Or *impractical.*

upon, on. See *in, into.* Much depends on sound and something on idiom (*Upon* my word! *on* the house).

utilize. Means *use,* but some appear to find it more indicative of calculated action. Often merely pretentious.

used to. So written except in the negative (didn't *use* to) when customary past action is meant. In passive constructions of the verb *to use* (It is used for painting; it was used for painting), the negative form does not change (it is not *used* for painting).

various, different. A useful, but not essential distinction, assigns *various* to general distributive meaning (various members agree) and *different* to discrimination (He gave it to different members each time), but cultivated colloquial practice uses the words interchangeably.

who, whom. Traditionally, *who* is used as subject of verb, *whom* as object of verb and preposition. Colloquially, *who* is superseding *whom,* especially in questions (Who are you speaking to? Who did you give it to?), but edited written prose does not admit the locution intentionally. One sign of the confusion these pronouns produce appears in the substitution of *whom* for *who* in interrupted relative structures (This is the man whom I think would be most likely to help you). In such a sentence the strength of *I think* seems to attract the object-form even though the subject-form is needed to govern the verb *would be.* Like *Between him and I,* this mistake generally comes from a self-conscious effort to be correct, coupled with ignorance of grammatical form.

-wise, -ways. In many words, interchangeable (*endways, endwise*); in a few, only *-wise* occurs (*clockwise, likewise, otherwise*). Recently, the fashion has grown for attaching *-wise* to every noun in sight (policy-*wise,* money-*wise,* statistics-*wise*).

without. A preposition, not a conjunction, in cultivated usage: He goes *without* me. "He won't do it *without* I come" should be corrected to "He won't do it unless I come" or "He won't do it without my coming." *Without hardly* is a kind of double negative and should be corrected to *with hardly* or *almost without.*

yet. When *yet* is used adverbially, it takes the perfect tense forms (He has not done it yet, *not* He didn't do it yet).

❋ *Mechanics*

THIS BRIEF CHAPTER on mechanics is intended to be simply a convenient source of information about the technical matters most frequently troublesome to college students.

1) *CAPITALIZATION*

1) *Names.* Capitalize proper nouns and the adjectives derived from them. Darwin, Darwinian theory; France, French policy; Republican party; Roman Catholic Church. When such adjectives come to be part of the name of an object in common use, capitalization generally disappears: china cups, india rubber, italic type, french fries, bermuda shorts, graham cracker.

2) *Honorifics.* Capitalize titles of honor which are followed by a proper noun: Rabbi Wise, President Hayes, Professor Wilson, Mr. Eliot. Capitalize titles of honor when they refer to a specific person: the President of the Board of Overseers, the Mayor of Cleveland. *But:* A corporation consists of a president, secretary, treasurer, board of directors . . . .

3) *Titles.* Capitalize the first word, the last word, and all other words except articles, one-syllable prepositions, and conjunctions in the titles of books, stories, poems, plays, essays, lectures, paintings, sculptures, motion pictures, and songs: *Twenty Thousand Leagues Under the Sea, Ode on a Grecian Urn, The Adoration of the Magi, Moonlight and Roses.* Within a sentence do not capitalize "the" if it is the first word in the title of a newspaper or magazine: the *London Times,* the *American Scholar.*

4) *Courses of Study.* Capitalize as for 3) if the course of study has a formal title: Economic Theory, Drama since Ibsen. Do not capitalize such terms otherwise: Capitalism represents a change in economic

theory from . . . . ; the development of the drama since Ibsen shows the influence . . . .

5) *Geographic Areas.* Capitalize words referring to geographic areas: the Far West, the Near East, the Old South. When the reference is adjectival, the word is sometimes capitalized and sometimes not, depending on the tastes of the writer or the practice of a publisher: a Western sandwich, a western sandwich; but if the reference is to an area of land or water whose boundaries are clearly fixed, capitalization will occur: the Atlantic coast. Words indicating direction only are not capitalized: They will go west this summer. (*But:* They will visit the West this summer.)

6) *The Deity.* Capitalize nouns and pronouns referring to a deity: Our God Who made heaven and earth sets His laws in the hearts of men; Jehovah; Lord; Saviour; Allah; Zeus.

7) *Historical Matters.* Capitalize the names of historical events, personages, places, institutions, artifacts, memorials, and documents: the French Revolution, General Taylor, Faneuil Hall, the Shenandoah Valley, the Washington Monument, the Bill of Rights.

8) *Family Relationships.* Capitalize words indicating family relationship when they are used in conjunction with proper names and when they are used as a substitute for proper names: Uncle Tom; my surprise at seeing Grandfather alone. Do not capitalize such words when they are used generically or when they are modified by possessives: the three sisters; my father, Mary's uncle (*But:* my Grandfather Perkins, Mary's Uncle John).

9) *Quotations.* Capitalize the first word of a quotation, if the quotation is itself a complete sentence, not if it is only part of a sentence: They answered together, "We have done nothing wrong." (*But:* They swore that they had done "nothing wrong.") If the quotation is interrupted, capitalize wherever a new sentence begins: "They have done it again," he observed, "and they deserve to win." "Don't put it there," he warned. "The water may damage it."

Do not capitalize

10) *Seasons.* fall, winter, spring, summer, autumn, springtime.

11) *Phrases or sentences following a colon.* The long months had restored his health: he was almost a new man. However, capitalization may occur if the colon is followed by a rule, a proverb, a sentence cited from a familiar text, an example, or the like.

12) *Parentheses within sentences, even if they are complete sentences.* He stepped further into the room (it was a library, he noted) and cleared his throat noisily in hope of attracting attention. Again, capitalization may occur if the parenthetical interruption is used for providing examples which are complete sentences.

2) SPELLING

Spelling is a matter of convention based on linguistic development. Without the convention, communication would be much more difficult than it is. For that reason the convention deserves respect. Although it is true that some people have what appears to be a genuine inability to spell even simple words correctly, the condition is so rare that no college student can use it as an excuse; if he has reason to think his disability is physical or psychological, he has an obligation to seek help from an oculist or a counselor.

The only "cure" for most bad spellers is the replacing of bad habits by good ones: each must discipline himself in proportion to his need. These procedures will help:

1) Always keep a dictionary within reach as you write; consult it, during revision of your text, whenever you are in doubt about the correct spelling of a word.

2) Check the spelling of words you seldom use.

3) If you habitually misspell some words, make a list of them and keep it where you can consult it readily.

4) Learn by heart the distinction between such similar-sounding words or frequently confused words as these:

accept, except	diary, dairy
affect, effect	dual, duel
all ready, already	eminent, imminent
altar, alter	euphemism, euphuism
assent, ascent	foreword, forward
breath, breathe	formally, formerly
capital, capitol	genteel, gentle, gentile
censure, censor	genus, genius
choose, chose	hear, here
climactic, climatic	hoard, horde
coma, comma	idle, idol
compliment, complement	illicit, elicit
conscience, conscious	illusion, allusion
corps, corpse	immanent, imminent
costume, custom	ingenious, ingenuous
coarse, course	irrelevant [irrevelant]
council, counsel, consul	it, it's
deceased, diseased	knew, new
decent, descent, dissent	know, no
desert, dessert	later, latter
device, devise	loose, lose

moral, morale
of, off
past, passed
peace, piece
psychological, physiological
plain, plane
pore, poor, pour
precede, proceed
precedents, precedence
presence, presents
principal, principle
prophecy, prophesy
quiet, quite
raise, raze
receipt, recipe
recent, resent
respectively, respectfully
rite, right
route, root, rout
sense, since
sight, site, cite

sleight, slight
stationary, stationery
statue, statute, stature
straight, strait
suit, suite
their, there, they're
then, than
threw, through
to, too, two
vain, vein, vane
venal, venial
vice, vise
weak, week
weather, whether, wether, whither
which, witch
whose, who's
wrack, rack
wrapped, rapt
wry, rye
your, you're

5) If you are not certain about the spelling of words containing one of the following combinations, *always check by dictionary*. There are "rules" for each combination, but if you have not learned them by now, the likelihood is that you will master the combinations only by forcing yourself to check until they stick permanently in your mind.

a. *ie* and *ei* (*believe, receive, weigh*)
b. final consonants before a suffix (*refér, referring; trável, traveling*)
c. final vowels before a suffix (*arrange, arrangement; desire, desirable; change, changeable*)
d. final *y* in plurals and verb forms (*lady, ladies; alley, alleys; stay, stayed; pay, paid*)
e. final *o* in plurals (*radio, radios; potato, potatoes*)
f. final *fe* in plurals (*wife, wives*); final *ff* in plurals (*sheriff, sheriffs*); but final *f* in plurals is variable (*shelf, shelves; chief, chiefs*)
g. plurals of compounds (*courts-martial, handfuls, menservants*)

6) Compound adjectives are hyphenated when they precede the noun unless the first part of the compound ends in *-ly* (*second-class citizen; poorly paid worker*).

7) Words at line end divide by syllable only (*pay-ing, be-gin-ning, un-pre-ten-tious, knowl-edge*).

8) Possession is indicated for personal nouns (not for personal *pronouns*) by an apostrophe with or without an inflectional *s*.

a. Singular nouns not ending in *s* take *'s*.

Gibbon's *Decline and Fall*

b. One-syllable singular nouns ending in *s* take *'s*.

James's pragmatic philosophy

c. Multisyllable nouns ending in *s* take only an apostrophe.

Collins' *Ode to Evening*

d. Plural nouns ending in *s* take only an apostrophe.

the Goncourts' journals

e. Plural nouns not ending in *s* take *'s*.

Gentlemen's Magazine

Possession may also be indicated by prepositional phrases (the pragmatic philosophy of William James) and is preferably so indicated when the relationship is not so much one of possession in the sense of owning as that of whole-to-part (the streets of Paris, the paintings of the Romantic Movement, the speeches in the Senate).

3) PUNCTUATION

Unlike spelling, punctuation is less a matter of convention than of common sense. Properly used, it indicates relationships within sentences and between sentences so that the reader may proceed without uncertainty. Improperly used, it misleads the reader.

1) THE PERIOD ·
a. Declarative and imperative sentences end with a period.

b. Abbreviations require a period.

2) THE COMMA ·   Nine tenths of the errors in punctuation on students' papers are due to misuse of the comma. These are the principal situations in which errors occur.

a. The use or omission of commas to set off appositive words and phrases depends on the relationship intended. If the appositive is an adjunct (Charles the Bald, Peter the Hermit), commas are omitted. If the appositive limits or restricts the word to which it stands in apposition, commas are likewise omitted:

Europeans acclaimed the novelist James Fenimore Cooper as they had once acclaimed Scott.

If the appositive is simply supplementary—if it adds information but does not limit or restrict—commas separate it from the word it supplements:

> The author of *Pathfinder,* James Fenimore Cooper, was a native of New York State.

Note that, if the appositive expression is to be set off by commas, it must be *completely set off:*

> The last part of *Dead Souls,* Gogol's greatest work, appears to be irrevocably lost. NOT: The last part of *Dead Souls,* Gogol's greatest work appears to be irrevocably lost.

b. Restrictive clauses (those that materially qualify the referent) are *not* set off by commas:

> The chapters that remain show the powerful genius of that great novelist. (Restrictive)

> The remaining chapters, which have been translated into a dozen languages, show the powerful genius of that great novelist. (Non-restrictive)

In the first example the phrase "that remain" limits the word "chapters." The subject of "show" is not merely "chapters" but "chapters that remain." In the second example the "which" clause adds information but does not limit "chapter" and does not govern "show." (See Glossary on *that, which.*)

2. Clauses joined by the conjunctions *and, but, or* ordinarily take a comma before the conjunction, unless both clauses are short.

> He wrote the essay, and I read it as soon as he brought it to me.

A comma is always helpful when *for* is used as a conjunction:

> I read it at once, for the publisher was calling for copy.

d. Commas separate items in series; their use before "and" in such a series is optional.

> The titles of books, stories, plays, and moving-pictures should be underlined in manuscript.

> A wordy, abstruse, pretentious statement is seldom clear. *But:* A wordy, abstruse, pretentious introductory sentence may easily discourage a reader.

> (In this example the adjective "introductory" has a different relationship to "sentence" from that of the other adjectives; "introductory sentence" is a unit of the same kind as "moving-pictures," but does not have enough use to gain the hyphen of "moving-pictures.")

e. Participial phrases are *completely* set off by commas—

> Reading the report again, he discovered the important detail he had missed.

> He discovered, by reading the report again, that he had missed several important details.

> He spent the remainder of the day at home, reading the report once again.

—unless they follow the main clause and are very short:

> He came home singing lustily.

f. Dependent clauses that explain or give a reason for the main clause are sometimes set off by commas:

> Ortega rejects this definition, for he believes "mass" is not a matter of number but of mental habit.

> BUT: He uses the term "mass-mind" whenever he refers to the mental habit of rejecting the unique or the original.

When dependent clauses *precede* the main statement, they are always set off by commas unless they are very short (note the punctuation of this rule):

> Whenever Ortega refers to the mental habit of rejecting the unique or the original, he uses the term "mass mind."

g. Commas set off parenthetical expressions of various kinds:

> Albert Einstein, the distinguished mathematician and physicist, was also an amateur musician. (appositive)

> He said that, like other scientists, he found mathematics and music a congenial combination. (additive)

> He insisted, moreover, that the two have fundamental similarities. (connective)

> Both are, in their purest form, entirely abstract; both use an entirely symbolic, that is, nonrepresentational, idiom. (qualifying; explanatory)

h. Occasionally, commas are needed where syntax does not require them simply to prevent misreading or to indicate a pause essential for correct reading:

> In the open air drama takes on the dignity of its surroundings.

> CORRECTED: In the open air, drama takes on the dignity of its surroundings.

> What must be must be.

> CORRECTED: What must be, must be.

i. Commas are used to separate numbers, dates, and addresses:

> There were 19,170 more votes cast this year than last.

> He was born on February 22, 1936, in Washington, D.C.

> We are moving from Middletown, Connecticut, to Middletown, New York; our address there will be 29 Park Street, Middletown 14, New York.

j. Degrees and titles are separated from the names of their bearers by commas:

> This report is the work of Samuel E. Jones, M.D., a friend of the late Consul General, M. Georges Faivre.

k. All forms of direct address are set off from the text proper:

> And these, my friends, are answers to your questions.

> If you want to come along, John, you are welcome to do so.

l. Commas set quoted words off from other parts of sentences that contain them, unless the quoted words are interrogative or exclamatory:

> "Virtue," she said, "is not the prerogative of bachelors."

> "Isn't it?" he asked ironically.

> "No, it isn't!" she retorted with vehemence. "You men are all alike," she went on. "You think you own the universe."

3) THE SEMICOLON • The semicolon is a connection between independent clauses not joined by a conjunction:

> History makes men wise; poetry makes them witty.

In such use, it suggests closer relationship and a more studied balance between units than is indicated by separate sentences. It may also separate a series of long, dependent clauses:

> When a man has read deeply in history; when he has come to appreciate the subtle illumination of poetry; when he has mastered the knowledge of nature, animate and inanimate; when he has examined the moral and religious thought of all time: then, and only then, can it be said of him that he has a liberal education.

There is often confusion about the use of the semicolon with such conjunctive words as "however," "therefore," "nonetheless," consequently." If such words introduce a clause, a semicolon precedes them; if they interrupt a clause, they are set off by commas:

> He made up his mind without any investigation at all; therefore, his discovery of the truth taught him the folly of hasty judgment.

If he had investigated the matter, he would not have said what he did say. He blurted out his opinion, however, without making any inquiry at all.

4) THE COLON • The colon is often confused with the semicolon. It has so definite a function in writing that every student should learn its particular uses and practice them frequently.

a. The colon may introduce an enumeration:

> Although he is known primarily as the author of the novel *Moby Dick,* Melville wrote sixteen books in all, demonstrating his skill in four different literary forms: the novel, the short story, the account of travel, and poetry.

b. The more important structural use of the colon is in expanding, explaining, or illustrating what precedes it:

> *War and Peace* is the giant of Russian fiction: by sheer comprehensiveness it overshadows all other novels in the language. (explaining)
> Like a giant, it gazes down on the panorama of Russian life: the debt-ridden extravagance of urban aristocrats, the poverty and obduracy of the peasants, the disorderly yet impassioned life of the military, the cynicism and anguish of the spiritually uprooted. (expanding)

> And its gaze is not only wide but penetrating: it reveals the quiet nobility of Andrei as superbly as it displays the tumult and confusion of the battle of Novgorod. (illustrating)

c. If the enumeration or expansion or illustration is the grammatical object of a preposition or the grammatical object or complement of a verb, the colon does not occur:

> The nations attending the conference are England, Denmark, France, West Germany, and the Netherlands.

> The cake is made of a rich batter filled with candied cherries, ginger, citron, and nuts.

5) THE DASH; PARENTHESES • These two marks of punctuation are most frequently used to set off matter not grammatically related to its context. Of the two, the dash is the less formal.

> Both men contributed—Beethoven the more powerfully of the two—to the enlargement of musical form.

> Beethoven's third symphony (the *Eroica*) provoked a storm of protest.

The dash is also used—and too often so used—to produce emphasis:

> To Beethoven, protest meant nothing, favor meant nothing; his life was focused entirely on one passion—music.

6) QUOTATION MARKS • Although the liberality with which quotation marks are used varies from writer to writer, general publishing practice has more or less established the conventions listed below.

a. Quotation marks are necessary for setting off phrases or passages not one's own (see the section entitled "Plagiarism"). They enclose *only* the quoted words:

> Plutarch tells us that, although the Athenians continued to observe Solon's laws, they nonetheless "expected some change and were desirous of another government."

> "Hence it was," Plutarch goes on, "that through the city. . . ."

Note that the commas fall *before* the quotation mark. That is true also of periods, even if a single quoted word occurs at the end of the sentence:

> Plutarch is not specific about what the Athenians expected; he limits himself to the general word "change."

The placement of other marks of punctuation in relation to quotation marks will depend on the sense of the passage:

> How does Plutarch know that "all expected some change"?

When a quoted passage continues for more than one paragraph, quotation marks are set at the beginning of *each* paragraph but at the end of the *last* paragraph only. If the citation is longer than seven or eight lines, a more common practice is to indent the quoted passage, *omitting quotation marks entirely.*

b. The terms of a formal definition and any other use of a word as though it were an object require quotation marks or italics:

> In the title *Brave New World,* the word "brave" means something like "good" or "noble."

> His "Yessir" was immediate but a shade contemptuous.

c. Quotation marks may also indicate that a word is being used in a special sense, usually one which the author has established beforehand or feels will be readily understood by his reader:

> He is genuinely an "amateur" tennis player, who plays for love of the game, not for money.

d. Colloquial words and slang expressions, if used in a context that does not readily accommodate them, are often set off by quotation marks. The purpose of the usage seems to be largely protective, the author making sure by this means that the reader knows his choice of language to have been deliberate.

Apparently teen-agers no longer "dig" that crooner as they once did.

In our part of the country such "toney" people seldom have much to do with the hill dweller.

e. The use of quotation marks to set off passages of dialogue from description and explanation has a long tradition in English. The convention is simple enough to illustrate, but it is no longer so invariably observed, even in novels, as it once was:

"You can do it, I think," he said, "but you will have to do it alone."

BUT: He said that you could do it but that you would have to do it alone.

A few contemporary writers omit the quotation marks, substituting a dash before the beginning of a speech or using no mark of punctuation at all:

—You can do it, I think. But you will have to do it alone, he added.

Or: He looked at her steadily. You can do it, he said, but you will have to do it alone.

Both of the foregoing examples get around the difficulty posed by the running together of "I think" and "he said" which is so neatly taken care of by quotation marks, but the fact that a difficulty arises may illustrate a sound reason for retaining the convention.

7) BRACKETS · Brackets are commonly used as a means of indicating additions to a cited text which have been supplied by the citer of the text.

The third of Haney's letters on the subject was more specific. It included full information about the location of the mine and an account of the operations so far completed. Then, in a sudden burst of candor, it concluded:

It is now only May [the letter is dated May 16] and already I have taken enough silver out of this hole to make me comfitable [*sic*] for the rest of my life.

(The bracketed "*sic*" is a device for indicating to the reader that the misspelling of "comfortable" occurred in the original text and is not a proofreader's or author's oversight.)

If a parenthetical expression occurs within another parenthetical expression, the internal one is set off by brackets.

8) SUSPENSION POINTS · In citing a text, a writer may wish to omit parts that are irrelevant to the purpose for which it is being cited. An omission is indicated by the simple device of inserting suspension points, or ellipses, at the proper place in the text:

The fourth and final letter has undertones of tragedy, but it begins with characteristic cheerfulness:

> Today I am going back to see Melia [Haney's only living sister] and I plan to take what I have got saved back with me. There is enough . . . for both of us, and some to spare . . . . It is a long trek, and I don't like to go it alone, but I must. Anyone who can stick it out here for ten months sure don't need to worry much about lasting through a little ten-day ride on horseback.

The first appearance of suspension points in the passage above uses only three since the omission occurs within a sentence. The second appearance uses a fourth to indicate the period at the end of the sentence from which the last part has been omitted.

In order to accommodate the text he cites to the sentence introducing it, a writer may break into the middle of a sentence or paragraph, or he may break off before the end. To indicate such interruptions he uses suspension points.

> In all the writing of these hardy adventurers there is something melancholy, a feeling—as one of them put it—of ". . . a hollowness inside that ore won't fill, a hole bigger'n a mine shaft and twicet as dark."

If a writer quotes a passage long enough to indent but still less (either at beginning or end) than the complete paragraph in the original, he indicates the omission of sentences in the same way that he indicates the omission of words from a sentence: by three suspension points before the quotation or four points after it.

❂ *The Use of Sources*

1) A DEFINITION OF PLAGIARISM

THE ACADEMIC COUNTERPART of the bank embezzler and of the manufacturer who mislabels his product is the plagiarist, the student or scholar
who leads his reader to believe that what he is reading is the original
work of the writer when it is not. If it could be assumed that the distinction between plagiarism and honest use of sources is perfectly clear in
everyone's mind, there would be no need for the explanation that follows; merely the warning with which this definition concludes would be
enough. But it is apparent that sometimes men of good will draw the
suspicion of guilt upon themselves (and, indeed, are guilty) simply because they are not aware of the illegitimacy of certain kinds of "borrowing" and of the procedures for correct identification of materials other
than those gained through independent research and reflection.

The spectrum is a wide one. At one end there is a word-for-word copying of another's writing without enclosing the copied passage in quotation marks and identifying it in a footnote, *both* of which are necessary.
(This includes, of course, the copying of all or any part of another student's paper.) It hardly seems possible that anyone of college age or more
could do that without clear intent to deceive. At the other end there is
the almost casual slipping in of a particularly apt term which one has
come across in reading and which so admirably expresses one's opinion
that one is tempted to make it personal property. Between these poles
there are degrees and degrees, but they may be roughly placed in two
groups. Close to outright and blatant deceit—but more the result, perhaps, of laziness than of bad intent—is the patching together of random
jottings made in the course of reading, generally without careful identification of their source, and then woven into the text, so that the result is a
mosaic of other people's ideas and words, the writer's sole contribution

274

being the cement to hold the pieces together. Indicative of more effort and, for that reason, somewhat closer to honesty, though still dishonest, is the paraphrase, an abbreviated (and often skillfully prepared) restatement of someone's else's analysis or conclusion, without acknowledgement that another person's text has been the basis for the recapitulation.

The examples given below should make clear the dishonest and the proper use of source material. If instances occur which these examples do not seem to cover, conscience will in all likelihood be prepared to supply advice.

THE SOURCE •

The importance of the *Second Treatise of Government* printed in this volume is such that without it we should miss some of the familiar features of our own government. It is safe to assert that the much criticized branch known as the Supreme Court obtained its being as a result of Locke's insistence upon the separation of powers; and that the combination of many powers in the hands of the executive under the New Deal has still to encounter opposition because it is contrary to the principles enunciated therein, the effect of which is not spent, though the relationship may not be consciously traced. Again we see the crystallizing force of Locke's writing. It renders explicit and adapts to the British politics of his day the trend and aim of writers from Languet and Bodin through Hooker and Grotius, to say nothing of the distant ancients, Aristotle and the Stoic school of natural law. It sums up magistrally the arguments used through the ages to attack authority vested in a single individual, but it does so from the particular point of view engendered by the Revolution of 1688 and is in harmony with the British scene and mental climate of the growing bourgeoisie of that age. Montesquieu and Rousseau, the framers of our own Declaration of Independence, and the statesmen (or should we say merchants and speculators?) who drew up the Constitution have reechoed its claims for human liberty, for the separation of powers, for the sanctity of private property. In the hands of these it has been the quarry of liberal doctrines; and that it has served the Socialist theory of property based on labor is final proof of its breadth of view.

> CHARLES L. SHERMAN, "Introduction" to John Locke, *Treatise of Civil Government* and *A Letter Concerning Toleration.*

1) WORD-FOR-WORD PLAGIARIZING •

It is not hard to see the importance of the *Second Treatise of Government* to our own democracy. Without it we should miss some of the most familiar features of our own government. It is safe to assert that the much criticized branch known as the Supreme Court obtained its being as a result of Locke's insistence upon the separation of powers; and that the combination of many powers in the hands of the executive under the New Deal has still to encounter opposition because it is contrary to the principles enunciated therein, the effect of which is not spent, though the relationship may not be consciously traced. The framers of our own Declaration of Independence and the statesmen who drew up the Constitution have re-echoed its claims for human liberty, for the separation of powers, for the sanctity of private property. All these are marks of the influence of Locke's *Second Treatise* on our own way of life.

In this example, after composing half of a first sentence, the writer copies exactly what is in the original text, leaving out the center section of the paragraph and omitting the names of Montesquieu and Rousseau where he takes up the text again. The last sentence is also the writer's own.

If the writer had enclosed all the copied text in quotation marks and had identified the source in a footnote, he would not have been liable to the charge of plagiarism; a reader might justifiably have felt, however, that the writer's personal contribution to the discussion was not very significant.

2) THE MOSAIC •

The crystallizing force of Locke's writing may be seen in the effect his *Second Treatise of Government* had in shaping some of the familiar features of our own government. That much criticized branch known as the Supreme Court and the combination of many powers in the hands of the executive under the New Deal are modern examples. But even the foundations of our state—the Declaration of Independence and the Constitution—have re-echoed its claims for human liberty, for the separation of powers, for the sanctity of private property. True, the influence of others is also marked in our Constitution—from the trend and aim of writers like Languet and Bodin, Hooker and Grotius, to say nothing of Aristotle and the Stoic school of natural law; but the fundamental influence is Locke's *Treatise,* the very quarry of liberal doctrines.

Note how the following phrases have been lifted out of the original text and moved into new patterns:

crystallizing force of Locke's writing

some of the familiar features of our own government

much criticized branch known as the Supreme Court

combination of many powers in the hands of the executive under the New Deal

have re-echoed its claims for human liberty . . . property

from the trend and aim . . . Grotius

to say nothing of Aristotle and . . . natural law

quarry of liberal doctrines

As in the first example, there is really no way of legitimizing such a procedure. To put every stolen phrase within quotation marks would produce an almost unreadable, and quite worthless, text.

3) THE PARAPHRASE ·

PARAPHASE: Many fundamental aspects of our own government are
ORIGINAL: Many familiar features of our own government are

apparent in the *Second Treatise of Government.* One can safely
apparent in the *Second Treatise of Government.* It is safe to

say that the oft-censured Supreme Court really owes its exist-
assert that the much criticized . . . Court obtained its being as

ence to the Lockeian demand that powers in government be kept
a result of Locke's insistence upon the separation of powers;

separate; equally one can say that the allocation of varied
and that the combination of many powers

and widespread authority to the President during the era of
in the hands of the executive under the

the New Deal has still to encounter opposition because it is
New Deal has still to encounter opposition because it is

contrary to the principles enunciated therein . . . . Once more it
contrary to the principles enunciated therein . . . . Again we see

is possible to note the way in which Locke's writing clarified
the crystallizing force of Locke's writing.

existing opinion.

The foregoing interlinear presentation shows clearly how the writer has simply traveled along with the original text, substituting approximately equivalent terms except where his understanding fails him, as it does with "crystallizing," or where the ambiguity of the original is too great a tax on his ingenuity for him to proceed, as it is with "to encounter opposition . . . consciously traced" in the original.

Such a procedure as the one shown in this example has its uses; for one thing, it is valuable for the student's own understanding of the passage; and it may be valuable for the reader as well. How, then, may it be properly used? The procedure is simple. The writer might begin the second sentence with: "As Sherman notes in the introduction to his edition of the *Treatise,* one can safely say . . ." and conclude the paraphrased passage with a footnote giving the additional identification necessary. Or he might indicate directly the exact nature of what he is doing, in this fashion: "To paraphrase Sherman's comment . . ." and conclude that also with a footnote indicator.

In point of fact, this source does not particularly lend itself to honest paraphrase, with the exception of that one sentence which the paraphraser above copied without change except for abridgement. The pur-

pose of paraphrase should be to simplify or to throw a new and significant light on a text; it requires much skill if it is to be honestly used
and should rarely be resorted to by the student except for the purpose,
as was suggested above, of his personal enlightment.

4) THE "APT" TERM •

> The *Second Treatise of Government* is a veritable quarry of liberal doc-
> trines. In it the crystallizing force of Locke's writing is markedly apparent.
> The cause of human liberty, the principle of separation of powers, and the
> inviolability of private property—all three, major dogmas of American
> constitutionalism—owe their presence in our Constitution in large part
> to the remarkable *Treatise* which first appeared around 1685 and was
> destined to spark, within three years, a revolution in the land of its
> author's birth and, ninety years later, another revolution against that land.

Here the writer has not been able to resist the appropriation of two striking terms—"quarry of liberal doctrines" and "crystallizing force"; a perfectly proper use of the terms would have required only the addition of
a phrase: The *Second Treatise of Government* is, to use Sherman's suggestive expression, a "quarry of liberal doctrines." In it the "crystallizing
force"—the term again is Sherman's—of Locke's writing is markedly apparent. . . .

Other phrases in the text above—"the cause of human liberty," "the
principle of the separation of powers," "the inviolability of private property"—are clearly drawn directly from the original source but are so
much matters in the public domain, so to speak, that no one could
reasonably object to their re-use in this fashion.

Since one of the principal aims of a college education is the development of intellectual honesty, it is obvious that plagiarism is a particularly serious offense, and the punishment for it is commensurately severe.
What a penalized student suffers can never really be known by anyone
but himself; what the student who plagiarizes and "gets away with it"
suffers is less public and probably less acute, but the corruptness of his
act, the disloyalty and baseness it entails, must inevitably leave a mark
on him as well as on the institution of which he is a member.

2) *MAKING A BIBLIOGRAPHY; USING FOOTNOTES*

Essays written for college courses generally require the use of
"sources": books, periodicals, and newspapers containing information
relevant to the topic of the essay to be written. The citation of such
sources occurs in one or both of two places: in footnotes; in a bibliography appended to the essay.

Very simply, a bibliography lists the books, periodicals and newspapers, and other documents actually used in the preparation of the

essay; a footnote indicates very precisely the source of a quotation or specific statement occurring in the text of the essay. For both, a more or less standardized system has been developed so that readers anywhere can turn quickly from the footnote or the bibliographical listing to the proper source and be sure that they have at hand the correct volume of the correct edition of the cited work. This section provides, in a form as abbreviated as clarity permits, the fundamental information you will need about these two tools of scholarly work.

BIBLIOGRAPHY •

A bibliography lists the books, periodicals, and newspapers, and other documents actually used in the preparation of an essay. (There are bibliographies, to be sure, which do more than that, but for present purposes the definition given above is accurate.) It is, therefore, a record for the reader of the kind and amount of research done in preparing the essay and, as such, it enables him not only to verify the documentation but also to make at a glance an estimate of the probable value of the paper. It is this latter function which occasionally leads the writer to make one of two errors in the compilation of a bibliography: (1) the listing of everything read during the period of research, whether or not it has any relevance to or value for the essay, a completeness that is both pretentious and wasteful of the reader's time and energy; (2) the listing of important or important-sounding volumes which have not been read at all or have only been "looked into," clearly a dishonest procedure.

The following examples illustrate the common kinds of bibliographical entry.

1) Lunt, W. E. *History of England.* New York. 1947

The author's name is given as it appears on the title page of the book itself, but with surname first so that alphabetization of entries will be obvious.

The title is italicized. (This is the equivalent of underlining in typescript and manuscript.)

The place of publication and date of publication are listed in that order.

2) Crosby, John. "Speechlessness at Great Length," New York *Herald Tribune,* CXI (July 23, 1951), p. 13.

The title here is set in quotation marks because it is only an article, a part of a larger work. Italicizing is reserved for the larger work (New York *Herald Tribune*). The simple rule for capitalization of titles explains usage here and elsewhere: *capitalize all words in a title except articles and one-syllable prepositions and conjunctions, and always capitalize the first and the last word.*

The volume number is given in Roman numerals to distinguish it from the numbers that follow. It is necessary for periodicals and newspapers because back numbers are bound by volumes for library storage.

The date of the issue and the page on which the article can be found provide all the additional information that is needed for quick access to the source. Commas separate each piece of information from the next.

3) "Haiti." *Encyclopædia Britannica,* 14th ed. (1936), XI, 81–83.

As is common in encyclopedias, the author of this article is not indicated. The entry therefore begins with the title of the article.

It is important that the edition be noted because the content of the article might be different in another edition and the location of it within the set would almost certainly be different.

4) Turgot, Anne Robert Jacques. *Œuvres de Turgot,* ed. Eugène Daire. 2 vols. Paris, 1844.

The title appears exactly as on the title page (is not translated).

In this case the author's name is implicit in the title, but is listed nonetheless so that the entry may be alphabetically placed. The man who prepared the *Œuvres (Works)* for publication is listed after the abbreviation "ed." ("edited by").

Note that the number of volumes has been stated. This is customary procedure if the work has more than one volume. Some bibliographers give the number of pages in one-volume works, but that is not necessary. Page numbers *are* given, however, in the second and third examples above because the source cited forms only part of a larger work whose other parts are not necessarily germane to the topic.

A final note: the items in a bibliography should be arranged alphabetically, the first word in an item determining its alphabetical placement, unless the first word is an article (the, a, an); in that case, the following word is the basis for alphabetization.

FOOTNOTES •

A footnote indicates very precisely the source of a quotation or specific statement occurring in the text of the essay. (It may also give incidental or supplementary information, of course.) There is some variation in the form of footnotes from one publishing house to another and even from one scholarly society to another. The instructions that follow, however, have the authority of most of the university presses in the United States and conform, as do those on bibliography, to the style sheet of the Modern Language Association. Only the most commonly used terms are presented for study. These few simple generalizations deserve prior attention and observance:

1) Number the footnotes consecutively throughout an essay.
2) Place the footnotes for each page at the bottom of that page; or, if you want to save yourself a great deal of space calculating, assemble them all on a separate sheet at the end of the essay.
3) Make sure, in the final draft, that the numbers in the text correspond to the numbers attached to relevant footnotes.
4) Indicate the presence of a footnote by an Arabic numeral in the text. Ordinarily, this numeral should come at the end of a sentence. It should always be raised above the line of text:

> Jones vehemently denied the report.[6] When the . . .

When footnotes are infrequent, an asterisk or other symbol may be used in place of numbers.
5) Use footnotes sparingly. Their purpose is to inform the reader, not to impress him.

The following series of footnotes satisfies the most common situations. A full explanation follows the series.

[1] Theodor Wilhelm and Gerhard Graefe, *German Education Today* (Berlin: Terramare, 1936), pp. 3–5.
[2] James Bryant Conant, "The Advancement of Learning in the United States in the Post-War World," *Science* XCIX (February 4, 1944), 91.
[3] Ibid., p. 92.
[4] *Jahrbuch des Reichsarbeitsdienstes,* 1937–38 (Berlin, 1937), S. 34.
[5] Conant, p. 94.

Explanation. The first footnote is a reference to three pages in a book published by Terramare in Berlin and written by two men. Their names appear in the order in which they are found on the title page. Note that they are not reversed so that the surname comes first as in bibliographical entries; this is simply because there is no purpose in making the adjustment necessary for alphabetization when arrangement is by order of occurrence in the text.

The second note refers to one page in an article that appeared in volume ninety-nine of *Science* magazine. In such an instance it is not necessary to name the publisher or place of publication if the magazine is at all well known, but it is advisable to give the date of issue as well as the volume number. Note that the page reference for a publication does not use the abbreviation "p." (for "page") or "pp." (for "pages") if the volume number is given. In the first example (where there is no volume number indicated because the work is published in a single volume) the abbreviation *is* used.

The third note is a reference to a different page of the same work as that referred to in (2). "Ibid." is an abbreviation for the Latin word *ibidem* meaning "in the same place" and always points back to the immediately preceding work.

The fourth note refers to a yearbook, a compilation of statistics (in this case, concerning state work projects). Such a volume is the work of a host of men, and there is no point in indicating either editor or author for any particular section. The abbreviation "S." stands for "page" in German.

The fifth note is also a reference to the article by Mr. Conant. This time, however, "Ibid." could not be used since another reference intervenes. Therefore, the author's name and the page number alone are given.

These additional footnote abbreviations occur frequently in scholarly texts:

cf.	*compare*	loc. cit.	*in the place cited;* (different from op. cit. because it refers to the same *passage,* not simply to the same work, as previously cited)
ch.	*chapter*		
et al.	*and others*		
ff.	*following*		
l.	*line*		
ll.	*lines*	passim	*throughout the work, here and there*
v.	*see*		
viz.	*namely*		

Just as honesty requires quotation marks around any statement copied directly from a written source, it requires a footnote to indicate the place from which information has been gathered or from which paraphrased reconstructions are woven into the text.

A fine bibliography and careful footnoting, no matter how ably prepared, will not make up for deficiency in reasoning, style, and substance of the essay proper, but they do enhance the value of good scholarly writing because they act as auxiliary agents in the process of communication.

❀ INDEX

❖ INDEX